CARLISLE

The Parents' Perspective

APPLIED SOCIAL PROBLEMS
AND INTERVENTION STRATEGIES

A series of books edited by Albert R. Roberts, Rutgers—The State
University of New Jersey, New Brunswick, New Jersey, USA

Volume 1
THE PARENTS' PERSPECTIVE
Delinquency, Aggression and Mental Health
Paul Lerman and Kathleen J. Pottick

Forthcoming

Volume 2
HUMAN SERVICES AND THE MEDIA
Developing Partnerships for Change
Edward Allan Brawley

This book is part of a series. The publisher will accept continuation orders which may
be cancelled at any time and which provide for automatic billing and shipping of each
title in the series upon publication. Please write for details.

The Parents' Perspective
Delinquency, Aggression and Mental Health

Paul Lerman

School of Social Work, Rutgers University
New Brunswick, New Jersey

and

Kathleen J. Pottick

School of Social Work, and Institute for Health,
Health Care Policy, and Aging Research, Rutgers University

with the assistance of Radha Jagannathan
School of Social Work, Rutgers University

 harwood academic publishers

Australia • Austria • Belgium • China • France • Germany • India • Japan • Malaysia •
Netherlands • Russia • Singapore • Switzerland • Thailand • United Kingdom • United States

Harwood Academic Publishers
Poststrasse 22
7000 Chur, Switzerland

British Library Cataloguing in Publication Data

Lerman, Paul
  Parents' Perspective:Delinquency,
  Aggression and Mental Health. - (Applied
  Social Problems & Intervention
  Strategies Series, ISSN 1070-6585;Vol.1)
  I. Title II. Pottick, Kathleen J.
  III. Series
  364.36

  ISBN 3-7186-0581-3   (hardcover)
        3-7186-0582-1   (softcover)

Contents

Introduction to the Series

Books in the *Applied Social Problems and Intervention Strategies* series will document both the prevalence of and remedies/intervention strategies for the most pervasive social problems of our times. During the past few years, significant new information has emerged on treatment modalities, social service delivery models, coalition building efforts, social policy reforms and social change. Each book will examine the development and the effects of societal and community responses to specific social problems such as abuse, juvenile delinquency, divorce, family violence, suicide, substance abuse, AIDS and homelessness.

Albert R. Roberts

Preface

Among the most serious issues on the public policy agenda today are the growing problems of youths, especially urban youths. However rampant the problems, effective solutions seem to be scanty. Traditionally, academics have relied on adolescent self-reports, official records, teachers, or mental health professionals to understand the variety of legal and psychological problems that adolescents might have. And they have constructed recommendations for action on the basis of these sources. This book veers away from these traditional sources. It turns to the parents of the youths themselves to give them a platform to systematically talk about how they understand the problems and what they have done to try to solve them. Legal and mental health professionals have always relied on parents to provide information on the status of their youngsters. But large-scale research has not followed suit; oddly enough, parents have been relatively underutilized as sources for information on youths with legal and mental health problems. We try to rectify this situation by firmly grounding our survey questions, quantitative and qualitative analyses, interpretations, and policy recommendations in things that we hope will matter to the parents and, ultimately, to the youths themselves.

In the process of conducting the research and writing the book, we learned firsthand how parents see the problems of their children. Importantly, this allowed us to disentangle the relationships between legal and mental health problems in theoretically and programmatically meaningful ways. There are many, many ways that youths can misbehave, getting in trouble with parents, teachers, and authorities. Our society has grown accustomed to the term "acting out" to describe virtually all types of disliked behaviors. This is a psychological orientation to youths' problems, for it assumes that misdeeds are usually signs or symptoms of an underlying "disorder." We believe that the psychological aspects of rule violations should be examined independently by accepted methods of scientific research and not merely assumed as "facts."

Youths who get in trouble may have an associated mental disorder, but the mere existence of rule-violating behavior cannot be accepted as evidence that emotional disturbance exists. Instead we might expect, at a minimum, that distinct indications of a "disorder" also exist independent of the symptoms. Otherwise we are in the position of stating that the symptoms alone constitute the disorder. In medicine, for example, a high thermometer reading may be a "fever" sign of any one of a number of diseases — or the result of drinking hot liquids, an overexercised body, or sunstroke. Independent signs are expected to exist to ascertain which disorder is associated with the higher temperature.

Examining Unresolved Issues

Public policy and social science research have continually been influenced by these ongoing efforts at categorizing the misdeeds of youths. The fields of sociology and criminology currently refer to "juvenile status offenders" as non-criminal deviants, not to be confused with delinquents. Studies using official or youth self-report data attempt to scrupulously avoid mixing status and criminal behaviors in any measures of "delinquency." However, there is still debate within criminology as to whether status offenses constitute a "pure" category or are inextricably associated with criminal-type offenses. By using a different data source, parents' reports, this study can contribute new information in studying and assessing this issue. This issue is, of course, independent of whether the offenses are signs of a psychiatric disorder.

The field of mental health continues to have an expansive definition of the "behavior and personality problems of childhood." The nosology of the *Diagnostic and Statistical Manual of Mental Disorders, Third Edition, Revised* (DSM-III-R) has come under some criticism for its overinclusiveness, especially for children diagnosed with "conduct disorder" (Wakefield, 1992). While empirical studies, such as those conducted by Achenbach and his colleagues (1983), assume that the behavior factors are indicative of a psycho-pathological "syndrome," this assumption requires further examination. Clinicians and researchers affiliated with psychiatry or psychology have assumed that deviant behaviors are, by themselves, symptomatic of a mental disorder. Sociologists and criminologists are socialized to believe that deviant behavior can be a normal response to an array of social experiences or conditions. Surprisingly, researchers from this tradition have failed to critically examine the evidence of whether or not patterned youthful deviance is invariably associated with a psychological disorder. To the extent that psychological variables are, in fact, found to be associated with one or more specific behavior factors, then theories of deviance would have to take such information into account. The examination of psychological variables, in concert with sociological variables, can expand our understanding of the causes of youthful deviance. In the process of conducting an explanatory analysis, this study can add to an interdisciplinary dialogue.

Our study examines whether problems that are more clearly psychological are indeed associated with legal delinquency or non-delinquent aggression. Further, past empirical studies rely on samples that are primarily white, whereas our study is based on a sample that is 78% black.

Parents as Third-Party Help-Seekers

Another unsolved issue is how to help the children and their parents. Parents are third-party help-seekers. Children rarely seek help for themselves. Moreover, parents of youths in trouble are frequently nonvoluntary help-seekers. Models of help-seeking have assumed voluntary, first-party help-seeking. The study tackles this problem straight on, and tests a formal model of help-seeking that was developed by Brickman and his associates (Brickman et al., 1982). We look at how parents think about the causes and solutions to the problems of their sons and daughters, and their past experiences with formal help-giving agencies. The nature of the problems, their beliefs about them, and their past helping efforts should influence how formal help is sought and utilized. What are the chances that families will actually become clients and that services will be utilized? The actual delivery of services can be influenced by the way service agencies are organized to receive clients. Programs that are based on systematically acquired information from parents about help-seeking successes and disappointments should be more effective. Our study makes recommendations for programs and policies that are linked directly to our findings.

In the process of conducting this study and writing the book, we relied on many people and learned a great deal from them. From the 226 parents who are represented in this book, we learned of their fears for their children and the frustrating attempts they have made to divert them from trouble. We owe them a great debt. Our interviewing team of nine devoted, meticulous, and gritty women travelled throughout Newark to the human service agencies to talk to these parents personally and were always ready to serve the study in any way they could. The study, quite literally, could never have been done without them: Geneva Mason-Allaway, Ann Clark, Rosa Conceicao, Louise Conklin, Joyce Swain Drake, Carolyn Krone Ferolito, Joanne Morris-Hearns, Brigitte King, and Lois Thompson. Two able interviewers, Jane Fassler and Mary Owitz, talked to clinicians by telephone, securing response rates of well over 90% for a six-month follow-up. They cared deeply about the study, and we are grateful. Soundaram Ramaswami and Radha Jagannathan coded the data competently; and Radha continued in the study to assist with data analysis with outstanding proficiency and competence and thereby deserves special mention. We had others involved in research assistance along the way, most notably: Deborah Fudge, Katherine Kraft, Fred Rasmussen, and Margaret Micchelli. All of them provided interesting insights and careful analytic work. A special word is in order for Maria Lajonchere, the secretary for the project. She was tireless in her efforts on behalf of the study, keeping track of everything and everybody.

We are especially appreciative of the cooperation of each of the 13 human service agencies that participated in the study, and each of the 68 clinicians who gave so generously of their time and professional judgment.

Rosemary C. Sarri provided helpful comments on an earlier version of the manuscript, and George W. Downs offered particularly instrumental advice for organizing the manuscript and presenting the findings. We thank them very much for their time and thought.

We also want to thank the National Institute of Mental Health for their financial support for the study (R01 MH 39195-01), and Charles Windle, our project officer, who helped the project along the way. Our gratitude is extended to Rutgers University's Institute for Health, Health Care Policy, and Aging Research, and its director, David Mechanic, for offering financial, intellectual and technical support through the NIMH-funded Center for Research on the Organization and Financing of Care for the Severely Mentally Ill (R01 MH 42917-02).

We are thankful to our families for their support. Jonathan Storm deserves special recognition for his contribution in helping us recruit respondents. A journalist, he wrote a recruitment letter that proved to be significantly better than ours. Thus, he has contributed to an important literature on survey methods with hard-to-reach urban respondents. Carla Lerman, as usual, provided intellectual and emotional support. And Barbara Christenberry superbly copyedited the manuscript.

Finally, we thank William Dietz and Robert Donnelly, who typed different versions of the manuscript with care and fortitude.

1

Overview

This book describes and analyzes the results of a study of how urban parents view the problems of their adolescent children, and how they have tried to cope with and seek help for them. It focuses on parents living in and around Newark, New Jersey in the county of Essex who are seeking help for one of their children with a youth problem.[1]

With a population of 275,221 in 1990, Newark is one of the major metropolitan areas in the United States. It also is considered one of the worst places to live. It has a violent crime rate of 39.6 per 1000, compared to the national rate of 8.56. Its median household income in 1989 was $21,650, while the median household income in the entire state of New Jersey was $41,234. Of the 91,552 households in 1990, over 22% (20,206) receive public aid. People live in crowded and oftentimes dangerous conditions. Nearly 70% of the 102,473 total housing units are rentals. Between 1970 and 1990, it lost 106,709 inhabitants, 28% of its 1970 population of 381,930. Its black population (160,885) is 85% of the total, and its Hispanic population (71,761) regardless of race, is 28% of the total. In two years, school expenditures per student declined from $8,025 (1988–1989) to $7,330 (1990–1991), a change—unadjusted for inflation—of 8.7% (New Jersey Municipal Data Book, 1993; U.S. Bureau of the Census, 1992).

[1]The study was called **The Essex County Youth Study**. We refer to it throughout the book as **ECYS**.

1

There are many such communities in the United States. This book is meant to shed light on the types of problems experienced by adolescents in these communities. We are expressly interested in legal delinquency, nondelinquent aggression, and psychological problems. Because we rely on parents to tell us their problems with their children, we also find out much about parents in urban communities: their concerns, frustrations, attributions and coping efforts. We recognize that efforts to help urban adolescents have failed in many respects. If clinicians are not constrained by lack of information about the complexity of the problems (which they frequently are), they are constrained by a lack of a systematic technology to help solve them. We view parents as third-party help-seekers; adolescents rarely seek help for themselves. If we understand parents' concerns, frustrations, and coping efforts, we can help in more informative ways by involving parents in ways that they request and that are meaningful to them. More importantly, by documenting how urban parents seek help, become clients, and utilize services, this study can help create new technologies for change that can be evaluated systematically.

Specifically, the book focuses on three concerns of parents, professionals, and lay social observers pertaining to youths in trouble with adults. The first concern addresses the question: What are the problems of urban youths? We are interested in describing the problems holistically. Rather than categorizing youths by legal criteria or diagnostic classification, we seek to understand the way problems "go together." Recent studies refer to the "co-morbidity" of problems, but it is not necessary to use clinical terminology to describe empirical findings about clusters of multiple behavioral problems. We aim to understand the interrelationships between delinquency, aggression, and psychological problems.

The second concern answers the question: Why do the specific patterns occur? Since we rely principally on the reports of parents about the behaviors of their adolescent sons and daughters, we intend to broaden our understanding of attributions that parents make to explain the problems of their children. Parents offer information about family members, peers, the neighborhood, and the relative disadvantages experienced by youths growing up in deprived urban areas. We are interested in assessing whether the causes, as perceived by parents, are the same for delinquency, aggression, and psychological problems.

The third area of concern is this: how do parents function as third-party help-seekers? Just as parents make judgments about the causes of problems, they also make judgments about the way they think the problems ought to be solved. In the book we describe who or what parents believe should be responsible to help solve the problems of their adolescents. We also ascertain how parents have personally tried to cope with the problems of their children and whether they have preferences for specific types of solutions.

Predominantly, we approach the data quantitatively, and we use statistics because we want to know how the phenomena we study are distributed throughout the population we sampled. In addition, each chapter that presents results of the study begins with parents' responses to open-ended questions. We believe the qualitative record is an important addition, and we adhere to traditional scientific standards in our presentation of the qualitative data by randomly selecting 10% of the parents to illustrate their personal, individual answers to our survey questions.

Before describing the study's sample, design, methods, and organization of the findings, we discuss the ideas that guided the direction of the empirical analyses.

Past Approaches to Describing Youths' Problems

Most studies of behavioral problems of youths are undertaken with the aim of making a contribution to the "explanation" of the problems. While we share this aim, we believe that explanations require specification of, and agreement on, the phenomenon that is the object of explanatory research. Before the 1960s, researchers relied on official police, court, or correctional records as a means of specifying the concept "delinquency." They constructed theories to "explain" the rate of occurrence of delinquency and geographic distribution of youths who had come to the attention of the juvenile justice system. Theorists of delinquency used the official records of delinquent behavior to define delinquency. They tended to emphasize, with only a few exceptions, explanations that featured the ideas of social class, social disorganization, culture conflict, anomie, differential opportunity, and differential association (see, e.g., Shaw and McKay, 1942; Sutherland, 1947; Whyte, 1943; Cohen, 1955; Cloward and Ohlin, 1960; Miller, 1958). Early findings suggested a relationship between delinquency and lower socioeconomic status.

In 1958, the landmark study of "unrecorded delinquency," which was based on youth self-reports, challenged the assumption about the disproportionate illegal behaviors committed by lower class youths (Short and Nye, 1958). In fact, until the development of the youth self-report method for measuring illegal deviant behaviors, it was assumed by most theorists that the actions of lower class youths, particularly those residing in inner-city areas, were appropriate primary targets of research. Over two decades, from 1960 to 1980, researchers relying on the youth self-report method to understand delinquency have had difficulty in obtaining significant correlations between measures of social class and self-reports of illegal behaviors.

However, in that time, new theoretical models began to emerge to explain the variance of those youths measuring high on self-reports. The new models, based on the responses of youths, emphasized the role of the family in socializing and controlling youths, and the importance of commitment and bonding to conventional persons and social institutions (Hirschi, 1969). The most dominant theory in criminology and sociology pertaining to delinquency (of all types) has been Hirschi's (1969) social control theory. According to Hirschi, youths are likely to be delinquent unless prevented from doing so by their "bonds" to the following: 1) attachment to parents, teachers, and other conventional adults; 2) commitment to respected and conventional goals, and activities such as school; 3) a high involvement in conventional activities; and 4) having a strong belief in conventional norms. If these "bonds" are weak, then the youth becomes "free" to engage in delinquency. Of the four critical bonds proposed by Hirschi, it is evident that three consist of psychological attributes pertaining to: 1) positive feelings about adults (i.e., attachments); 2) beliefs about the worthiness of long-term goals and activities linked to goals (i.e., school completion and achievement); and 3) moral beliefs about right and wrong behaviors (i.e., conventional norms). The theory of social control advanced by Hirschi (1969) would not have been so persuasive for such a long period of time had it not been for the development of the self-report method.

Recently, improvements in sampling and methods of collecting self-reports have revealed social class differences in delinquency. Using a representative national youth sample, and more precise self-report items, Elliott and his colleagues (Elliott and Ageton, 1980; Elliott and Huizinga, 1983) identified a relationship between measures of social class and delinquent activities. Improved sampling and measurement, as well as interest in the potential multiple problems of youths, has expanded research using the self-report method.

Expansion of Self-Report Method

Although official records and youth self-reports result in differences regarding which youths are delinquent, and where they are likely to be found, both methods share one important attribute in common. Both focus on identifying behaviors that are explicitly illegal. Until very recently, delinquency researchers relying on self-reports were unconcerned about measuring mental health problems or antisocial (but legal) behaviors such as lying, cheating, or bullying others. Some researchers have initiated the use of self-reports to measure drinking, marijuana and smoking, suicide, depression, and school and community misbehaviors, together with illegal behaviors, and they have found that self-reports of illegal behaviors are correlated with a variety of self-report measures of other behaviors and mental health problems (White and LaGrange, 1987; see also Loeber, Stouthamer-Loeber, Kammen and Farrington, 1991; Dembo, Williams, Whitke, Schneider, Getrell, Berry and Wish, 1992).

The emergence of multiple measures of problems of youths can be directly linked to research in the field of alcohol and drug abuse (Jessor and Jessor, 1977 and 1984; Jessor, 1987; Kandel, 1978; White, Johnson, and Garrison, 1985). Researchers show that relationships between distinct types of behavioral and psychological problems are indications of a common "behavior proneness" that requires similar explanatory variables to account for the varied behaviors. Jessor, for example, reports that a multiproblem "behavior structure" is influenced by the psychological and social characteristics of youths, the perceived environment, family socialization, and parental demographic characteristics (Jessor, 1987). This array of multiple causes is, of course, much broader than the few causes offered by the sociological "social control" theory advanced by Hirschi.

The concurrent cluster of adolescent problem behaviors is of interest to delinquency, alcohol and drug abuse, and mental health researchers alike, and the interdisciplinary term to describe this phenomenon to be explained is co-morbidity (Robins and McEvoy, 1990; Institute of Medicine, 1989). The finding that youths have multiple and overlapping problems has stimulated a fertile, interdisciplinary exchange of explanatory theories and operational indicators of co-morbidity.

The Achenbach Child Behavior Checklist

The Achenbach Child Behavior Checklist (CBCL) (Achenbach and Edelbrock, 1983, 1987) is one of the most widely used interdisciplinary reporting instruments in the child development literature. Achenbach's checklist measures delinquent and nondelinquent behaviors, as well as somatic and emotional complaints. The instrument has been tested on a variety of samples—clinic and court referrals, institutionalized delinquents, and random samples of "normals." Using a 118-item list of specific behaviors and emotional problems, Achenbach and his colleagues have factor analyzed data from 2300 parents of youths referred to 42 East coast mental health clinics and a random sample of about 1500 parents of nonreferred (i.e., "normal") youths residing in a metropolitan area. Both boys and girls are studied, and the youths range in age from 4 to 16 years. Using the clinic and normal samples, Achenbach has established norms for each sex for distinct age groups: 4–5, 6–11, and 12–16-year-olds. Focusing on 12–16-year-olds (the age range used in the current study), Achenbach and Edelbrock (1983) find 9 specific factors for males and 8 for females. Analyses for each sex yield distinct delinquent and aggressive factors, as well as factors reflecting psychological problems.

Using cut-off scores of clinic-referred youth at the 98th percentile, Achenbach and Edelbrock (1983) demonstrate that the measures are reliable and valid. For example, on the delinquent scale, only 3% of normal boys scored above the cut-off scores, whereas 35% of clinic-referred boys scored that high. A similar result was obtained for girls on the delinquency scale: 2% for normals, as compared to 41% for clinic referrals. On the aggressive scale there was a difference of 4% vs. 26% for boys, and 2% vs. 27% for girls. The other scales provide comparable and significant differences.

Achenbach has expanded the pioneering work with a Dutch sample (Achenbach and Edelbrock, 1987). In addition, he has teamed up with four other colleagues (Achenbach, Conners, Quay, Verhulst, and Howell, 1989) to produce an expanded checklist of 215 behavioral/emotional items, 115 of which have counterparts with the Achenbach CBCL. For simplicity in this book, the expanded checklist is called the Achenbach, Conners and Quay checklist, abbreviated ACQ. The ACQ was completed by American parents of 1750 boys and 1088 girls at ages 6–11, and 954 boys and 689 girls at ages 12–16 referred to 18 mental health clinics in different parts of the country. The sample was 80% white, 14% black, and 6% other. Comparison with Achenbach's earlier work and the Dutch sample disclosed that the following "syndromes" replicated well for each sex at ages 6–16: aggressive, delinquent, attention problems, anxious/depressed, somatic complaints, and withdrawn (Achenbach et. al., 1989). Similar syndromes were found with a new national sample of 2200 non-referred American children aged 6–16 (Achenbach, Howell, Quay, and Conners, 1991).

Reliability of Achenbach's Self-Report Method

How reliable are self-reports when compared to the reports of others, such as teachers, parents, and peers? A meta-analysis of 118 studies of ratings by parents, peers, and the youths on comparable items reveals that correlations between informants of the same status averaged about .60. However, correlations between youths and other types of informants were much lower—an average correlation of .22 (Achenbach & Edelbrock, 1987). Specific correlations between youths reporting on their own behaviors and other informants who provide information about the subjects' behaviors are as follows: for parents/youths an average of .25; for teachers/youths an average of .20; for mental health workers/youths an average of .27; and peers/youths an average of .26. These correlations are statistically significant, but they are certainly not as reliable as correlations between ratings by pairs of parents about youths (an average of .59), pairs of teachers about youths (an average of .64), or pairs of observers about youths (an average of .57). On a test—retest of the youths about themselves the correlations average .74. In the absence of external validation, however, we prudently assume that reports of youths about their behavioral problems are only mildly correlated with the reports of other knowledgeable informants like parents, teachers, or other independent observers, and even their peers (Achenbach et al., 1987).

Parents and teachers achieved a correlation of only .27 in the meta-analysis conducted by Achenbach and his colleague (1987). As Achenbach and Edelbrock (1987) note, self-reports of youths and other informants are relatively low, and may indicate that the target variables differ from one situation to another, rather than that the reports of different informants are invalid or unreliable (p. 213). For the same reason, we argue, low correlations are found between illegal behaviors documented in official police files and self-reports of illegal behaviors. The Philadelphia Cohort Study, initiated by Wolfgang and his colleagues, found that official police records and self-reports correlated .25 (Wolfgang, Figlio and Sellin, 1972; and Tracy, 1987). This result is comparable to the one found in the meta-analysis of youths and adult informants by Achenbach (1987). The police may not have known about the illegal behaviors of many of the Philadelphia informants, and many youths noticed by police may not be likely to report their activities truthfully. Additionally, there is research to suggest that the demeanor and public language of youths can be used as cues for defining deviance, and arresting youths (Piliavin and Briar, 1964; Lerman, 1967).

Youths' Self-Report and Black-White Differences

Understanding behavioral problems of youths takes on additional meaning when one considers that the most widely cited theory to explain delinquency, that is, Hirschi's social control theory, was originally based on a sample that deliberately excluded *all* of the more than 1000 black youths "because of the unreliability of the Negro data" (Hirschi, 1969, p.79, fn. 23). Other, more recent research using data from the National Youth Study (NYS) (Elliott and Ageton, 1980; Elliott, Ageton, Huizinga, Knowes, and Carter, 1983) has addressed this omission. In their face-to-face interviews with youths in a confidential context and with a broad list of behavioral items, they demonstrated that the black/white difference in predatory types of crimes against persons, such as simple assault, aggravated assault, sexual assault, and robbery, was substantial. The National Youth Study did not report relationships between youth self-report and official records, but the differences between black and white youths that they discovered is similar to differences found in our best studies of delinquency from official records (Wolfgang, Figlio, and Sellin, 1972; Shannon, 1982). The National Youth Study's measures and procedures have undoubtedly set a higher standard for using youth self-reports. Nevertheless, it still is unable to demonstrate that youth self-reports are reliably associated with a knowledgeable second source of information about problematic youth behaviors. In addition, the National Youth Survey focuses on delinquent behaviors, and not on concurrent mental health.

Our study improves upon the former ones in several ways. First, our sample is predominantly black, and we have sufficient numbers of nonblacks to make meaningful comparisons. Second, because we rely on the standard Achenbach Child Behavior Checklist (CBCL)(Achenbach and Edelbrock, 1983,1987) (see methods section in this chapter for full description), we are able to compare the behaviors of blacks in our sample with whites in studies conducted by Achenbach. Achenbach samples are 80% to 90% white, with a higher socioeconomic status than our sample (Achenbach et al., 1989, p. 304).

Using Parent-Reports to Understand Problems and Help-Seeking

The springboard for our book is the parents' reports of their adolescents' problem behaviors as measured by Achenbach's Child Behavior Checklist (CBCL) (Achenbach & Edelbrock, 1983). Our study is unable to make a direct contribution towards improving the reliability and validity of youth self-reports, per se. Instead, by using a different source of unofficial information—that is, parents as informants—we can contribute to expanding our knowledge about strategic issues that have emerged in the study of the problems of urban youths. Theoretically, the potential relationships among delinquency, aggression, and psychological problems is of vital concern to us from service and policy perspectives, and we explore ideas about the coexistence of multiple problems of youths as researched by Jessor and Jessor (1977) and others (Donovan & Jessor, 1985; Jessor and Jessor, 1989; Osgood et al., 1989; Dembo, Williams, Whitke, Schneider, Getrell, Berry, and Wish, 1992; White, 1992).

Using the CBCL as the means to identify delinquency, aggression, and psychological problems, we explore their common and independent causes. Prevention policies can be better developed from knowledge of causation. We use two sources of information to explain the adolescents' problems. One source is the parents' perspective itself since we asked them directly what they believe caused the problems. The other source is information from the survey that can help us explain problems of youths, such as their associations with bad peers or lack of guilt.

We are interested in parents' ideas about causation, but also in their ideas about solutions. In the book, we test the theory of attribution developed by Brickman, Rabinowitz, Karuza, Coates, Cohn & Kida (1982), which posits that desired solution strategies are related to individuals' notions of who or what is responsible for causing and solving problems. Is the attribution of responsibility more influential, we ask, to the way parents want the problems solved than the nature of the problem itself? Brickman would suggest that it is, and our data are analyzed to answer this question.

Since this is a study from the parents' point of view, it does inform us of their efforts as third-party help-seekers. We investigate the usefulness of a model of help-seeking developed by Gross and McMullen (1983) to view how parents seek help, how their children become clients, and how help is utilized. We are explicitly interested in understanding the utility of the help-seeking model to describe third-party help-seeking, especially under involuntary conditions, since the model has not been tested on parents to our knowledge.

This study contributes to knowledge on delinquency, aggression, and mental health among both black and white youths. We hope it can provide strategic information to policymakers and clinicians about the problems faced by urban youths as they are seen through the parents' perspective. Moreover, it should offer guidance to diagnosticians, epidemiologists, and service providers to systematically help urban youths.

Methods of the Study

Design of the Interview Schedule

The interview schedule appears in Appendix A. The schedule follows the researchers' interest in obtaining multiple assessments of problems in the lives of urban youths as described by parents, and asks parents to report how they think about and handle the problems of their adolescent children. Respondents were chosen to represent parents seeking help from local social agencies. Parents were introduced to the interview as participants in a study of Essex County Youth. The interview began with the standard Achenbach Child Behavior Checklist (CBCL)(Achenbach and Edelbrock, 1983, 1987), and then asked a variety of questions about the "main problem" of concern to them: why they are concerned, when they noticed it, how they noticed it, and what they personally tried to do about the problem. We began the interview with the CBCL because the checklist often is administered as a single instrument, and we wanted to replicate as closely as possible the test conditions of the CBCL. If Achenbach behavior items were asked first, we could compare the Newark youths with the larger clinical and nonclinical samples of adolescents studied by Achenbach and Edelbrock (1983), and be fairly confident that similarities or differences were not due to the order of the questions.

After administering the CBCL, the interview focused on the "main problem" of concern to them so that we could provide a specific, and therefore more reliable, referent for their experiences. We designed the interview to flow from their opinions about the main problem, to their ideas about agencies, to information about themselves and how they lived. In these three sections we solicited their ideas about the causes of, and solutions for, the problem; their assessments of help they received from informal sources, such as friends and family, and formal sources, such as medical doctors, social workers, and clergy; and their understanding of their child's relationship with the natural parents and other people in their home.

The flow of the interview was from general open-ended questions to more specific closed-ended questions. The funneling procedure allowed parents to generate their own responses so that they were not influenced by the content of more specific questions. For example, parents were asked this open-ended question: "Looking back to when the main problem first got *started*, why do you think it began?" Closed-ended questions followed: "Considering everything you know about what caused (*Name's*) problem to get started or get worse, how responsible would you say the following people are—a lot, some, a little, or not at all? Parents were asked about themselves, their spouse, their child, friends of their child, brothers and sisters and other relatives. Another question, which focused on external causes such as school, neighborhood, income, discrimination, and crowded housing, used the same format. This procedure is designed to provide an unbiased venue for the parents to think about their adolescent's problem and their feelings and ideas about it, and therefore, to maximize the likelihood that parents are responding to their own frame of reference.

Illustration of the Funnel Technique in the Interview

A summary of one of the interviews from the 10% random sample of parents is presented here to illustrate the flow of the interview and the advantages of the funnel technique. This particular interview took one hour and seven minutes. The child being discussed is a 13-year-old boy.

In response to several questions about the outside activities of her son, she reports that he skates and bikes for sport, but has no hobbies and is in no organizations, teams or clubs. She says that he does chores, like taking out the garbage, washing dishes, cleaning his room, and doing chores for neighbors. She told us that there were three problems on the Achenbach Child Behavior Checklist that she saw as connected, and as the *main* problem of her child: He lies or cheats, steals at home, and destroys things belonging to his family or other children. We asked her to tell us what concerned her about the main problem, and she said, "Because you can't trust a person who lies, steals and cheats, and it's pretty bad when you can't trust your own child...I'm afraid if he grows up like that, I'm afraid he'll get hurt." There were several instances of stealing over the last six years which she described in detail. She reported that people in her son's family had stolen things.

The open-ended question asking why the problem got started prompted this response: "Maybe because I couldn't buy him everything he wanted so he could go to a store and steal it. He had plenty of toys." This was coded under the large category of "conditions of the environment theme" with specific reference to "poverty."

In response to the next open-ended question asking whether there was anybody responsible for the main problem getting started, she said,"he did it on his own—him and a friend." We asked whether there was anything that made the main problem get *worse* after it first got started: "Yes, as time went on he felt he could take money out of a drawer." We then asked the closed-ended question about what people caused the problem to get started or get worse, with response categories of "a lot," "some," "a little," or "not at all." There she reported that her son is responsible "a lot," and that his father is responsible "some." She said she does not know his friends personally, so she could not say how responsible they were. She herself and other relatives are "not at all responsible." He has no brothers or sisters to assume any responsibility for the problem.

The closed-ended question about the potential external causes of the problem revealed that she felt that family heredity—"maybe on his father's side of the family" was responsible for causing the problem a lot. Influences that affected the problem "some" were TV, movies, newspapers; kind of school; not having enough religious faith; and not enough family income. Bad health, type of neighborhood, discrimination, and crowded apartment or house, she reported, did not cause the problem at all. When the mother answered the open-ended question about the causes of the problem, she only mentioned income. The closed-ended format secured more information on external influences.

Notice that the closed-ended questions illuminate and broaden the open-ended one. The question asking about the responsibility of people showed us that the mother perceived that her son was more responsible for the problem than anyone else. It also showed us that she viewed the child's father also as responsible. Using a Likert scale, ranging from "a lot" to "not at all" assures that the respondent is not influenced to answer in a particular direction. Without biasing her answer, the question provided the mother a chance to think about how much responsibility the child's father might have, a person that did not come to mind in her response to the open-ended question. Thus, the closed-ended format provides insights into a wider range of influences on the problem that would not otherwise be generated spontaneously.

Sampling Strategy

Two different samples from human service agencies were drawn for the study. One sample was prospective and interviews with parents took place in local service agencies after the required intake interviews, but before any services were delivered. The study was described to parents by the clinician, and, if the parents agreed to participate, they were introduced to the Rutgers interviewer who secured the permission letters and conducted the interview in the agency. The prospective, agency-based sample consisted of 126 parents. The second sample was retrospective. Parents were contacted directly by letter after a clinical intake interview had been scheduled to request their participation in the study. These interviews took place in a neutral location on the Rutgers–Newark campus, away from the local agencies. Letters were sent to all parents who had been scheduled for an intake interview, regardless of whether they had showed up for it. One hundred interviews were secured in this way. Respondents who were referred because of domestic violence or an allegation of abuse or neglect were deliberately excluded from the sample.

All of the parents had used services at either one of six state–funded Community Mental Health Centers (CMHCs) or one of seven human service agencies subcontracted to the county–funded Family Crisis Intervention Unit (FCIUs) to work with the Juvenile Courts. In New Jersey, youths with mental health problems not in need of hospitalization can receive mental health services from two different service delivery systems: the state-funded community mental health centers (CMHC) and the county-funded Family Crisis Intervention Unit (FCIU). Youths can enter the CMHC as walk-ins or by having been evaluated at, and referred by, one of seven emergency mental health screening centers distributed across the State. The FCIU is a diversionary service of the Family Courts, by linking status-offending youths to services at free-standing local agencies under contract to the county. The purpose of the FCIU is to help families resolve behavioral problems within a short period of time. The FCIU has contracts with the CMHCs to refer youths with more serious mental health problems. Out of a total of eight community mental health centers in Essex County, we received the cooperation of six of them. Out of a total of eight family crisis units, we received the cooperation of seven. Thus, the study includes thirteen separate social agencies, representing over 80% of all of the youth-serving agencies in and around Newark, New Jersey.

The sampling strategies, including the difficulties that were encountered in conducting the survey in the agencies and a detailed comparison of the different methods, are reported in Lerman and Pottick (1988) and Pottick and Lerman (1991). We provide a brief description of the sampling methods and results to assist readers to assess the interviewed samples.

The agency-based strategy was relatively ineffective in securing potential respondents and inefficient in securing completed interviews. For example, we interviewed 36% out of 218 potential unduplicated individual cases in the family crisis system and only 20% out of 168 unduplicated cases in the mental health system; these are disappointing rates in both instances. Analysis reveals, however, that there are no significant differences in available demographic characteristics between the cases we interviewed and those we lost in either service system, using comparisons of adolescent's age, sex, number of problems mentioned, parent's race, zip code, and referral source. We did discover, however, that the interviewed family crisis sample is not geographically representative of the larger population of mental health and FCIU service users.

The second strategy of contacting FCIU parents directly by letter after parents had been offered a clinical intake and interviewing them in a neutral location (i.e., on the Rutgers–Newark campus) was more effective in securing respondents, and more efficient in securing research interviews. Also, the Rutgers–Newark sample was more geographically representative of the larger population of FCIU service users than the agency-based strategy. We began by randomly splitting the potential sample of 219 cases into two groups and verifying addresses to end up with approximately equal subsamples. In order to test different survey techniques to increase response rates, two major manipulations were introduced. The Wave I sample of 113 potential respondents received an academic-style letter requesting their participation, based on Dillman's (1978) recommendations. The Wave II sample of 106 potential respondents received a cover letter with the same information composed by a metropolitan newspaper writer. The second manipulation targeted the kind of final follow-up, either a final letter (Wave I) or a personal phone call (Wave II). Significantly different interview completion rates of 30% for Wave I and 53% for Wave II indicate that procedures including a journalistic-style letter and a personal phone call are more effective (Lerman and Pottick, 1988; Pottick and Lerman, 1991). Using the journalistic-letter and phone call, we were able to secure response rates similar to national household surveys on nonclinical populations in urban areas (Veroff, Douvan, and Kulka, 1981).

The agency-based and Rutgers–Newark samples differ in several respects. The agency-based sample is more dependent on welfare than the research-team sample (58% vs. 30%). It also contains proportionately more inner-city respondents than the research-team sample (41% vs. 13.5%). And, it contains more adolescents under 15 years old (55% vs. 33%). In all other respects, the samples are similar. The research-team sampling design obtains a broader geographic distribution of respondents to include those who live outside the central parts of the city. In addition, it expands the socio-demograph-ic profile of the sample. Moreover, Wave II of the research-team strategy secures respondents who are more critical of services and pessimistic about problems than the agency-based design. For example, respondents in the Rutgers–Newark sample feel less understood by human service workers than those in the agency-based design (p< .001), tend to believe that the agency would be less helpful (p<.001), and tend to think that the problem will take longer to solve (p<.05) (Pottick and Lerman, 1991).

It is possible that conducting the research interview outside of the agency allowed parents to feel freer in describing negative feelings about their personal and agency experiences. In addition, parents may have had more information with which to evaluate the nature of the problem because they were interviewed up to eight months after their contact with the agency in the Rutgers–Newark design.

Follow-up data were obtained on the agency-based sample of 126 parents through telephone interviews with clinicians conducted after four weeks and then again at six months about problems, services and outcomes. We secured 119 surveys at four weeks and 116 surveys at six months, representing 94% and 92% follow-up rates. Of the 126 agency-based parent interviews, 36 were from the community mental health system and 90 were from the family crisis system. All 100 of the Rutgers–Newark interviews were from the family crisis system since there was no readily available central source from which to draw names in the mental health system. No follow-up data from clinicians were secured for the Rutgers–Newark sample. While parents were paid for taking the time to be interviewed ($10.00 in the agency-based sample, and $20.00 in the Rutgers–Newark sample), clinicians were not paid.

The Interviewing Situation

Interviewers were trained in interviewing techniques using the standard *Interviewer's Manual* (1977) developed at the Survey Research Center at The University of Michigan's Institute for Social Research. Interviewers were recruited from churches, volunteer organizations, and personal networks. From twenty final candidates who we personally interviewed, ten were selected to undergo training. Nine were chosen: five black women, three white women, and one Portuguese woman who was capable of speaking Spanish or Portuguese. The black and white women were middle-aged, married, with children. The Portuguese woman was young and unmarried. The black women were retired from blue-collar jobs, while the white women were nonworking. The interviewers were matched to respondents' race or ethnicity when possible, and the interview was translated into Spanish for Hispanic respondents.

All interviewers were provided written instructions for each question. Instructions guided them in asking questions uniformly, and helped them to clarify questions and probe neutrally for answers. Neutral probing was especially critical for interviewing parents who were seeking help for their children's problems. Interviewers understood that parents might be sensitive to others' opinions about them as parents, and that responding with other-than-standard-neutral-probes might make them feel guarded, and thus, might jeopardize the validity of the study.

Eight of the nine interviewers stayed with our field operations for the full year of data collection, despite complicated field procedures. Since we were securing many respondents prospectively, the interviewers were informed only a few days ahead of time that they would have to travel to one of the thirteen social agencies to interview a parent after their clinical intake interview. Potential research cases in the agency-based sample were lost for a variety of reasons. Thirty-five percent out of 547 scheduled agency appointments for a clinical intake did not occur because the parent did not show up for the intake, and therefore, could not be interviewed for the research. Another 35% cancelled their clinical appointments, which meant they could not be interviewed for the research. Only a small minority of about 10% refused to be interviewed for the research. Nevertheless, of the 547 scheduled appointments, only 23% resulted in a research interview. We paid interviewers for their time to get to the agency, but lost cases disappointed them. That did not appear to dampen their commitment to the project, however. Most of the interviewers had an affection for Newark, having grown up in and around it. They told the principal investigators that they felt the parents' perspective on their adolescent children and their lives was an important one to record, and that many parents spontaneously asked for copies of the results.

To introduce the interview, the following statement was read to all respondents:

Hello, I'm (interviewer's name) and I'm working for a Rutgers University research study on young people in Essex County.

Thank you for giving us permission to ask you some questions. We want to find out how parents think about young people and the problems that youths might have while growing up.

Everything we talk about will be strictly private and confidential. Nobody in your family will ever be identified by name.

If we should come to any question you don't want to answer, just let me
know and we'll skip over it. I think you will find the questions interesting and will want to give them careful thought.

At the end of the interview we would like to fill out a form so that Rutgers can send you a check for taking the time to talk to us.

The interviews were conducted between September 1985 and
August 1986, and they each took about one hour and fifteen
minutes to complete. No interviews were terminated prematurely.
As noted, a few parents refused to be interviewed after their clinical
intakes, and we lost cases for reasons that have already been
discussed. How the final sample was selected will be addressed in
the next section.

Description of the Sample

The sample of 226 respondents represents low-income, minority,
and urban parents of youth in some sort of trouble. The mean age of
the youths is 14.5 years; 59% are boys and 41% are girls. Seventy-
eight percent of the sample is black and about 77% of the households
are headed primarily by women. Sixty-three percent live in Newark
itself and about 46% had received welfare in the month prior to the
interview. Boys and blacks are somewhat over-represented in the
sample because the study has a larger number of respondents from
the family crisis system than from the mental health system. Boys
and blacks are more likely than girls to be involved in court referrals.
The mean number of children in the household is 2.8, and the mean
number of adults in the household is 1.7. The mean amount of
schooling of the parent is 11.7 years, and the majority of the parents
are Protestant (60%). A father or stepfather lives in only 27% of the
households. Two-hundred and six of the 226 respondents (91%)
were women. Forty-two parents are from the CMHC system and 184
are from the FCIU system.

The sample represents a traditionally hard-to-reach service and
research population. It is difficult to locate a study with more than
200 cases of low income, minority parents with adolescents identified as having mental health problems. While the final sample was
not secured through consistently standard and uniform procedures,
a source of unique data has been collected. As long as we generalize
cautiously and compare carefully, the analysis should tell us much
about parents and their adolescent children. If we permitted

ourselves to ignore all samples that were less than ideal, then many seminal contributions of scholars like Weber, Piaget, and Freud would have been dismissed without consideration of the merit of their contribution. The analysis that follows is justified by the findings, interpretations, and contributions to interdisciplinary discourse.

Coding

Highly detailed coding schemes were developed for each of the open-ended questions. To do this, we took a random sample of 25 of the first 100 interviews and recorded each of their responses to every open-ended question on separate index cards. Abstract categories that captured their responses were developed. An example will illustrate the outcome of this procedure. We asked parents why they thought the problem began. This was coded in five general categories with several subcategories within each one. The five general categories in answer to this question were: 1) missing/absent father theme; 2) peer-related theme; 3) child-related theme; 4) parent/family-related theme; 5) external themes of work, school or conditions of environment. Responses that did not fit under these categories were recorded as "other." Any mention of a theme received a score of 1, and all other responses received a 0; each theme was coded in this "dummy variable" fashion. Each respondent was coded for three different possible responses to this question. Respondents who mentioned two subcategories of one general category of why the problem began were coded for each subcategory, but they were coded only once if they mentioned a second reason within one subcategory.

Analysis

Standard univariate statistics are used to describe the sample of youths and parents, and we use traditional bivariate statistics of correlation and chi-square where appropriate to the level of measurement to describe relationships of interest among the major measures of the study. Attention is directed to the Achenbach Child Behavior Checklist (CBCL) (Achenbach and Edelbrock, 1983, 1987), and it is analyzed in several ways. First, three different procedures developed by Achenbach to measure youths' behaviors are applied to this sample so that comparisons between the Newark youths and youths in Achenbach's samples can be systematically made. Achenbach's procedures are described in detail in appendix B. In a second stage of analysis, we deviated from Achenbach's procedures to clarify delinquent, aggressive, and psychological problems for both boys and girls. Accepting the CBCL to measure behaviors, does not necessarily mean that the item responses cannot be assessed from analytic perspectives quite distinct from the way it has been used by Achenbach. Thus, factor analysis, which will be described in detail in chapter 3, is used to uncover the latent behavior patterns of youths in the study, and stepwise regression analysis is conducted to explore predictive models for the behavior patterns and help-seeking decisions. The sample size is relatively small for the number of theoretically important variables investigated. Therefore, an incremental procedure is used to develop best fitting models. First, we test partial models using theoretically related variables. Then, we take the best fitting variables from the partial models, and test a final, full model with demographic controls.

Preview of the Book

The book is organized into two major parts. Part I (Chapters 2–4) focuses on the problems of urban youths, and Part II (Chapters 5–8) focuses on parents as third-party help-seekers, describing their coping efforts and use of the human service system. Part I consists of Chapters 2–4, and Part II contains Chapters 5–8. Chapter 9 summarizes and interprets the results.

Chapter 2 reviews past studies that describe and explain multiple problems of youths. There, we pay particular attention to traditional psychiatric problems associated with delinquency and aggression. Chapter 3 describes the behavioral problems of the youths in the sample: their delinquency, aggression, and mental health problems. Here, we develop a classification scheme that allows us to view delinquency and aggression in the context of traditional psychiatric disorders. In chapter 4 we explain the causes of the youths' delinquent, aggressive, and psychological problems.

Chapter 5 focuses on the role of parents as third-party help seekers, and describes the conditions under which parents seek help for the problems of their children. Chapter 6 addresses the problems involved in youths becoming clients. Chapter 7 demonstrates how mental health services are utilized by youths with different types of delinquent, aggressive, and psychological problems. Chapter 8 assesses the preferences of parents for solutions to the problems of their children, including alternatives not offered by local agencies. It also tests the theory that specific preferences concerning solutions are a function of attributions of responsibility for the causes of, and solutions to, problems. A summary of the results, together with our interpretations, is located in Chapter 9. There, we address the practice and policy implications of the findings for helping urban youths, and make specific recommendations for creating a pro-social youth service policy in urban areas.

2

Past Research

Many terms have been used in the past to describe problematic behaviors of children and adolescents. Historically, behavioral categories reflect the cultural opinions and values of specific eras. Here are some examples:

- a "stubborn child" (1646)

- boys and girls with "vicious propensities" (1824)

- a child who "violates any law" of a city, village, or the State is a "delinquent child" (1898)

- youth exhibiting "behavior and personality problems of childhood ... made manifest by disorders of behaviors, such as tantrums, stealing, seclusiveness, truancy, cruelty, sensitiveness, restlessness, and fears" (1930)

The "stubborn child" category was included in the 1646 legal code of the Massachusetts Bay Colony. The statutes made it a capital offense for youths 16 years of age and older to disobey their parents. The law was copied into the legal code of other colonies. The legal category, without capital punishment, became the forerunner of juvenile court codes referring to "incorrigibility," "ungovernability," and "beyond the control" of parents (Sutton, 1988).

The first juvenile correctional facility built in America in 1824, The House of Refuge, promised to provide a "prompt and energetic corrective" to the "vicious propensities" of boys who are offenders, petty criminals, vagrants, or "homeless." In addition, girls who were in danger of acquiring habits of "fixed depravity" were to be admitted to a separate wing of the House of Refuge (Bremner, Barnard, Haraven, and Mennel, 1970, p. 679).

The first juvenile court statute, enacted in Illinois in 1898, expanded the concept of delinquency to include violations of "any law"—civil or criminal. This could include truancy, begging, cigarette smoking, loitering, or other "offenses." By 1932 virtually every state had juvenile court statutes that encompassed criminal and noncriminal behaviors (Bremner et al., 1970). Beginning in the 1960s, states began to distinguish between criminal type offenders and "juveniles in need of supervision" (Lerman, 1977). Two types of youths in trouble with adults were legally differentiated as delinquents and status offenders.

The mental hygiene movement of the 1920s provided the impetus for viewing the psychological side of delinquency. Child guidance clinics evolved to deal with "maladjustments" of youths. By 1931 there were more than 230 clinics functioning as adjuncts of the juvenile courts in communities across the country. Summarizing the decade of growth, the director of the Division on Community Clinics of the National Committee for Mental Hygiene told the first International Congress on Mental Hygiene that clinics classified a spectrum of troublesome behaviors as symptoms of "disorders of behavior" of childhood (Bremner et al., 1970, pp. 1054–1055; Richardson, 1989).

Public policy and social science research, as well as clinical interventions by a variety of human service personnel, have continually been influenced by these ongoing efforts to categorize the problems and misdeeds of youths. The fields of sociology and criminology currently refer to "juvenile status offenders" as non-criminal deviants, not to be confused with "delinquents." Juvenile status offenses refer to behaviors that are deemed illegal if committed by a minor, but would not be considered criminal if engaged in by an adult. By contrast, youths are classified as delinquent if the behaviors they engage in could be classified as criminal offenses, similar to adults. Studies using official records and youth self-reports attempt to scrupulously avoid mixing status offenses and criminal behaviors as they measure delinquency. And, as was discussed in Chapter 1, the interdisciplinary dialogue between researchers in criminology and those in mental health has only recently begun.

This chapter focuses on: 1) current approaches to clinical diagnostics, 2) evidence for the coexistence of delinquency, aggression, and psychological problems among adolescents, 3) known predictors of behavioral problems of adolescents, and 4) help-seeking by adults for their children.

Current Approaches to Clinical Diagnostics

Rutter (1986) pinpoints the problem of clinical diagnosis for adolescents: it is hard to disentangle normal adolescent developmental problems from serious mental illness. Moreover, the purpose of diagnosis, from a medical standpoint, is to prescribe treatment. If treatment does not follow from diagnosis, then why bother to diagnose? Because most mental health researchers and clinicians believe that effective solutions to problems can be developed once problems are understood, much effort has been devoted to creating valid and reliable measurement instruments for diagnosis.

In attempting to categorize the "behavior and personality problems of childhood," the revised, third edition of the Diagnostic and Statistical Manual of Mental Disorders (DSM-III-R, 1987) refers to three types of "disruptive behavior disorders":

1. Conduct disorders

2. Attention–Deficit Hyperactivity disorders

3. Oppositional Defiant disorders (American Psychiatric Association, 1987, pp. 49–58)

Conduct disorders refer to stealing, running away, lying, cheating, fire-setting, truanting, burglary, and types of physical and sexual aggression. Attention-deficit hyperactivity disorders refer to the following types of disturbances: fidgets, easily distracted, blurts out answers, difficulty in remaining seated or sustaining attention. The authors of DSM-III-R note that these behaviors often coexist with, or are a precursor to, the other disruptive behavior disorders. Oppositional defiant disorders refer to behaviors such as arguing with adults, temper tantrums, defiance to adult requests, and angry, resentful and annoying acts.

Clinicians have relied traditionally on interviews with the "client," that is, the child or adolescent, and/or informants, such as parents, or less frequently, teachers, to describe a particular youth's problems. Ideally, judgments to make diagnostic assessments should utilize a variety of data sources and assess functioning on emotional, relational, and social levels, as well as specific symptom levels (American Psychiatric Association, 1987).

Since the 1970s a growing number of clinicians have attempted to improve the reliability of clinical diagnoses by employing standardized interview instruments as part of intake procedures. In their review of five interview schedules used with parents and youths, Gutterman, O'Brien and Young (1987) note problems regarding the reliability of the instruments and the validity of the diagnostic categories that emerge from them.

The DSM-III-R has attempted to partially address the issue of reliability by providing a list of critical items from which clinicians choose to make a diagnosis. For example, a youth must have engaged in 3 of 13 assorted delinquent, aggressive, and status offense items within the past 6 months to be considered a candidate for a diagnosis of "conduct disorder." Many of the items can be found in the Achenbach CBCL checklist, but there are no rules provided for why 3 or more items should be considered evidence of a disorder. Instead, clinicians are asked to assess other associated features: use of tobacco, liquor or drugs; sexual behavior; age at onset; degree of impairment; complications; and predisposing factors (American Psychiatric Association, pp. 53–54) to support the diagnosis. In contrast to the DSM-III-R approach, the studies reported by Achenbach and Edelbrock (1983) and Achenbach, Conners, Quay, Verhulst, and Howell (1989) reveal that an aggressive behavior syndrome is distinguishable from a delinquent behavior syndrome, and should not be automatically combined in one conduct disorder. Similar conclusions are reached by Lewis, Lewis, Unger, and Goldman (1984) from their study of 114 psychiatrically hospitalized adolescents in two hospitals where they compared youths who had been diagnosed with conduct disorders versus those who had other diagnoses. They found that adolescents diagnosed with conduct disorder have a multiplicity of symptoms of other psychiatric disorders, and there were no major symptomatic differences between the conduct disorder and non-conduct disorder groups. Only violence distinguished adolescents ever diagnosed as having conduct disorder from other adolescents. But violence alone is not a valid diagnostically distinguishing characteristic because it is a nonspecific symptom and may be present in varying degrees in a number of other syndromes, such as schizophrenia, manic-depression, and epilepsy. They conclude that the conduct disorder diagnosis tends to obscure other potentially treatable psychopathology, and they recommend that violent behaviors be eliminated explicitly from the criteria for conduct disorder.

The field of clinical diagnostics is in a state of scientific flux, even though insurance companies continue to rely on DSM-III-R categories. In the area of diagnosis of children and adolescents, validity and reliability of clinical disorders have proven to be even more difficult to ascertain than in the adult population. Nonetheless, and to their credit, researchers in a variety of disciplines struggle to obtain reliable and valid indicators of real emotional distress, and attempt to explore potentially concurrent problematic behaviors, such as smoking, drinking, drug use, delinquency, and aggression.

Evidence of Multiple Problems of Youths[1]

Adolescents with multiple problems, including mental health, substance abuse and delinquency, have been shown to be intractable in treatment and at high risk for continued problem behaviors as adults. Adolescents with multiple problem syndromes are often treated in service systems which emphasize one facet of the problem. As Hawkins (1985) has said: "Agency labels and boundaries become meaningless when we realize that mental health agencies, substance abuse programs, the criminal justice system, and schools are all dealing with the same individuals" (p. 4).

Delinquency and Mental Health Problems

Studies on the evidence of psychiatric disorders among delinquent populations have relied almost exclusively on the DSM-III-R diagnostic instrument. This is unfortunate because the instrument, as we will show in Chapter 3, is overly inclusive and may obfuscate important distinctions in the problems of youths.

Using the DSM-III-R tools, several researchers have revealed that many delinquent youths meet standards for mental disorders, particularly for the diagnosis "conduct disorder." For example, one study by Adam, Kushani, and Shultz (1991) applied DSM-III and

[1]This section of the chapter was researched and written by Fred Rasmussen, research assistant and doctoral candidate in sociology at Rutgers University, under a National Institute of Mental Health grant (#MH 43450–05) awarded to Rutgers University's Institute for Health, Health Care Policy and Aging Research.

DSM-III-R diagnostic criteria in evaluating 100 juvenile justice center residents. Using the DSM-III criteria, 99% of the subjects met the diagnostic requirements for conduct disorder. When the somewhat more stringent DSM-III-R standards were applied, 86% of the subjects met the conduct disorder diagnostic criteria.

McManus (1984) found that 90% of male and female seriously delinquent incarcerated adolescents (N=71), who were evaluated for psychopathology, were assigned a DSM-III diagnosis of conduct disorder. Male delinquents were significantly more likely to be assigned an aggressive conduct disorder diagnosis, but no more likely than females to receive an undersocialized diagnosis. If the adult diagnostic category of antisocial personality disorder were applied to this group of adolescents, 54% of the delinquent sample studied would meet the DSM-III diagnostic criteria, including 45% of the females.

In a study of committed female juvenile offenders, a rarely analyzed population, all of the subjects were diagnosed with conduct disorder according to DSM-III criteria. Although the sample was very small (N=15), no relationship was noted between the conduct disorder diagnosis, other types of psychopathology present, or the types of offenses committed by the subjects (Meyers, 1990).

A number of studies report the similarities in psychopathology between delinquent and psychiatric treatment populations. Shanok (1983) identifies similarly severe psychopathology in a sample of court remanded delinquent (N=29) and nondelinquent (N=25) adolescent boys admitted to a public hospital psychiatric inpatient program. The delinquent patients were somewhat more violent than the nondelinquents, with twice as many engaging in aggressive acts, but socioeconomic and family background factors were similar.

Cohen, Parmalee, Irwin, Weisz, Howard, Purcell & Gest (1990) report similar findings in a comparison of sample groups of adolescents from an inpatient program at a state-operated psychiatric hospital (N=32) and from a state-operated juvenile corrections facility (N=36). Using the Child Behavior Checklist (CBCL, Achenbach & Edelbrock, 1983), the authors found no significant difference between the two groups. Only race differentiated the groups, with blacks overrepresented in the corrections sample. Further analysis, however, indicated that the white adolescents in the corrections groups had higher problem behavior scores, while the blacks in the corrections group had lower problem behavior scores. The white adolescents in the corrections group also scored higher on externalizing and internalizing scales, suggesting that they may have had serious behavioral and emotional difficulties. The issue of race emerges as a critical factor in this study, and questions arise regarding the differential placement of adolescents based on race.

Lewis (1980) identifies race as the most powerful factor distinguishing two groups of adolescents—one from a correctional school (N=63), and the other from an inpatient unit of a state psychiatric hospital (N=35). Psychiatric symptoms reported in the two groups were similar, but a significantly greater proportion of black adolescents were present in the correctional group. Girls were also more likely to be hospitalized and boys were more likely to be incarcerated.

In a more recent study, however, Kaplan and Busner (1992) report that there was no racial bias in the 1988 admissions to the child and adolescent public mental health system (N=1,474) or correctional facilities (N=1,405) in the state of New York. Even though the data presented in this study indicate that whites comprised 62% of the mental health admissions and only 23% of the admissions were blacks, while 56% of the corrections admissions were blacks and 28% percent were whites, the authors contend that there was no racial bias because the two systems functioned as independent entities. They argue that the two systems have different points of entry, and only a very modest proportion of cases (17%) are referred by the courts to the mental health system. The authors conclude that because of the different points of entry and the autonomy of the two systems, the disproportionate number of blacks in the juvenile justice system does not imply racial bias on the part of the mental health system. This analysis does not address fully the potentially similar symptoms of psychopathology present in the two groups, nor does it attempt to explain the larger proportion of blacks in the juvenile justice system.

Several of the studies reviewed above suffer from relatively small sample size, and as a result, findings of no difference in psychiatric symptomology between juvenile justice and psychiatric populations may be an artifact of the statistical power of the analyses. An additional study with larger samples by Westendorp et al. (1986), however, also analyzes variables which differentiate placement of adolescents into juvenile justice and mental health systems. Consecutive admissions to six mental health treatment programs in a 12-county catchment area (N=221) and consecutive placements in various programs by the juvenile court (N=55) were compared.

Placement in both systems represented the entire range of programs available from the most to least restrictive.

Results of this analysis show that the measurements of psychopathology were of little overall value in differentiating these two groups of adolescents, indicating strong similarities in the prevalence of mental illness within the two samples. Subject and family demographic variables were more discriminating between the two groups. Race, gender, and marital history of parents were the strongest predictors of placement in one of the two systems. Race differences reflected the greater number of black adolescents in the juvenile justice system, and gender differences mirrored the relative absence of girls in the juvenile justice group. The preponderance of adolescents in the mental health group with intact families consisting of two married and never divorced parents contrasted with the higher incidence of divorced/single parent families in the juvenile justice groups.

These findings focus attention on the importance of including juvenile justice system populations in the overall assessment of the magnitude of child and adolescent mental health problems.

Risks of Problems

Research on factors that put youths at risk for delinquency, aggression and psychological problems has been conducted within different disciplines, most notably, criminology (delinquency and aggression) and mental health (internal, psychological and conduct disorders/externalizing problems). Within the field of criminology, Hirschi's theory of social control (1969) and Jessor and Jessor's theory of the generality of deviance (1977) have produced research suggesting the causal links to delinquency. In mental health, psychodynamic and child developmental psychological theories have produced research on causation of mental health problems.

Hirschi's (1969) theory of social control, as was discussed in Chapter 1, argues that youths are prevented from engaging in delinquent activities as a function of their bonds with conventional persons and social institutions. Until recently an array of self-report studies provided empirical support for Hirschi's theoretical orientation, but these studies were all conducted with cross-sectional samples (i.e., samples studied at one point in time, rather than over a period of time). Using large-scale, longitudinal data, The National Youth

Study (NYS) has been unable to demonstrate the potency of parental attachment, goal commitment, and involvement in conventional activities on delinquent behaviors. Elliott and his colleagues were only able to obtain significant results for measures of moral beliefs about breaking the law and association with delinquent peers (Elliott, Huizinga, & Menard, 1989). When a general measure of delinquency was used in the National Youth Study, none of Hirschi's variables were capable of accounting for any of the variability in problem behaviors; instead, prior delinquency, association with delinquent peers, and male gender were the only variables that emerged in a multivariate analysis.

Because of the rich and unique data offered by the National Youth Study, several researchers have reanalyzed the data. In one reanalysis, Agnew (1991) responded to criticisms made by Hirschi regarding Elliott et al.'s findings. Improving on the methods of Elliott et al. (1989), Agnew (1991) retested the Hirschi model by: 1) selecting the most reliable and valid measures pertaining to the four "bond" dimensions of control theory; 2) employing contemporaneous, rather than lagged, statistical analyses; and 3) correcting any statistical errors associated with each measurement. The results of this careful reanalysis confirmed the original major conclusions of Elliott and his colleagues: "next to prior delinquency, association with delinquent peers is the best predictor of delinquency" (Agnew, 1991, p. 148).

The second major reanalysis of the National Youth Study made new distinctions on the variable to be explained, that is the measure of serious delinquency. Smith, Visher, and Jarjoura (1991) proposed that delinquent behavior on twelve items be assessed from three perspectives: 1) whether youths participated in delinquent behavior at any time period, regardless of the number of events or the frequency of offending; 2) the frequency of engaging in one or more of the twelve behavior items regardless of the time period; and 3) the persistence of the behaviors over three distinct annual time periods. Using statistical methods different than those used by Elliott and his colleagues, Smith's group found that four variables were likely to account for variability in all three types of serious delinquency—participation, frequency, and persistence: 1) male gender; 2) association with delinquent peers; 3) use of alcohol; and 4) moral beliefs against breaking the law.

The results of all of the above analyses on the National Youth Study provide evidence that association with delinquent peers is the strongest risk factor associated with delinquency (aside from prior delinquent involvement). Moral belief also is somewhat involved in the risk for delinquency, but this is the only social control variable that has emerged in the varied analyses of the National Youth Study data. On the basis of these results, as well as the persistent occurrence of association with delinquent peers in many other studies, criminologists and sociologists are now rediscovering the significance of "differential association" with conventional and/or deviant persons and differential learning environments (first advanced by Sutherland in 1947, as well as Sutherland and Cressey, 1955 and then updated by Burgess and Akers, 1966). Given the continued importance of the peer variable in past and recent studies, systematic attention needs to be paid to the consequences of hanging out with bad peers in research on youths engaging in problem behaviors.

While research using the National Youth Study data base has been useful in expanding our understanding of delinquent-type behaviors, there is a growing awareness that focusing primarily on social control bonding variables, peer associations, and other traditional sociological variables may be restricting. Researchers from other disciplines have contributed studies that focus on inappropriate or inadequate parenting, family interaction patterns, developmental stresses of pre-adolescence and adolescence, affective and other psychological disorders, and dispositions towards risks of delinquency (Quay, 1965; Jessor and Jessor, 1977; Patterson, Chamberlain, and Reid, 1982; Jessor, 1987; Loeber, 1988; Institute of Medicine, 1989; Zill and Schoenborn, 1990; Avison and MacAlpine, 1992; and Gore, Aseltine and Colten, 1992).

Jessor (1987) has posited that the personality and perceived environment systems always provide the strongest associations with problem behaviors, and that they are relatively equal in strength. He suggests that deviant behaviors may be part of a "behavior system," whereby one set of deviant problems make it more likely that the other deviant actions will occur. This "behavior system" is influenced by personality system variables and the perceived environmental system that provides social support and controls. These two systems are, in turn, influenced by socialization and the demographic and social structure. Each of the "systems" can yield increases or decreases in psychosocial risk factors for occurrence of problem behaviors.

There is uncertainty whether parent-reports would follow the same theoretical predictions. In areas of uncertainty, it is useful to balance research guided by theory, and research guided by a search for new or distinctive information. Jessor's theory has provided sufficiently provocative empirical results to justify attention to it in our data set of parents of urban youths. Thus, we adapt the theoretical orientation provided by Jessor and categorize all parental responses into three primary "risk categories": 1) attributions of the adolescent's responsibility and the personal problem (indicators of the perceived "personality system"); 2) attributions of socialization responsibility (indicators of the family system); and 3) attributions regarding the perceived environment (indicators of influences outside the home).

While Jessor's work has expanded how investigators view the nature of deviance, it has not forwarded a deep understanding of the relationship between internal, psychological problems and deviance. Mental health researchers, coming from a different vantage point, have not addressed this relationship fully either. But, some research does exist to suggest that there are different risks involved in internalizing disorders (such as depression, anxiety) and externalizing disorders (such as delinquency, aggression). Williams, Anderson, McGee, and Silva (1990), in an analysis of sample data from a cohort study of 1,037 children born in Dunedin, New Zealand between April 1, 1972 and March 31, 1973 interviewed biannually since age 3, finds that different risks are involved in internalizing, externalizing, and multiple disorders. The following risk factors predicted behavioral and emotional disorders: being a boy and the child of a mother with depression; having reading difficulties; and solo motherhood, and marital changes (weak predictors). Externalizing and multiple disorders were more common among boys, and internalizing disorders were more common among girls. Mother's depression predicted internalizing disorders, while low IQ predicted externalizing and multiple disorders. Cumulative disadvantage was related to behavioral disorder and girls in particular may be susceptible to adverse family background factors.

The above research strongly suggests two directions for study. One is that research needs to focus on whether the coexistence of internal, psychological problems is most likely to occur with aggressive or delinquent behaviors. The other is that research must address whether internal, psychological problems are subject to the same influences as legal delinquency or non-delinquent aggression.

An understanding of the structure of problems, and a delineation of risk factors associated with them, can provide the foundations for more precise psychosocial theories of problems of youths (Institute of Medicine, 1989).

Help-seeking

In 1986, 2,967 mental health organizations, or 62% of all mental health organizations in the United States, including territories, offered psychiatric services (Sunshine, Witkin, Atay, & Manderschied, 1986). Over one-half million children and adolescents received outpatient services in that year (Pottick, Hunsell, Gaboda & Gutterman, 1993). Service delivery is based on two processes: service provision and service utilization. There is evidence that minority populations are more likely to experience problems of access to care than other groups, and they encounter institutional, cultural, language, and economic barriers (Sue, 1977; 1988), although recent empirical studies show that the situation is improving (O'Sullivan, Peterson, Cox, & Kurkeby, 1989; Sue, Fujino, Hu, Takeuchi, & Zane, 1991; Wu & Windle, 1980). The utilization of services by minority populations, especially minority youths, is on the national policy agenda in order to ameliorate the problems of differential access to services and promote better mental health.

The theory of help-seeking which focuses on the conditions under which individuals are likely to look for both informal and formal help for themselves is a framework that has received a great deal of attention in the medical field, especially in relation to adults. The models, described below, suffer from two limitations in relation to children. First, as we pointed out in Chapter 1, children rarely seek help for themselves. Rather, parents serve as third-party help-seekers. Models of help-seeking assume first-party help-seeking. Second, help, especially for children, is sometimes imposed, rather than sought after. Under these conditions, parents are reluctant, involuntary help-seekers in behalf of their children. The models assume voluntary help-seeking. Research on help-seeking for children and adolescents must take these situations into account in order to fully understand and explain differential help-seeking and utilization. While we were able to find research on children's reactions to aid (Eisenberg, 1983; Shell & Eisenberg, 1992), we were unable to uncover research explicitly investigating the differential processes of parental help-seeking for different problem behaviors of children and adolescents. It is possible that different problems lead to different strategies for coping, and requests by parents for solutions. Knowledge of different help-seeking patterns will help us better understand utilization outcomes in order to better provide services.

The model of help-seeking, accounting for involuntary adolescents whose parents seek help for them, is presented below.

Models of Help-seeking

Gross and McMullen (1983), building on the work of Piliavin (1972), depict the help-seeking process as a model of phased decision-making activities. The proposed sequence of major decision stages are as follows:

1. Problem awareness;

2. Assessment of the problem as normal or not;

3. Assessment of the importance of the problem;

4. Initiation of efforts at self-help;

5. Search for help from intimates, professional contacts, and others;

6. Selection of outside helper.

While the authors are aware that it is unlikely that help-seekers follow this quasi-rational sequence in an exact, serial, fashion, the distinctions are analytically useful and may capture the kinds of early decisions that must be resolved before subsequent actions can be carried out. The logic of the model suggests that parents must first be aware that a problem exists. Without accepting the existence of a problem, why begin a search for remediation? However, before efforts are expended on coping with the problem, parents may very well ask whether the problem is a normal occurrence. If it is conceived as a normal part of development, for example, there may be no felt need or desire to pursue the issue; the problem can be ignored.

From a parent's perspective, if the adolescent's problem is defined as non-normal, then the issue of its relative importance emerges. Compared to other concerns, is this problem sufficiently important or relevant to warrant further action? If so, then a variety of self-initiated parental behaviors can be attempted, such as advising, remonstrating, or a manipulation of rewards and punishments. If these efforts are successful, then there may be little or no perceived need to work any further on the problem. In the event that change is not forthcoming, then parents may voluntarily begin to secure the advice, counsel, and support of family members, friends, professional contacts, or others. These intimate and formal contacts may, in turn, provide suggestions on seeking new forms of help.

As we discussed, the help-seeking model is based on a voluntary search for solving the problems presented by youths. But this assumption leaves out the likely possibility that police, teachers, or child welfare agencies may bring problems to the attention of parents, and that parents may be required to respond to a formal agency referral or summons.

Help-seeking and Attributions

Because Americans generally value independence over dependence, taking help can be perceived as an undesirable behavior. For parents of adolescents with problems, accepting help may take on many meanings: it may embarrass them with relatives or friends, or even jeopardize their standing in a community. It may make them question their competence to carry out the parenting role. Taking help is a type of moral issue, at the center of which is the concept of responsibility (Shaver, 1985). All moral issues attempt to allocate responsibility. Theory on giving and receiving help, as a function of responsibility, has been developed in the field of social psychology by Brickman et al. (1982). In their seminal article published in the *American Psychologist* in 1982, Brickman and his colleagues posit that we can determine the kind of help that is preferred if we know how "actors" (i.e., help-seekers) allocate responsibility for causes and solutions to problems. The model proposes that the self can accept a high degree of responsibility or a low degree of responsibility for the cause or the solution. The differential allocation of responsibility by actors for causes and solutions are hypothesized to lead to four types of coping efforts:

1. A *moral* type of coping requires a great amount of personal striving and use of personal will by the actors. It is activated when responsibility for both causing and solving the problem is attributed to the actor;

2. A *compensatory* type of coping requires effort and conscientiousness by actors to work on the problem if others also provide extra resources or a strong learning environment. It is activated when actors believe they have little responsibility for causing the problem, but simultaneously do accept responsibility for solving it.

3. An *enlightenment* type of coping requires outside authorities to exercise discipline in helping with the problem. It is activated when actors believe they are responsible for causing their problem, but are unable or unwilling to take responsibility for solving it;

4. A *medical* type of coping requires experts to tell actors what to do as part of a treatment plan. It is activated when actors believe they are not responsible for causing their problem and are also not responsible for solving it (Brickman et al., 1982).

While a degree of empirical support has been reported in the social psychological literature, there has not been a test of the proposed models with parents as third party help-seekers (Depaulo, Nadler, and Fisher, 1983) or with parents who involuntarily participate in the human service delivery system. The present study offers a unique opportunity to test the utility of the ideas set forth by Brickman and his associates. To our knowledge, there is no existing literature about parental attributions of responsibility as they relate to specific coping efforts. Knowing more about parent attributions should enable us to expand our understanding of the role of parents as third party help-seekers for their children's problems. Research needs to address how parents attribute responsibility for their adolescents' problems, how it may influence the way they conduct themselves as third-party help-seekers, and how it may influence their sons or daughters towards becoming cooperative clients of an agency. A fuller knowledge about coping preferences could contribute to better practice theory, as well as to a social science paradigm about helping and coping with the problems presented by youths.

The chapters to follow attempt to increase our understanding of diagnostic nosology and co-morbidity of problems of urban youths, as well as third-party help-seeking in urban service delivery environments. This information should be of interest to policy planners, clinicians, researchers and the lay public in efforts to improve delivery of services to urban youths in trouble.

3

The Problems

INTERVIEWER: *What is there about the*
main problem that particularly concerns you—
Could you tell me why you are concerned?

I'm concerned about his lying and cheating because I was always told a liar be-
comes a thief, and I really want it to stop before it reaches that far.

Mother of 15-year-old boy

His anger is what troubles me the most. I don't know why it exists, but I know it is
there. He doesn't talk about it with me....There are so many things about his behav-
ior that I don't understand.

Mother of 16-year-old boy

She tried to kill herself three years ago. I just found out about it recently. She tried
again October 23. The next time she might succeed.

Mother of 16-year-old girl

This chapter answers one major question. What are the patterns of problems described by the parents of these youths? Several strategies are used to answer this question. First, we compare our sample of predominantly black youths with the clinical and non-clinical samples of predominantly white youths described by Achenbach et al. (1983, 1987). Then, we reanalyze the CBCL to clarify the relationships between delinquency, aggression and internal, psychological problems for both boys and girls. We develop a four-group typology of youths: those who are high on delinquency and high on aggression; those who are high on delinquency and low on aggression (pure delinquents); those who are high on aggression and low on delinquency (pure aggressives); and those who are low on delinquency and low on aggression. How youths with these combinations of problems do in terms of internal, psychological problems is then described. Additionally, we look at the differences between the problems of youths referred to the specialty mental health system and the court-referred family crisis intervention unit (FCIU) agencies. Finally, we explore the similarities and differences between the patterns of behavior among our inner-city youths and patterns identified in other national studies using both youth self-reports and parent reports.

Mean Scores of ECYS and Achenbach Clinic Samples

In order to compare the range and types of behavioral problems exhibited by the ECYS sample, parent reports were first scored by using Achenbach's scoring procedures (see Appendix B). The methods generate three distinct types of scores: 1) a total behavior score; 2) a specific factor or scale score; and 3) a general internal and external score. The total behavior score uses the 118 specific items plus one general "any other problem" item. Each of the 119 items is scored as "not true" (0); "somewhat or sometimes true" (1); or "very true or often true" (2). The results are added together for a final score. The procedures are the same for all ages and sexes, and do not distinguish between types of behaviors. It is meant to be a general measure of total numbers of behavior problems that is weighted for frequency of occurrence. The rationale for combining the scales is made on the basis of moderate to high intercorrelations of specific scale scores, despite the fact that they are independent.

The specific factor or scale score relies on the results of factor analyses conducted for each sex, according to the age groups of 4–5, 6–11, and 12-16. The factor analysis is conducted by first scoring each of the 118 items as having occurred or not; the frequency distinction between sometimes and often is deliberately ignored. The dichotomous scored items (i.e., 0 vs. 1 or 2) are then entered into a statistical factor analysis that identifies items sharing a sufficient commonality to distinguish them from other groupings. Achenbach uses a decision rule that items must reach a factor loading of at least .30 to be included in the factor. A factor is a hypothetical construct that can best be described by the items that share a high proportion of the variance of this commonality. Illustratively, delinquency is an idea or construct that could refer to many specific legal violations. But in the Achenbach factor analysis, it was found that nonlegal, as well as legal, forms of deviance were statistically associated and formed a reliable factor. The empirically derived factor was labeled "delinquency" in order to capture the dominant content of the specific items. Once the items are categorized for each factor they are scored, using the frequency weights of 0, 1, or 2. Duplicate scoring of items is permitted for different specific scales, as long as there are no duplicates within the scale. Each sex, according to the Achenbach procedures, yields distinct factors and specific factor scale scores.

The internal and external factor scoring is based on the results of a second-order factor analysis for each sex. Here, the frequency scores of each item in each specific scale is subjected to a new factor analysis in order to determine if there is any commonality between scales. For each age and sex group, the specific scales are entered into the new factor analysis to determine whether the weighted scores of the scales behave in a common manner. Achenbach obtained second-order factors that successfully group most of the scale scores into two distinct dimensions: internal and external. Internal scores are behaviors and feelings that refer to fearful, inhibited, or "over controlled" items. External scores refer to aggressive, antisocial or "under controlled" behaviors. Scales that could not be statistically distinguished as internal or external are labeled as "mixed." Items are scored as 0, 1, 2 on internal, external, or mixed dimensions. Duplication of items is permitted between dimensions in order to conduct the second-order factor analysis. The resultant factors contain duplication of items.

All youths in our study are scored using each of Achenbach's three scoring procedures. Table 3–1 compares Achenbach's clinical youths, aged 12–16 years, with ours on scores for total behaviors, and specific, and second-order factors. If we first examine the bottom line of part A, the total mean scores of ECYS and Achenbach clinical boys are presented. The ECYS boys receive a total mean score of 54.8, whereas the Achenbach clinical sample receive a score of 53.1. This difference is not statistically significant. However, both sample scores are significantly different from Achenbach's "non-clinical" sample of boys who score only 17.5 (table not shown). The ECYS and clinical samples could have been drawn from a similar population of youths with behavior and emotional problems, since their total scores are statistically similar. Similarly, the difference between the ECYS total mean score for girls (60.5) and the Achenbach total mean score for clinical girls (55.8) is not statistically significant; again they could have been drawn from similar populations. The results indicate that the total mean number of problem behaviors identified on the CBCL is comparable for both boys and girls in the ECYS sample of Newark youths and other clinical samples of youths residing in diverse communities. This result is noteworthy since the ECYS sample is 78% black, whereas Achenbach's clinical sample is approximately 80% white.

Differences between the two samples do, however, emerge when specific scale scores are compared. Table 3–1 presents a comparison of the Achenbach (ACH) clinical sample raw score results reported in the *Manual*, and the ECYS findings, by scale types for each sex. For boys, Achenbach's factor analysis yielded 9 factors, using 88 of the original 118 specific items; the girls yielded 8 factors, using 90 specific items. In Table 3–1 each of the factors are labeled according to the names provided by Achenbach; he created the names to fit the strongest items found within each factor. Following Achenbach, ECYS youth are scored for each item associated with a specific factor as 0, 1, 2; the results for each respondent are summed to allocate a scale score. For example, the first male factor, somatic, uses 15 items to arrive at an ECYS sample mean score of 3.9 compared to an ACH clinic mean score of 4.5. When subjected to a T test comparison of means (using the published standard deviation and the ECYS deviation), the result is statistically nonsignificant.

For the boys, 3 of the 9 scale scores yield statistically significant results—scale numbers 5, 6, and 7. Scale 5 is associated with an "internal" dimension of behavior. Items included in scale 5 include: bragging and boasting; can't get his/her mind off certain thoughts; daydreams; fears might do something bad; repeats certain acts over and over; and four other items. Achenbach refers to this combination of items as "obsessive-compulsive"; it is also included in the broader "internal factor," since the reported behaviors and feelings refer to "fearful, inhibited, overcontrolled" items and this scale shared a common variance with other scales (1 through 5).

Scale 6, "hostile-withdrawn" behavior, refers to such items as: acts too young for his/her age; complains of loneliness; destroys his/her own things; destroys things belonging to his/her family or other

Table 3.1 Comparison of Achenbach Clinical Sample and Essex County Youth Study Raw Scores, By Scale Types for Each Sex[a]

A. BOYS

Scale Type Name	ECYS Mean (N=134)	Clinical Ach Mean (N=250)	Probability Level
1. Somatic	3.9	4.5	NS
2. Schizoid	3.0	3.0	NS
3. Uncommunicative	9.5	9.1	NS
4. Immature	3.1	3.1	NS
5. Obsessive–Compulsive	5.2	4.4	<.02
6. Hostile–Withdrawn	6.5	8.0	<.01
7. Delinquency	8.8	6.6	<.002
8. Aggressive	15.8	16.1	NS
9. Hyperactive	9.0	9.0	NS
Internal (Scales 1–5)	22.2	21.4	NS
External (Scales 7–9)	28.3	26.5	NS
Total Score (All Items)	54.8	53.1	NS

B. GIRLS

Scale Type Name	ECYS Mean (N=92)	Clinical Ach Mean (N=250)	Probability Level
1. Anxious–Obsessive	10.2	11.7	<.05
2. Somatic–Compulsive	2.0	2.9	<.02
3. Schizoid	3.1	2.7	NS
4. Depressed–Withdrawn	9.4	9.4	NS
5. Immature–Hyperactive	8.2	7.2	NS
6. Delinquent	13.3	11.5	<.02
7. Aggressive	17.5	15.5	NS
8. Cruel	4.4	4.0	NS
Internal (Scales 1–4)	22.7	24.4	NS
External (Scales 6–8)	30.9	26.9	<.02
Total Scores (All Items)	60.5	55.8	NS

[a]Each comparison is based on a T test of means, using the standard deviations associated with each measure for each sample.

children, and other related items. On a second order factor analysis that included all 9 male factors, scale 6 was labeled a "mixed" factor because it loaded equally well on being grouped with internal scales 1–5 or external scales 7–9 (i.e., items referring to aggressive, antisocial, or undercontrolled behavior). Scale 7, "delinquent" behavior, refers to a total of 13 items that include: destroys own things and things belonging to others; disobedient at school; lies; steals; and truants.

While the ECYS males are significantly lower on the hostile-withdrawn factor, and higher on the obsessive and delinquent factors, they do not differ statistically on the more general second order factor groupings. Scales 1–5 are included in the internal dimension; scoring of all the items included in these scales (without duplication) yielded a mean score of 22.2 for ECYS boys and 21.4 for ACH clinical males. This is an insignificant difference. The difference on the external dimension score is also not significant. We can conclude that the ECYS boys exhibit a similar range of both internal and external problems when compared to the ACH clinical order, despite the sharp difference in ethnicity/race.

The ECYS girls score significantly lower on the first two internal scales, "anxious–obsessive" and "somatic-compulsive," but the total internal dimension score (for the combined scales 1–4) is not statistically different from the ACH clinical females. Anxious-obsessive behaviors by girls refer to the 19 items that include: can't get his/her mind off of certain thoughts; complains of loneliness; cries a lot; easily jealous; and fears certain animals, situations, or places. The somatic-compulsive scale refers to 8 items that include: fears going to school; feels dizzy; has aches or pains; and other symptoms without known medical causes.

The ECYS girls are statistically higher on the delinquent scale (13.3 to 11.5). While the scores on the other external scales (i.e., aggressive and cruel) are not statistically significant, the cumulative higher mean score that results from combining the scale items comprising the external dimension yields a difference that is statistically different (30.9 to 26.9). Because of the difference on a summary external scale, but not on the internal scale, we can conclude that the ECYS girls have stronger differences with their Achenbach clinical peers on external behaviors than do the ECYS boys. However, ECYS boys and girls display scores on general internal problems that make them indistinguishable from the clinical baseline youth used by Achenbach.

High Cut-off Scores of ECYS and Achenbach Clinic Samples

Besides comparing the ECYS samples by their mean scores on the factors obtained by Achenbach, it is also possible to assess the percent of youth that score above a specific cut-off score. For each specific factor, as described earlier, Achenbach chose the score that emerged as the "cut-off" at or above the 98th percentile for each clinical sex/age group. The 98th percentile was chosen as the "norm" because it approximates two standard deviations above the mean and serves as an empirical, non-judgmental, means for choosing a "serious" score (Achenbach and Edelbrock, 1983, p. 64). For the broader scales of total behavior score, and internal and external scores, he uses the 90th percentile because the number of items are larger.

Table 3–2 depicts the percent of each sex scoring above the chosen norm for two Achenbach sample groups (normal and clinical) and two ECYS sample groups (mental health and family crisis). By breaking the ECYS into two groups, it can be determined whether ECYS youth differ by referral system, as well as with each of the Achenbach samples.

The differences between the Achenbach "non-clinical" sample and the other samples are consistently large for each scale for both sexes. The differences with the normal sample are all statistically significant. Differences with the normal sample appear to be cumulative, since the percent of ACH clinical and ECYS males scoring above the total cutoff score is 71%, 61.9%, and 74.3%, respectively, compared to only 10% for the non-clinical sample. Comparable results for total scores occur for the females.

There are no statistically significant differences between the Achenbach clinical sample and the ECYS mental health samples for each of the scale types, regardless of sex. However, there are three significant differences between the male Achenbach clinical and ECYS family crisis samples. ECYS family crisis males score significantly higher on the obsessive-compulsive and delinquency scales; they are significantly lower on the hostile-withdrawn scale. These three scales are the same ones that emerged in our first comparison of ACH clinical and ECYS boys. An extra asterisk has been added for the male delinquency scale because there also exists a significant difference between the ECYS mental health and family crisis samples. The family crisis males are clearly higher on the delinquency scale than all of the other male clinic sample groups—60.2% compared to 35% and 43.9% for the Achenbach and ECYS mental health samples,

Table 3.2 Percent Youth Scoring Above Cutoff Scores by Achenbach Normal and Clinical Samples and ECYS Samples, for Each Sex

Males 12–16

| | A. Achenbach Samples | | B. ECYS Samples | |
Scale Type Name	Normal (N=250)	Clinical (N=250)	M. Health (N=21)	Fam. Crisis (N=113)
1. Somatic	2.0%	20.0%	19.0%	14.2%
2. Schizoid	2.0	16.0	23.8	14.2
3. Uncommunicative	2.0	20.0	23.8	21.2
4. Immature	3.0	23.0	33.3	26.5
5. Obsessive–Compulsive	2.0	22.0	23.8	31.0*
6. Hostile–Withdrawn	2.0	33.0	33.3	24.8*
7. Delinquency	3.0	35.0	43.9	60.2**
8. Aggressive	4.0	26.0	14.3	22.1
9. Hyperactive	4.0	46.0	42.9	46.9
Internal (Scales 1–5)	10.0	62.0	52.4	68.1
External (Scales 7–9)	9.0	66.0	52.8	73.5
Total Score (All Items)	10.0	71.0	61.9	74.3

Table 3.2 (Continued)

	Females 12–16				
	A. Achenbach Samples			B. ECYS Samples	
Scale Type Name	Normal (N=250)	Clinical (N=250)	M. Health (N=21)	Fam. Crisis (N=71)	
1. Anxious	2.0 %	35.0	23.8%	19.7 %*	
2. Somatic–Compulsive	3.0	36.0	29.6	19.7*	
3. Schizoid	2.0	21.0	21.0	23.9	
4. Depressed–Withdrawn	2.0	43.0	43.0	35.2	
5. Immature–Hyperactive	2.0	37.0	37.0	45.1	
6. Delinquency	2.0	41.0	41.0	62.0 **	
7. Aggressive	2.0	27.0	27.0	31.0	
8. Cruel	1.0	35.0	35.0	46.5	
Internal (Scales 1–4)	5.0	58.0	47.6	46.5	
External (Scales 6–8)	4.0	52.0	38.1	66.2*	
Total Score (All Items)	10.0	74.0	71.4	77.5	

*N<.05 between Achenbach clinical and ECYS Family Crisis Samples, using T tests of proportions.
**N<.05 between Achenbach clinical and ECYS Family Crisis Samples, and between Mental Health and Family Crisis using T tests of proportions.

respectively. The ECYS boys, however, do not differ from the other
five clinical samples on the summary scores of internal or external
behaviors.

The females yield more differences than males. On two internal
type scales—anxious/obsessive and somatic—ECYS females score
significantly lower than the Achenbach clinical females. On one external type scale, delinquency, the ECYS females are significantly
higher. Similar to the boys, the ECYS family crisis females also score
significantly higher on the delinquency scale than the ECYS mental
health females. The cumulative external score (based on scales 6–8)
is also significantly higher for ECYS family crisis females when
compared to the Achenbach clinical sample of females. In this respect, they differ from the male comparisons. However, the cumulative internal score is the same for ECYS girls and the other two
clinical samples.

The analysis of Table 3–2 reaffirms that the nonclinical samples are
strikingly different from the ACH clinical or the ECYS samples, regardless of sex or ethnicity/race. The data also indicate that there are
no statistical differences between the ACH clinical and ECYS mental
health subsamples, regardless of sex or ethnicity/race. Any difference between the ACH clinical and the ECYS sample can be attributed to the youth associated with referrals to the family crisis center;
and this finding holds for both sexes. The strongest differences between the ECYS family crisis subsample and the ACH clinical sample are for the delinquency scales, for both sexes. This result
highlights the fact that the ECYS family crisis subsample is indeed a
more delinquent group than the clinical samples. The differences
might be expected, since a significant number of ECYS parents reported talking to the police prior to attending the local family crisis
agency, and there is a correlation of about .30 between talking to the
police and a high score on the ECYS delinquency scale. The differences on the other scales may be due to the unique differences between the ECYS and ACH clinical samples on specific types of
internal problems.

Gender-Neutral Behavior Scales

The procedures used by Achenbach to measure problem behaviors
has many advantages. However, there are also some disadvantages:

1. The scores for each sex are separate, and produce sex-specific scales that cannot be combined or compared;

2. The delinquency scores include an item relating to association with bad peers, which prevents an examination of peer relationships as an explanatory variable;

3. The scores for girls include an item relating to lack of guilt, which prevents the examination of psychopathic behavior as an explanatory variable;

4. The scores reflect a lack of sensitivity to legal distinctions between items;

5. The scores permit duplication of items in different factors.

Each point will be discussed briefly. Then, we will present the details of our analysis and our findings.

1. *Scoring each Sex Separately*—From the very outset of the reports on the CBCL, Achenbach has kept males and females distinct in computing factor analyses. While this approach may have advantages for clinicians, it appears premature for researchers to proceed in this fashion. There is no *a priori* reason why we should automatically assume that the behavior problems of males and females will be different at all ages, for all samples. There appears to be distinct advantages in finding those items common to both sexes and scoring accordingly; any sex differences in scores can then refer to a similar set of items.

If factor analysis of items were conducted for both sexes, then we could begin a comparison on the assumption of a core of similarity. Differences could be explored *after* the extent of similarity was assessed. Being delinquent, aggressive, withdrawn, or impulsive should refer to similar items, regardless of sex. Besides the theoretical parsimony of assuming similarity first, there is also the pragmatic fact that analyses can also compare similarities and differences in the variables that explain the variance in the scores of each sex. If these explanations differ, an unknown source of variability could be due to the difference in the measurements of the problems.

The recent (ACQ) study reported by Achenbach et al. (1989) also displayed an interest in seeking core items that cut across sex (and age) lines. However, this was accomplished in the ACQ study by conducting separate factor analyses of items for both sexes. In the analyses to be reported in this section, an opposite approach is adhered to—both sexes are combined in all factor analyses first, and then sex differences are explored.

2. *Separate Handling of Peer Item*—The influence of peers on the deviant behaviors of youth has been of interest to criminologists for many years. Even clinicians are aware that peers are important. The *Diagnostic and Statistical Manual* (i.e., DSM-III-R), used by psychiatrists and mental health workers, explicitly provides that a "conduct disorder" can be one of three types:

Code 312.20 group type

Code 312.00 solitary aggressive type

Code 312.90 undifferentiated type (American Psychiatric Association, 1987).

It is difficult to test for the significant contribution that peers can make to explanatory theories, if the item is automatically included in a list of delinquent behaviors to be explained. If the bad peer item is included then it can cause interpretive problems even for the authors of the checklists. Achenbach et al. (1989) caution readers of an abnormal psychology journal that the inclusion of the bad peer item—"hangs around with children who get in trouble"—in their revision of the CBCL does not mean that all the other problems of the delinquent syndrome always occur as a group activity (p.319). While this may be so, the inclusion of the item prevents researchers from examining the conditions under which peer factors exist or are theoretically important. The variable is too strategic as an explanatory—or independent—variable to be included in a factor analysis of dependent variables. In the analyses that follows, the bad peer item is deliberately excluded in all factor analyses of behavior items—so it can be used as an independent variable in subsequent analyses.

3. *Use of a Psychopathic Item*—There is also a long history of interest in understanding how lack of guilt about a deviant act influences youth behaviors. Reviewing 40 years of psychological research on "patterns of delinquent behaviors," Quay notes that "unsocialized aggressive" delinquents were once labeled "psychopathic" (Quay, 1986). In an effort to avoid a negative labeling of youth, this type of categorization was deliberately dropped (Ibid). However, items referring to trust and lack of guilt were maintained as self-report or parent report items. Achenbach included an item, "doesn't seem to feel

guilty after misbehavior" in his CBCL list. However, this item was not included in any of the scales for males because it did not emerge in the factor analysis as a significant item. The item was included in Achenbach's female factor analysis. In order to assess the relative influence of "lack of guilt" for both sexes, this item was treated as an independent variable and omitted from all factor analyses.

4. *Legal Distinctions Between Items*—Analysis of the CBCL delinquency and aggressive scales discloses that there are seven items that are probably illegal, criminal-type, violations: steals at home; steals outside the home; vandalism; destroys things; attacks people; threatens people; and sets fires. These items are mixed in with six juvenile status items: disobedient at home; disobedient at school; stubborn; runaway; truancy; uses alcohol or drugs. Since one of the aims of this study is to assess the overlap between legal and nonlegal offenses, it is important to carefully examine the relationship without any premature mixing of any items.

In order to understand the two classes of items more precisely, an analysis can conduct one distinctive factor analysis of only the illegal types of behavior (for both sexes) and a second factor analysis for the status offense items. On the basis of these factor analyses, distinctive patterns can be identified without any influences from all of the remaining CBCL items.

After this analysis is completed, the remaining nonlegal items can be subjected to a separate factor analysis. It is important to note that the legal delinquent and status items (as well as the bad peer and lack of guilt items) would not be included in this separate factor analysis. This procedure can assure that the nonlegal factors are created independently of the illegal and status factors. It is an empirical fact that factor analyses can yield different combinations of commonality, depending on the mix of the items (Camasso and Geismar, 1992). Therefore, to insure that an assessment of relationships between internal items and delinquent items is based on independent factors, the factors were generated in separate runs.

5. *Eliminating Duplicate Items*—By conducting the analyses in the proposed manner, it can be expected that some items will occur in more than one factor. Achenbach made the decision rule that items could occur in more than one factor. In the proposed analysis we will follow a different decision rule: there will not be any items that can occur in more than one scale. Independence of items used in the factors

can be achieved by selecting the items that are most strongly related to a factor. In the case of ties, the items that appeared to be similar in content to other items will be chosen. By eliminating duplications, each factor can be assessed as occurring independently and thereby provide unique behavior patterns to be explained.

Factor Analysis of Legal Items

The seven legal items are entered into an orthogonal factor analysis, using a varimax rotation method. This statistical procedure, as well as the rule of only scoring items as 0 or 1 (ignoring the extent or frequency) at the outset, emulates the technical steps used by Achenbach. The ECYS factor analysis yields two factors, accounting for 52.4 percent of the total variance of the seven items (see Appendix C for factor loadings). We label the first clear factor as "legal property" and the second as "legal assault." Each factor includes items that load .30 or better on one factor, but not on the other. Four items (# 81, # 82, # 106, and # 72) share a commonality that refers to theft in, and out of, the home, vandalism, and setting fires. The legal assault factor consists of three items (#57, #97, and #21), and refers to physically attacking or threatening people and destroying things belonging to others. Evidently, destroying things of others is distinguished from vandalism.

Separate factor analyses are conducted for boys and girls, to determine if a different mix of items would occur. We find that regardless of sex, two types of legal delinquency factors, property and assaultive delinquency, exist.

Factor Analysis of Status Offense Items

A factor analysis of status offense items is conducted with identical procedures to those employed in the analysis of legal delinquency items. Six status offense items fall into two distinctive patterns that account for 54.2 percent of the variance (see Appendix C for factor loadings). The first factor is labeled "disobedience," and contains the following items: stubborn (#86), disobedient at home (#22), and disobedient at school (#23). At an earlier time period disobedient behaviors were statutorily defined as referring to a "stubborn" or "incorrigible" child (Sutton, 1988). The three other items comprise the second factor, and are a mixture that we label "truant/runaway."

It contains item #101 (truancy/misses school), #67 (runs away from home), and #105 (uses alcohol or drugs). Again, separate factor analyses are conducted for boys and girls. It yielded a two-factor solution, with the same items appearing in each factor.

Factor Analysis of All Other CBCL Items

Setting aside the results of the two legal delinquency and two status offense factors, we subjected all of the remaining items that had emerged in the original Achenbach analysis to a factor analysis. The procedures used by Achenbach, as described in Appendix B, are employed: only rotated factors that result in at least six items with factor loadings of .30 or better, and a minimum eigenvalue of one, are retained as factors. The statistical procedures yield eight factors. The names that have been attached to the factors, and the highest loading items, are set forth in Table 3–3 (see Appendix C for factor loadings).

Table 3.3 Summary of Factor Analysis Results of All Other Items, Both Sexes

Factor Name	No. of Items in Factor	Undupli-cated No. of Items Used	Top Three Item Samples
Verbal Aggression	17	12	Argue, sulk, tantrum
Somatic	07	07	Nausea, cramps, vomit
Depressed	10	09	Sad, worry, nervous
Unliked/Cruel	07	05	Not get along, unliked, cruel
Strange ideas/ behavior	07	06	Strange ideas/ behaviors, suspicious
Withdrawn	07	05	Daydreams, stares, refuses to talk
Hyperactive	06	05	Restless, can't concentrate, poor, school work
Fearful/Perfectionist	07	06	Fear do bad, perfectionist, teases

A total of 67 items generate the eight factors that met the above standards. The eight factors account for 31.5% of the variance of all the items that are entered into the analysis. This is, of course, far lower than the 52% to 54% of variance accounted for in the analysis of legal delinquency and status offense items. Evidently, the greater mixture of items is associated with a much smaller degree of commonality than occurs with a smaller number of items chosen for theoretical reasons.

As noted in the third column, the number of items that are actually used for scoring is reduced for each factor in order to obtain unique factor items that do not overlap with one another. The total number of unduplicated items used in scoring the eight factors in the subsequent analyses totals 55 (a reduction of 12 items).

Examples of the types of behavior problems that are common to each factor are listed in the final column. As an illustration, hyperactive refers to behaviors like restlessness, can't concentrate, and poor school work. While the name of this factor, and others, are similar to ones employed by Achenbach, not all of the items displayed in Table 3–3 are identical items in factors published in the CBCL *Manual*.

Second-Order Factor Analysis

After identifying the two legal delinquency, two status offense, and eight nonlegal factors, we score each factor using the weights of 0, 1, or 2. The scored factors are entered into a second-order factor analysis. Unlike Achenbach's finding of a two-factor and mixed scale solution, the ECYS sample yields a clear three-factor solution. Instead of only one external type of behaviors, the ECYS analysis finds two: "mixed delinquent" and "multiaggressive" types of behaviors. The third factor refers to internal types of behavior problems, which we call "new internal," to distinguish it from the internal behaviors described by Achenbach (Achenbach and Edelbrock, 1983). Appendix C contains the statistical factor loadings for each of the three general factors.

"Multiaggression" contains four factors: verbal aggression; fearful perfectionist; unliked/cruel; and legal assault. The loadings range from .71 to .82, and are not accompanied by loadings above .30 on any one of the two other factors. It is of interest to note that the legal assault factor is associated with this general aggression factor, and not the factor that included all of the illegal and status items, mixed delinquency. A few psychological types of items are included within this aggressive factor (from the fearful/perfection scale), but the 26 items in this general aggression factor primarily refer to external-type behaviors.

"Mixed delinquency" refers to a mixture of property offenses, the two status offense scales, and the hyperactive scale. There is little overlap on the aggressive factor for the legal property and truant/runaway scales—but this is not the case for the hyperactive and disobey scales. Both of the latter two scales have moderate loadings on the multiaggression scales. However, the loadings are appreciably higher on the mixed delinquency scales. Therefore, the scales were scored on this dimension. These results are in general agreement with Achenbach, since virtually all of these items are included in the external scale reported by him.

"New internal" refers to the following specific factors: withdrawn; depression; strange ideas/behavior; and somatic. While all of the identified scales load the highest on this factor, only the withdrawn scale did not have any loadings above .30 on the other two general factors. Depression had a moderate loading with multiaggression, as did somatic; and strange ideas/behavior had loadings above .30 on multi-aggression and mixed delinquency. It is evident that some degree of overlap with the external factors exists for three of the four scales comprising the new internal factor, but they may be combined into an independent scale.

The reduction of 12 specific factor scales into three general factors, using a total of 68 items, occurs at a very satisfactory statistical level. Multiaggression accounts for 41.2% of the variance, and the other general factors of mixed delinquency and new internal account for 13.9% and 8.7%, respectively. The total variance accounted for is almost 64% which means that the three factor solution is empirically sound. Moreover, the alpha reliability coefficients for each of the three factors is high: .91 for the two external-type factors and .89 for the new internal factor.

Each of the three ECYS factors is strongly correlated with their counterparts in the CBCL general scales. The ECYS new internal factor has a correlation of .92 to .94 with the ACH internal scales (controlling for each sex); the ECYS multiaggression factor has a correlation of .85 to .91 with the ACH external scales (controlling for each sex); and the ECYS mixed delinquency factor has a correlation of .83 to .86 with the ACH external scales (controlling for each sex). While the results are comparable to Achenbach in distinguishing

broad patterns in internal and external behaviors and problems, the
ECYS results permit both sexes to be combined or compared in any
analyses. In addition, relationships between the three ECYS factors
can be easily examined for the total sample and each sex separately.

Before examining the overlap between delinquency, aggression
and internal mental health, the content of the delinquency and aggression factors will be compared with results from two national
studies that rely on parent and self-reports. In addition, the content
of the new internal factor and Achenbach's internal factor will be
compared.

Behavior Patterns in ECYS and National Samples

One of the major purposes of this study is to determine whether one
or more of the several behavior patterns identified in this study of inner-city youths are similar to patterns generated with samples of
youths with different ethnic/racial characteristics. Two major studies are worth examining in detail. One is the Achenbach et al. (1989)
study (ACQ) of a national sample of American parents reporting on
youths referred to mental health clinics around the country. The other is the National Youth Study (NYS) conducted by Elliott et al.
(1983), based on youth self-reports. Both studies were mentioned
earlier, but here we examine the specific content of behaviors found
in each study, and compare it with our results.

The Achenbach, Conners and Quay Study

The 1989 ACQ study identifies six "core syndromes," or patterns of
items, using factor analyses of responses by the parents of new and
old mental health clinic samples of American and Dutch males and
females aged 6–16. Scores on each core syndrome are then used to
compare the scores of a matched sample of American clinic and non-
clinic youth. The national American sample of 2,200 referred and
2,200 nonreferred children were demographically matched on the
criteria of: age; sex; socioeconomic class; ethnic/racial group; regions of the country; and type of adult informant. The Achenbach,
Conners, Quay (ACQ) instruments of 215 items was presented to
matched samples that are 80% white, 14% black, and 6% other. (A second analysis of ACQ items was reported in 1991, but this analysis
focused on identifying core syndromes that were comparable for
two out of three types of reporting instruments—youth self-reports,

teacher reports, and parent reports—for the ages of 4–16 (Achenbach, et al., 1991). Our comparisons rely solely on the 1989 analysis.

The six core syndromes identified by first order factor analyses
with the ACQ clinic samples were: aggressive; delinquent; anxious/
depressed; attention problems; somatic complaints; and withdrawn. The core syndrome of delinquency consisted of 11 items that
applied to both sexes for the ages of 6–16. According to a footnote,
some items displayed variability by age or sex; however, the total list
is quite similar to the earlier results obtained by Achenbach and
Edelbrock for 12–16-year-old boys and girls (1985).

The referred children were much more likely to score high on the
delinquency syndrome than the national sample of matched non-referred youth. Table 3–4 presents a list of the 11 items comprising the
ACQ delinquency syndrome and this study's mixed delinquency
items. The purpose of the comparison is to assess the similarity of the
patterns of the two lists (setting aside any weighted scoring difference).

Of the 11 ACQ items only two are omitted from the ECYS list—bad
companions and destroys others' things. As noted earlier, bad peers
is deliberately omitted in this study for theoretical reasons. Had bad
peers been included there is little doubt it would have appeared on
the ECYS list (see Chapter 4 for details). This means that only one
item—included as an item in the ECYS multiaggression factor—did
not appear on the ECYS mixed delinquency list. The ACQ list of comparable items conveys an image of delinquency that refers to disobedience and disaffection towards school and home, defiance of
property rules, cheating and lying, and precocious use of alcohol or
other drugs. This pattern of activities is quite likely to occur in the
company of peers who also get in trouble—probably for a similar set
of activities. This image of disobedience and disaffection, rule defiance, cheating and lying, and use of stimulants—quite likely in the
company of peers—is similar for ACQ and ECYS samples. This comparable image of "delinquent" youth is shared, even though the
ACQ sample is 80% white and the ECYS sample is 78% black. A core
pattern of varied delinquent activities appears to exist that cuts
across the boundaries of sex, ethnicity/race, social class, region of
the country, and even between American and Dutch youths. This is a
significant fact that needs to be taken into account in theorizing
about the causes of delinquency.

Besides the shared items in the core pattern of delinquency, ECYS
youth display additional characteristics: impulsiveness, restless-

ness, lack of concentration, poor school work, and traditional "incorrigible" behaviors (i.e., stubbornness and disobedience to parents). Hyperactivity, explicit disobedience to parents, and low school performance may be unique to the delinquency "syndrome" of ECYS youth, since these behaviors are not part of the 1989 ACQ core delinquency pattern. Instead, these types of behaviors are linked to the ACQ syndrome of either aggressive (for stubborn or parental disobedience) or attention problems for the other items.

As noted, aggression constitutes a distinct syndrome in the ACQ study, as it does in the ECYS analysis. However, vandalism—an item referring to the destruction of private or public property—is an integral part of the core patterns of delinquency and appears on the ACQ and ECYS lists in Table 3–4. The ACQ delinquency list also contains "destroys others' things," suggesting that property destruction may be a stronger part of the core pattern than is found in the ECYS mixed delinquency factor.

Table 3.4   Comparison of Items Used in National ACQ Delinquency Syndrome and ECYS Mixed Delinquency Factor

ACQ List of Delinquency Items[a]	ECYS List of Mixed Delinquency Items
Alcohol, drugs	Alcohol, drugs
Bad companions	———
Cheats, lies	Cheats, lies
Destroys others' things	———
Disobedient at school	Disobedient at school
Runs away from home	Runs Away
Sets fires	Sets fires
Steals at home	Steals at home
Steals outside of home	Steals outside home
Truancy	Truancy
Vandalism	Vandalism
(11 Items)	Restless
	Can't concentrate
	Poor school work
	Impulsive
	Stubborn, sullen
	Disobedient at Home
	(15 Items)

[a]See text for source

Table 3.5 Comparison of Items Used in National ACQ Aggression Syndrome and ECYS Multi–Aggression Factor

ACQ List of Aggression Items[a]	ECYS List of Multi-Aggression Items
Argues	Argues
Brags, boasts	Brags
Bullies, cries	Bullies, cries
Demands attention	Demands attention
Disobedient at home	———
Doesn't feel guilty	
Easily jealous	Easily Jealous
Impulsive	———
Loud	Loud
Screams	Screams
Show off	———
Starts fights	Starts fights
Stubborn, Irritability	———
Sudden mood changes	———
Sulks	Sulks
Swearing, obscenity	Swearing
Talks too much	Talks too much
Teases	Teases
Temper tantrums	Temper tantrums
(19 Items)	Destroys things
	Attacks people
	Threatens people
	Obsessive
	Doesn't get along
	Not liked
	Gets teased
	Whining
	Fear do bad things
	Fearful/anxious
	Perfectionist
	(24 Items)

[a]See text for source

Table 3–5 compares the 1989 ACQ list of aggression items with the ECYS multiaggression list. Of the 19 items found on the ACQ list, 13 can be found on the ECYS list. These items refer primarily to verbal types of aggression, but also include two types of nonlegal interpersonal aggression—cruelty, bullying and starts fights. It is clear, however, that the ECYS multiaggression factor also includes items that are clearly illegal (and more serious) types of interpersonal violence—attacks people and threatens people. The other ECYS items (listed below the legal assault items) are also absent from the ACQ list. A reasonable inference is that the ECYS sample shares verbal aggression and physical aggression, short of being illegal, with national samples. However, the ECYS samples tend to be more physically violent in expressing aggression. In criminological terms, the ECYS aggression syndrome is more likely to be associated with examples of aggravated or felony assault. The addition of the legal assault items may not be unique to the ECYS sample, since Achenbach's original CBCL analysis found that items referring to "attacks" and "threatens people" were integral parts of the 12–16-year-old aggression scales for males and females.

A comparison of the internal items of the ECYS and ACH factors indicates that the measurement of psychological problems may not be as stable across population groups for all types of problems. Even though the overall correlations between the ECYS and Achenbach general internal scale scores are extremely high (i.e., .92 to .94), when controlling for each sex, only two of the four ECYS factors appear to be highly congruent with the national ACQ study. Five somatic items are contained in the ACQ somatic scale and all five are contained in the seven item ECYS somatic scale. ECYS and ACQ agree on the following items: dizziness; aches and pains; headaches; stomach pain; and vomit often. In addition, ECYS somatic includes rashes, and nausea.

The ECYS depression factor has a high similarity to the ACQ anxious/depressed scale for seven of the nine items contained in the ECYS scale. These congruent items are: feels worthless; too guilty; unloved; lonely; nervous and tense; sad and depressed; and worrying. However, the ACQ scale containing these items also contains six more items that refer to "anxious" types of feelings that are not on the ECYS depressed list: fearful and anxious; fears impulses; needs to be perfect; fears school; feels persecuted; and self-conscious. The first three of these items are in the ECYS fear/perfection scale (that was found to be part of the ECYS multiaggression scale, in a second factor analysis). The ECYS items not included in the ACQ anxious/depressed syndrome referred to "cries a lot" and "moody" (an item contained in the ACQ aggression and ECYS multiaggression factors).

The other ECYS factors are less congruent with the ACQ lists. The

ECYS contains three of nine items contained in the ACQ withdrawn scale. These are: prefer to be alone, refuses to talk, and stares blankly. The ECYS list also includes daydreams and confused in a fog. The missing ACQ withdrawn items are: secretive; self-conscious; shy–timid; underactive; unhappy, sad, depressed (also appearing in the anxiety/depressed scale); and withdrawn.

The last ECYS factor, strange ideas and behaviors, contains six items, and two can be found in an ACQ schizoid scale: strange behavior and repeats acts over, compulsive. Missing from the ECYS lists are hears things, says strange things, and sees strange things. The ACQ schizoid scale, it is important to note, had the lowest correlation of all the factors within and between sex and age groups, and was therefore eliminated as one of six core syndromes.

A final internal factor identified by the ACQ analysis referred to attention problems. The nine items contained in the ACQ attention list did not emerge as a single, coherent, factor in the ECYS analysis. However three of the items are included in the ECYS mixed delinquency factor (i.e., can't concentrate, poor school work, and impulsive); another three of the items are included in the ECYS withdrawn factor (i.e., stares blankly; confused; and daydreams). The three remaining ACQ attention items not contained in any ECYS list are: acts too young, can't sit still; and poor coordination, clumsy.

This detailed analysis of the ACQ and ECYS results provide confidence that the combined mixed delinquency, multiaggression, and new-internal factors are quite reliable at the more general behavioral/emotional levels. While mixed delinquency and multiaggression factors can be used either alone, or in combination, it appears that the analysis will have to be more cautious in using the more specific, internal scales. Somatic and depression factors have their counterparts in a variety of samples, but the reliability for the other two factors—across samples—appears to be weak.

The National Youth Survey

The National Youth Survey (NYS) is a national, longitudinal and panel self-report survey of youths aged 11–17 which was initiated in 1977 by Elliott and colleagues. As of 1983 these youths had been interviewed a total of six times. The study furnishes important longitudinal data on self-reported behaviors, attitudes, beliefs, and activities of youths. The results of the unique study have been published in two major books (Elliott et al., 1985 and 1989), numerous articles, and mimeographed reports.

Elliott and his colleagues use 47 self-report items. Nearly all describe explicitly illegal behaviors that attempt to measure the delinquency of American youth. Some of the items are similar to CBCL items, while others are an approximation. They include types of illegal delinquency activities that are not in the CBCL. Table 3–6 compares 16 items used in the NYS and comparable CBCL items used in the ECYS. The percent of NYS youths who report that they have engaged in the behavior during the past year is compared to the percent of ECYS parents who report that their adolescent has engaged in the behavior during the past six months. The NYS data are based on the initial wave, conducted in 1977, for 11–17-year-old boys and girls because this is the age group closest to the 12–16-year-olds in the ECYS sample.

Section A compares items that are closest in wording. Except for the comparison of damaging school property and vandalism, the ECYS parents report a much higher level of behaviors that could be "illegal" for minors. This could be expected, since the NYS sample is a representative sample of all American youth, whereas the ECYS sample represents youth in trouble who are known to mental health or family crisis agencies located in and near a large city. The frequency distributions indicate that parent reports are certainly capable of capturing critical dimensions and amounts of potential illegal behaviors. The biggest differences refer to skips school, stealing inside home, runs away, and attacks people.

Section B refers to NYS items that are more specific than the approximate ECYS items. Except for the comparison of "hit students" and "started fights" the ECYS parents report a higher rate of occurrence of potential illegal behaviors. In order to assess the relative magnitude of two ECYS items used as indications of risk variables, the occurrence of "doesn't feel guilty" and "hangs around with children who get in trouble" are also noted at the bottom. Comparisons in part B provide evidence once again that parents are indeed reporting a substantial amount of deviant and potentially illegal behaviors. In addition, a clear majority of ECYS youth do not feel guilty and hang around with bad peers—59% and 66%, respectively.

Unlike the designers of the ACQ national study of parent reports, the principal investigators of the NYS study of self-reports did not submit the list of 47 items to a factor analysis. Instead items were

Table 3.6 Comparison of Prevalence of Similar Behaviors in National Youth Survey and Essex County Youth Samples (in Percent)

A. Closest Wording Items	NYS(11–17 yrs)[a]	ECYS (12–16 yrs)	%
1. Skipping classes	31 %	Skips school	65 %
2. Stole less than $5	18	Stole outside of home	27
3. Damaged family property	24	Destroys things of family or others	33
4. Damaged others' property	18		
5. Steal from family	16	Steals inside the home	32
6. Damaged school property	16	Vandalism	15
7. Run away from home	06	Runs away	34
8. Attacks to seriously hurt	06	Attacks people	21

B. Approximate Wording	NYS(11–17 yrs)[a]	ECYS(12–16 yrs)	%
1. Cheated on school test	49 %	Lies or cheats	73 %
2. Hit students	48	Starts fights	46
3. Lied about age to buy alcohol	27	Lies or cheats	73
4. Public drunkenness	14	Uses alcohol or drugs	25
5. School suspension	10	Disobedient at school	72
6. Obscene calls	11	Swearing, obscene	49
7. Forced students to give $	03	Cruel, mean, bullies	46
8. Forced others to give $	03	Threatens people	23
9. (No similar item)	—	Doesn't feel guilty	59
10. (No similar item)	—	Bad peers	66

[a]Delbert S. Elliott, Suzanne S. Ageton, and David Huizinga, 1980. *The National Youth Survey Project Report No. 11*, Boulder, Colorado: Behavioral Research Institute, Mimeograph.

grouped by *a priori* categories into felony assault, robbery, felony theft, minor theft, status offenses, school delinquency, and other groupings and then analyzed for statistical reliabilities. A summary scale of 35 items (including 13 of the 16 items reported in Table 3–6) was constructed by the NYS researchers, using a statistical measure of reliability. A reading of the broad list of 35 items indicates that many types of minor and serious forms of illegal behaviors are indeed inter-correlated.

For purposes of testing theories of delinquency emanating from sociology and criminology, Elliott and his colleagues deliberately exclude 13 of the 35 items that refer to less serious and status behaviors. The list of 22 items is created on *a priori* grounds, in order to focus on "more serious forms of delinquency" (Elliott et al., 1989, p.11). The list of 22 types of serious delinquency refers to eight property items, 10 aggressive items, and four general behaviors (referred to by Elliott et al. as a "Grand Delinquency C Scale"). A tighter list of the most serious offenses, referred to as "Index Offenses," includes six aggressive and three property offense items.

The image of delinquency conveyed by the NYS study could be as inclusive as the combination of 35 illegal property, aggression, status, and other behaviors, or as narrow as the list of nine index items. Without additional statistical analysis, it is difficult to assess what cluster of behavior items form a unique pattern. If factor analyses had been performed with the national sample in the NYS, it is likely that the image of delinquency would, at a minimum, also consist of multiple types of illegal behaviors and a separate aggressive pattern. This inference is based on the results of recent factor analyses of self-report items with a known delinquent population by Barton and Butts (1990). A factor analysis of 26 behavior items (similar in wording to the NYS study), obtained in interviews with 412 adjudicated male delinquents, yielded a four-factor solution:

1) *Minor Offenses* – ranging from runaway and truanting to stealing and damaging property worth less than $50;

2) *Property Offenses* – ranging from stealing or damaging property between $50 and $200 to property violations of over $200;

3) *Violent Offenses* – ranging from threatening to hurt someone with a weapon to inflicting injury so the victim required hospitalization; and

4) *Drug and Alcohol Offenses*

In addition, a factor analysis of the NYS items in a longitudinal study of children aged 7–9 and 11–15 living in Denver in a high official delinquency area yielded a four-factor solution: 1) theft offenses; 2) assault offenses; 3) status and 4) public disorder offenses and all others (Huizinga, Esbensen and Weiher, 1991).

Patterns of Delinquency and Aggression

The delinquent and aggressive behaviors that emerge in our sample of inner-city youths are similar to ones found in national samples, international samples, and among youths from different racial and ethnic backgrounds. The measure of mixed delinquency contains virtually all of the items found in the national study of parent reports, and there are also similarities in the identification of an aggression factor or syndrome. These are important findings in and of themselves. But a closer investigation of the delinquent and aggressive behaviors can expand our understanding of youthful deviance even further. Specifically, it is strategically useful to understand the behaviors contained in the core pattern of delinquency in terms of their broader meaning, such as the developmental stage at which they emerge, their consistency, and how they evolve.

Research using the CBCL and the ACQ forms of parent reports, provides convincing evidence that delinquency, particularly during adolescence, ages 12–16, consists of a core pattern of specific behaviors. Achenbach, Conners, and Quay have established that specific illegal behaviors are found to coexist with noncriminal, status-type, behaviors in national samples of clinic and non-clinic American and Dutch boys and girls. The ECYS analysis confirms that a core pattern of items can be found in a sample of predominantly black youths who have used youth service systems meant to help them with mental health problems.

It is of critical importance that we appreciate that the dominant core pattern consists of a *combination* of items referring to the following diverse criminal and noncriminal types of behaviors:

1. *Disobedience and disaffection from school* (i.e., disobedient at school and truancy);

2. *Disaffection from home* (i.e., runs away and steals at home);

3. *Disobedience of property rules* (i.e., steals outside the home, vandalism, sets fires, and destroys things belonging to others);

4. *Dishonesty* (i.e., cheats and lies);

5. *Use of Alcohol or Drugs*

From a child development perspective, "serious delinquency" would mean the coexistence of virtually *all* of the behaviors comprising the pattern for at least six months. From our data we cannot pinpoint precisely at what age the core pattern emerges. The ACQ study reported that the "syndrome" of delinquency was found in the 6–11 and 12–16 age groups, but footnoted seven of the eleven items to indicate that they were found only in one age or sex group (Achenbach et al., 1989, p.312). The four items that are consistent across age and sex are cheating and lying; stealing at home; stealing outside the home; and hanging out with youths who get in trouble. Core behaviors of dishonesty, theft, and association with bad peers emerge in pre-adolescence and persist at least until the age of 16. The other items become a consistent part of the core pattern after the age of 12. Thus, the delinquency pattern is responsive to adolescent development. Similar evidence about the development of a delinquent syndrome exists from data in the NYS. Frequencies of virtually all behaviors comprising the delinquent pattern increased substantially during adolescence. In the NYS, the increases in the percent of youth at ages 11 and 15 reporting a behavior during the past year follow:

1) cheating on school tests – from 31% to 64%

2) lied about age – from 7% to 37%

3) stealing less than $5 – from 8% to 25%

4) stolen from family – from 14% to 17%

5) skipped classes – from 5% to 47%

6) public drunkenness – from 1% to 20%

7) school suspension – from 2% to 14%

8) damage school property – from 8% to 24%

9) runaway from home – from 4% to 6%

Similar differences can be found for other NYS cohorts, both within, and across sample years (Elliott et al., 1983, Age tables K and O).

The evidence strongly supports the inference that the core pattern

identified by the ACQ study expands during adolescence; it includes a larger number of behaviors and an increase in the frequency
of their occurrence. The 1991 ACQ study finds that delinquent patterns increase with age. Evidently, the age of 6–11 is associated with a
pattern that primarily includes dishonesty (i.e., cheating and lying),
breaking property rules (i.e., stealing both inside and outside the
home), and hanging with bad peers. The last item is surprising, since
the impact of peer influence is usually associated with adolescence.
The following parts of the core pattern are more often added between the ages of 12–16: disobedience and disaffection from school
(i.e., truancy and disobedient at school); use of alcohol or drugs; and
disobedience from home (i.e., running away).

An understanding of the peer item, as well as other items in a core
pattern, can be gained by noting that younger children are likely to
be less consistent in their behaviors. For example, Edelbrock, et al.
(1985), studying children's self-reports in structured interviews,
find that test-retest intra-class correlation of items varied substantially as follows: .43 for 6–9-year-olds; .60 for 10–13-year-olds; and
.71 for 14 to 18-year-olds. The source of this unreliability may be
due to a variety of influences. But most developmental psychologists would cite maturational processes of cognitive and moral
growth and behavioral consistency as sources. These maturational
processes can affect reliability and validity scores. Maturation pro-
motes greater congruence between moral attitudes and beliefs and
behaviors. Peers often are important during adolescence because
the urge for conformity is linked to an ability to be cognitively and
behaviorally consistent. Lerman (1967) found that knowledge of
argot words and delinquent behaviors become more consistent
with age.

If it is important to understand the emergence and expansion of
the core patterns of behaviors from a developmental perspective, it
is also useful to note that specific samples of youths may add behaviors to their patterns of "mixed delinquency." Earlier in the chapter,
we showed that ECYS youths scored significantly higher for separate male and female delinquency scales than the clinic samples studied by Achenbach. By combining the sexes into a unisex factor
structure, and making distinctions between legal and nonlegal
items, we find that the ECYS sample replicates the ACQ core pattern
of delinquency found in more representative samples of clinic and
nonclinic youth. In addition to replicating the core pattern, ECYS
youths add items that reinforce the pattern (e.g., poor school work

and disobedience at home) and expand the pattern (e.g., impulsive, stubborn, and poor concentration).

The content of the factor structures found in the ECYS sample may refer to two types of patterned forms of delinquency: normal (cultural) delinquency and expanded delinquency. Normal delinquency is represented by core pattern items that probably occur, especially in adolescence, in all regions of America. The core pattern can be found in urban or suburban areas, among black and white youths, and in lower class, middle class, and upper class neighborhoods. This type of delinquency may explain researchers' inability to locate consistent or even clear-cut evidence of class and ethnic/racial differences in patterns of delinquency, based on either parent and self-reports. Normal delinquency is a natural part of American society for a significant number of American youths.

During adolescence many youths engage in one or more of the behavior items in the core pattern during a six month or 12 month period (see Table 3–6). The number of youths who engage in all or most of the behaviors during a period of time in the core pattern is currently unknown. As we presented earlier (see Table 3–2), 35% to 41% of adolescents ages 12–16 who were seen in mental health clinics scored at least two standard deviations above the national mean on the same delinquency factor. Based on national data on the number of youths using mental health facilities (National Institute of Mental Health, 1986), this would have meant that over 700,000 youths known to mental health clinics would probably have scored high on the core delinquency pattern.

The expanded delinquent pattern found in the ECYS sample probably occurs much less frequently. In content, the expanded delinquent type is similar to Cohen's (1955) description of the characteristics of "delinquent subcultures." He argues that a distinct pattern of behaviors is shared by youths growing up in lower class neighborhoods. Using official data, observations, and biographical descriptions, Cohen infers that the subculture pattern is primarily masculine, and tends to be versatile and non-specialized in content. Activities of theft, truancy, malicious mischief, and vandalism occur in a peer context. These activities are part of a pattern that also include behaviors that are impulsive, defiant of rules, and are often expressive and non-utilitarian (Cohen, 1955, pp.24–32). These are characteristics that can be ascribed to the deviant delinquency pattern found in the ECYS sample. The ECYS data, unlike the data on boys used by Cohen (1955), refer to a pattern of mixed delinquency that cuts across sex.

Cohen argues that many of the activities are performed maliciously, with an air of spite, contempt, and ridicule of conventional authority and adult rites. Assessing intentions is not an explicit focus of the CBCL, but youths scoring high on the core aggressive pattern engaged in cruel, mean, teasing, and taunting behaviors. An expanded aggression pattern, found among ECYS youths, includes attacks and threats on people. A combination of a high score on expanded patterns of *both* aggression and mixed delinquency factors could approximate the subcultural description offered by Cohen, especially if the aggressive and delinquent activities occur in the company of like-minded peers. Moreover, youths who are high on both aggression and delinquency resemble the description of an ideal type of "conduct disorder" (Institute of Medicine, 1989 p. 29).

The expanded aggressive-delinquent type could provide a third distinction among patterned delinquent activities. Based on the frequencies of attacking and threatening people, we would expect that a delinquent-aggressive behavior type would consist of fewer numbers than an expanded delinquency type. On the basis of existing evidence, it is reasonable to hypothesize that youths scoring high on both mixed delinquency and multiaggression (i.e., a delinquent-aggressive type) will be found in disproportionate numbers in lower income neighborhoods. The NYS study, for example, found that the "most striking and consistent class difference is the consistently higher general rate of felony assault for the lower class" (Elliott, et al. 1989, p.40).

The next section will provide an empirical test of a delinquent-aggressive typology. First, we create a four-fold classification of the total sample into specific delinquent-aggressive types. Then we test whether the expanded core pattern is more likely to be found among one or both of the high delinquent types. Subsequently, we explore whether this expanded core pattern is more likely to be linked with youth who are also higher on measures of legal assault and cruel behaviors. How peer relationships operate in each of the types is examined. Finally, the relationships between delinquency-aggressive behavioral patterns and internal mental health problems is investigated.

Delinquent-Aggressive Typology of Urban Youths

The delinquent-aggressive typology is created by cross-tabulating mixed-delinquent youths who score above and below the median with multiaggression youths who score above and below the median. The four types, and the number of youths classified into each category, are as follows:

1) Low delinquency/low aggression   (80 youth);

2) Low delinquency/high aggression   (34 youth);

3) High delinquency/low aggression   (36 youth);

4) High delinquency/high aggression   (76 youth);

Because of the moderately strong bivariate relationship between the two measures (r =.51), there are more youths classified into the low/low and high/high ends of the typology. Nevertheless, there are a sufficient number of youths in the mixed categories to test whether there are differences between high/high youths and other types. Table 3–7 compares mean scores on eight factors, a single peer item, and three demographic characteristics for each of the delinquency by aggression types.

The table presents the results of an analysis of variance to test whether any of the four means associated with each of the types are statistically different from each other. If the means are similar, they are noted by a similar letter; if the means are different, they are noted by different letters. The variance for each of the comparisons is displayed in the last column on the right. The highest mean score is noted with an A, the second highest with a B, and the third highest with a C.

The first group of comparisons focus on specific factors that make up the mixed delinquency score. The means of the two high delinquent score types, high delinquency-low aggression and high delinquency-high aggression, are no different in relationship to three of the four behaviors that comprise the core delinquency pattern—legal property offenses, truancy/runaway, and disobedient. The specific delinquency factor, hyperactivity, however, does not behave the same way. Rather, the most impulsive-type behaviors are found in the high delinquent-high aggression type and the second highest are found in the high delinquent/low aggression type (A vs. B). High delinquent types, regardless of aggression, score higher on all specif-

Table 3-7 Comparison of Mean Score Differences Between Delinquent/Aggressive Types on Specific Factors, Peer Associates, and Demographics[a]

	Delinquent/Aggressive Typology				
	Low Del/ Low Agg	Low Del/ High Agg	High Del/ Low Agg	High Del/ High Agg	Variance (R^2)
I. Specific Delinquent Factors					
1. Legal Property	B	B	A	A	26.5%
2. Truant/Runaway	B	B	A	A	30.8%
3. Disobey	C	B	A	A	51.8%
4. Hyperactive	D	C	B	A	58.5%
II. Specific Aggressive Factors					
1. Verbal Aggression	B	A	B	A	60.6%
2. Fearful/Perfection	B	A	B	A	38.4%
3. Legal Assault	C	B	C	A	29.6%
4. Unliked/Cruel	C	B	C	A	42.0%
III. Peer Associations					
1. Bad Peers	B	B	A	A	23.9%
IV. Demographics					
1. Gender (M/F)	B	A	C	B/C	6.1 %
2. Age	A	A	A	A	NS
3. Sample type (FCIU/MH)	A	A/B	B	A/B	4.0 %

[a] Any means with different letters are statistically different from each other at a probability level of .05 or less; conversely, any means with the same letters are not statistically different. The highest mean scores are noted by "A", followed by "B", the next highest, to "D". The letter allocations are based on the Waller–Duncan K ratio T test as an analysis of variance measure.

ic delinquent factors, including hyperactivity, than low delinquent types (C vs. D). We can conclude that the expansion of the core delinquency pattern occurs more strongly among high delinquent youth who also score high on aggressive behaviors, and to a lesser degree among high delinquent-low aggression youths.

The second group of comparisons on specific multiaggression factors reveal that there are no differences in the mean scores of the two high aggressive types on verbal aggression and fear/perfection (i.e., A for high delinquency-high aggression and A for low delinquency-high aggression); similarly, there are no differences among the low aggressive types for these two measures (i.e., B for high delinquency-low aggression and B for low delinquency-low aggression). The legal assault and unliked/cruelty measures do not behave in a similar fashion. There are distinct differences in the mean scores for the two high aggression types (A vs. B), and a further difference in the mean scores of the two low aggression types. We can conclude that the core aggression pattern is most likely to be expanded with legally assaultive and cruel behaviors by those youths who are simultaneously high on delinquency and aggression. By contrast, the high delinquency-low aggression youths are as unlikely to engage in legally assaultive and cruel behaviors as the least deviant youths, those who are low delinquent-low aggression types.

While the first two groups of comparisons reveal that the high delinquency-high aggression youths fit Cohen's description of a delinquent subculture, the scores on peer association indicate that any subculture of delinquency is unlikely to be homogeneous. Youths who hang out with peers who get in trouble (i.e., bad peers) are as likely to be found in one delinquent type as another. In fact, the data indicate that high delinquency is most likely to occur with bad peers, but high levels of aggression occur with or without peers. Delinquent-type behaviors, rather than aggressive-type behaviors, are most likely to be associated with bad peers. However, high delinquents who are also high in aggression express their higher degree of legally assaultive and cruel behaviors with peers.

The fourth group of comparisons provides information about critical demographic characteristics. Comparisons reveal that females are most likely to be low delinquency-high aggression types and males are most likely to be high delinquency-low aggression types (A vs. C). The most deviant type—high delinquency-high aggression—are either males or females and this group is indistinguishable from the least deviant type—low delinquency-low aggression (B vs.

B/C). There are no significant age differences between the types. There are service system differences, with the family crisis system more likely to be associated with high delinquency-low aggression youths and the mental health system more likely to be associated with low delinquency-low aggression youths (A vs. B).

In summary, we conclude that the most deviant youths, that is, ones scoring the highest on both delinquency and aggression, are likely to be more impulsive, legally assaultive, and cruel than other types of youths. However, the expanded behaviors are not necessarily related to bad peers, age, sex, or service system.

Delinquency, Aggression, and Mental Health

Besides understanding how core patterns of delinquency and aggression expand, the typology also may be used to understand the internal, psychological (or traditional mental health) correlates of delinquency and aggression. The prior work of Achenbach & Edelbrock (1983, 1987) and Achenbach et al., (1989) suggests that there are significant associations between many of the specific scales. As Achenbach et al. (1989) note: there well may be a "general psychopathology factor analogous to the G factor reflected in the positive correlations typically found among diverse measures of ability" (p.307). Without using the language of psychopathology, Jessor (1987) suggests that there exists a "behavior proneness," such that deviant behaviors are associated. Similarly, the National Youth Survey shows highly intercorrelated measures that were able to be combined into a general delinquency scale. Intercorrelations between delinquency and aggression exist in our data set, too, as we reported earlier, but the strategic issue is to determine what overlap occurs when all three factors are considered simultaneously.

Using the delinquent-aggressive typology, we examine the mean score difference between the types to investigate which types of youths are likely to have internal, psychological problems, as measured by the new internal factor. The mean new internal scores for each type are shown below. The letters in parentheses indicate whether the mean score of each measure is significantly different from the others.

1) Low delinquent-low aggression   7.375 (C)
2) Low delinquent-high aggression   15.194 (A)

3) High delinquent-low aggression   11.000 (B)

4) High delinquent-high aggression   16.618 (A)

There are sizable, and statistically significant, differences between the types. The two high aggressive types (with and without high delinquency) are associated with the highest new internal scores and they are statistically similar. The second highest new internal score is associated with high delinquency-low aggression, but it is distinguished from both the highest and lowest score (i.e., 11.000 (B) vs. 16.618 (A) vs. 7.375 (C)). The results clearly indicate that high aggression—with and without high delinquency—is the behavioral condition most likely to be associated with more internal, psychological types of problems.

These results provide firm evidence that delinquency, aggression and mental health are significantly associated, and it is clear that the strongest relationship occurs between internal, psychological problems and aggressive behaviors. Next we examine how different types of internal, psychological problems are related to aggression.

Table 3–8 presents the mean internal scores for each of the four delinquent-aggressive types. Strange ideas and behaviors are most highly associated with youths who are high delinquency-high aggression types; the two mixed types (i.e., low delinquency-high aggression and high delinquency-low aggression) have statistically similar, but lower mean scores. The lowest mean scores occur in the group of youths with low delinquency and low aggression.

Depression and somatic behaviors are highly associated with high levels of aggression, regardless of whether the youths are more or less delinquent.

Withdrawal is most likely to occur among youths of all types, except those who are low in delinquency and low in aggression. Thus, only when the level of deviance is small, that is, in the group of low delinquency-low aggression, will there be a diminished occurrence of withdrawn feelings.

The last line summarizes the associations that occur when all four indicators of internal, psychological distress are combined. The combined, overall, measure shows three levels of difference. Internal, psychological problems are most likely to be associated strongly with aggression in youths, regardless of their involvement in delinquent activities. Next, internal psychological problems are likely to reveal themselves in delinquent youths with less aggressive tendencies (the pure delinquent types). The least likely group to have inter-

Table 3-8 Comparisons of Delinquent/Aggressive Typology, by Specific Internal, Psychological Items and New Internal Factor Means[a]

	Low Delinquency		High Delinquency		
	Low Agg	*High Agg*	*Low Agg*	*High Agg*	R^2
1. Strange Ideas/Behaviors	C	B	B	A	27.3%
2. Depressed/Anxious	B	A	B	A	20.1%
3. Somatic	B	A	B	A	9.8%
4. Withdrawn	B	A	A	A	10.4%
New Internal Score	C	A	B	A	26.7%

[a] Means with the same letter are not significantly different, using the Waller–Duncan K–ratio T–test as an analysis of variance measure. "A" represents highest means; "C" represents lowest means.

nal psychological problems are youths with low delinquency and low aggression.

This analysis indicates that delinquency, aggression, and internal, psychological problems coexist. However, the associations are not similar for all types of psychological problems. Strange ideas and behaviors expand when youths are highly delinquent and highly aggressive. Strange ideas and behavior are moderately linked to both pure delinquency (high delinquency-low aggression) and pure aggression (low delinquency-high aggression), but the score increases when the thresholds of high delinquency and high aggression are reached simultaneously. A microanalysis of the six items comprising strange ideas and behaviors reveals that "suspicious," "repeats certain acts over," "compulsive," and "strange behavior," which have more significant correlations with aggression than other items, may be responsible for the relationship (analysis not shown). Thus, strange ideas and behaviors expand as delinquency and aggression expand.

This interpretation is similar to the one we posed earlier when we examined the expansion of delinquency and aggression. There, we argued that the core patterns of delinquency and aggression were expanded when the two overall measures of delinquency and aggression reached a critical threshold together. Then high amounts of disobedience, hyperactivity, legal assault, and unliked/cruel behavior were likely to occur.

Before ending this discussion on the interrelationships of delinquency, aggression and internal, psychological problems, it is important to point out that each of the four indicators of internal, psychological problems accounts for a different amount of variance. The amount of variance associated with strange ideas/behaviors and depression is stronger than the amount associated with somatic behaviors and withdrawal. As the earlier microanalysis of strange ideas and behaviors reveals that "suspicious," "compulsive," and "strange ideas and behavior" are more likely to be tied to aggression (particularly when high delinquency also occurs), another microanalysis on depression reveals that four out of nine depression items are most likely to be linked to aggressive behaviors: two refer to feelings of being unloved and worthless (i.e., "feels that no one loves him/her" and "feels worthless or inferior") and two refer to anxiety (i.e., "nervous, high stress, or tense" and "sudden changes in mood or feeling"). Other research has found that low self-esteem and severe anxiety are often linked to other types of emotional distress

(Avison and MacAlpine, 1992). Our study reveals that specific types of psychological problems are associated with behavioral problems—especially aggression.

Summary and Conclusions

This chapter began with one major question. What are the patterns of problems described by the parents of these youths? Several strategies were used to answer this question. First, we compared our sample of predominantly black youths with the clinical and nonclinical samples of predominantly white youths described by Achenbach et al. (1983, 1987). Additionally, we looked at the differences between the problems of youths referred to the community mental health system and the family crisis intervention unit (FCIU). And we explored the similarities and differences between the patterns of behavior among our inner-city youths and patterns identified in other national studies using both self (youth) reports and parent reports. Then, we reanalyzed the CBCL to clarify the relationships between delinquency, aggression and internal, psychological problems for both boys and girls. We develop a four-group typology of youths: those who are high on delinquency and high on aggression; those who are high on delinquency and low on aggression (pure delinquents); those who are high on aggression and low on delinquency (pure aggressives); and those who are low on delinquency and low on aggression. How youths with these combinations of problems do with regard to internal, psychological problems was then described.

Behaviors of Black Urban Youths

Our research is the first to compare findings reported by Achenbach for his predominantly white clinical and nonclinical samples with a predominantly black, urban sample. This is a significant comparison to report, since the ECYS sample was 78% black, whereas Achenbach's samples were 80% white. Using Achenbach's instrument and scoring procedures, it is clear that the scores of the ECYS boys and girls (ages 12–16) are much closer to Achenbach's clinical samples than to a randomly drawn nonclinical, metropolitan, sample. In fact, the total mean scores for all types of problems contained on the Child Behavior Checklist (CBCL) were statistically indistinguishable for the ECYS and Achenbach clinical samples regardless of sex. The ECYS and clinical samples could have been drawn from a similar population of youth with known behavior and emotional problems, despite the profound differences in the background characteristics of the two samples.

When the scores were categorized by whether the problems were of an internal (i.e., psychological, over inhibited) or external (i.e., uninhibited or antisocial) type, similar results occurred in the comparison of ECYS and Achenbach clinical males. The mean scores on these two measures were so similar that again the two samples could have been drawn from a similar population of youths with known emotional and behavior problems. The ECYS girls were also similar to their clinical peers on the internal measures, but they differed on the extent of their external problems. The ECYS girls scored significantly higher on this measure than the Achenbach clinical sample, although both the ECYS and clinical samples of girls were above Achenbach's nonclinical sample (66% to 52% to 4% scored above the cut-off scores, respectively).

When comparisons were conducted for specific types of scales, then statistically significant differences emerged for comparisons for each gender. While the total mean score of problems may be similar for ECYS and the clinical samples, the specific mix of problems can vary. Boys were higher on one specific internal and one specific external score, (obsessive-compulsive and delinquency, respectively) and lower on the mixed scale of hostile-withdrawn. A further analysis of the differences disclosed that the sharpest distinction between the ECYS and clinical sample occurred with the delinquency scale. The difference on the delinquency scale was due to the much greater percent of family crisis males that scored above the serious cut-off designated by Achenbach (60% to 35%, respectively).

The ECYS girls also had three statistically significant differences on specific scale scores; two internal scores were lower (anxious-obsessive and somatic) and one score was higher (delinquency). Similar to the boys, the sharpest discrepancy occurred for the delinquency scale. In particular, the family crisis females had 62% who scored above Achenbach's cut-off score, whereas the clinical sample had 41%.

The results of the ECYS and Achenbach clinical sample comparisons indicate that the parent report method can be used with both white and black parents. Not only is the range of problems comparable, but it appears that the total mean scores are similar. Despite this similarity between samples on total aggregate measures, it is also evident that the method can uncover statistically significant differences between different populations. Since the bulk of the ECYS respondents are linked to the family crisis system, the specific differences that emerged are probably associated with the delinquent types of referrals this system receives. We certainly would have expected these ECYS youth to have engaged in more behaviors that are associated with a police contact, and their parents report that this is the case by a very wide margin.

Besides displaying strength in eliciting reliable and valid responses from parents of diverse backgrounds, the parent report method—particularly as developed by Achenbach—has displayed other positive attributes. Distinctive samples—like the ECYS youth sample—can be compared with nationally established sex and age norms because Achenbach has used samples of youths with known problems and comparison samples of normal youths. The samples of clinical youths provide an opportunity to find the specific clusters of behaviors and feelings that cohered together as an empirical reality, while the normal samples provide a basis for establishing cut-off scores that could serve as the age/sex norms. In contrast, the best self-report study—NYS—has only examined a national random sample, but lacks a comparison sample of youths with problems to create empirically derived scales that can be used as a basis for erecting valid national norms of youth behaviors.

While the parent report method has displayed strengths that have yet to be demonstrated by current self-report efforts, it also has weaknesses that need to be identified. Because youths from the ages of 17 and upwards are likely to engage in behaviors and have feelings that are unknown to parents, the parent report method has refrained from establishing age/sex norms beyond the age of 16. Fortunately, self-reports of 17- and 18-year-olds have the highest reliability scores, and this method could be used as an alternative. Another problem that is restrictive for researchers—but may not be so for clinicians—is the Achenbach use of separate items and scores for each sex (at each age).

Assessing Core Patterns that are Gender-Neutral

In order to cope with the gender weakness of the Achenbach scoring, we conduct a new factor analysis of the CBCL items (except for the exclusion of "hanging out with bad peers" and "lacks guilt"). Unlike Achenbach's findings of a two-factor and mixed-scale solution for each sex, the total ECYS sample yields a three-factor solution appli-

cable without regard to gender. Instead of only a broad-based external measure of antisocial behaviors the ECYS analysis distinguishes
between a "mixed delinquent" and "multiaggressive" factor; the
third factor refers to psychological items and is labeled as a "new internal" factor. Each of the factors is strongly correlated with its counterparts in the CBCL general scales of internal or external for each
sex—thereby validating that the ECYS measures are quite comparable to age/sex results of Achenbach. In addition to this analysis, each
major ECYS problem type (i.e., factor) is compared to a recent national study using parent reports (for youth referred to 18 mental health
clinics) in different parts of the country. This study constructed
scales that were applicable to both sexes (the study was conducted
by Achenbach, Connors, Quay, et al.—or ACQ). The 1989 ACQ study
identified six district "syndromes" that were reliable for all age and
sex groups: aggressive; delinquent; anxious-depressed; attention
problems; somatic complaints; and withdrawn.

A comparison of the ECYS and ACQ delinquency scales (i.e., syndromes) disclosed a very close fit, since 9 of the 11 ACQ items were
also on the ECYS list. One of the missing items (bad peers) had been
deliberately omitted from the ECYS analysis in order to be used as a
potential explanation variable—but a separate analysis disclosed
that it was strongly associated with the ECYS delinquency measure.
The ACQ and ECYS items convey an image of a garden variety of delinquency that can occur anywhere in America—in inner cities, as
well as in middle class and suburban areas. The core delinquency
items refer to five types of deviant behaviors (illegal as well as legal):
1) disobedience and disaffection from school (i.e., disobedient at
school and truancy); 2) disaffection from home (i.e., runs away and
steals at home); 3) disobedience from property rules (i.e., steals outside the home, vandalism, sets fires, and destroys others' things); 4)
dishonesty (cheats and lies); and 5) uses alcohol and drugs. From a
research or child development perspective, the coextensive appearance of these multiple types of behaviors within a six-month period
would be a potent indicator of a delinquent pattern of behavior—whether measured in a random, clinical, or court-linked sample. In addition to the core items, ECYS youth display characteristics
that expand the types of items included in the core pattern (i.e., display poor school work, stubbornness, and disobedience to parents);
ECYS youth also elaborate the core pattern by including hyperactive
behaviors (i.e., display impulsiveness, restlessness, and lack of concentration). In the 1989 ACQ study, these types of hyperactive items

and the expanded delinquency items are included in the attention or aggressive core syndrome (with some overlap of items between syndromes).

A comparison of the ECYS and ACQ aggression scales discloses that 13 of the 19 ACQ items can also be found on the ECYS list. The core items refer primarily to verbal types of aggression, but also includes two nonlegal interpersonal, types of hostile behavior—"cruelty or bullying" and "starts fights." While a national core syndrome of verbal and physical aggression can be readily identified as likely to occur in middle class and inner city areas, the ECYS sample's multiaggression factor also includes items that are likely to consist of illegal types of interpersonal violence—"attacks people" and "threatens people." In criminological terms, the ECYS sample—in contrast to the 1989 ACQ clinical samples—is more likely to be associated with examples of actual or theoretical aggravated felonious assault; these are precisely the types of behaviors that the National Youth Study (NYS) found to distinguish between a national sample of black and white youth.

The comparisons of the three external-type ACQ core patterns with the ECYS results indicates that two of the patterns appear to be fairly stable across population groups. The delinquency core pattern is virtually similar for the ECYS and ACQ samples, and the aggression core pattern displays a high degree of convergence for the two diverse samples. However, the third ACQ external-type syndrome—attention problems—appears to be less stable across population groups. There are ECYS hyperactive items that appear on the ACQ attention list or that appear on the ACQ aggressive list; in addition, some of the items appear on both the ACQ aggressive and attention problem list.

A comparison of the internal items of the ECYS and ACQ factors indicates that the measurement of psychological problems may not be stable over population groups for all types of problems. Only two of the internal types of problems found in the ECYS sample are congruent with the ACQ national clinical sample—the somatic and anxious/depressed scales. The ACQ study contains five somatic items—and all of these are contained in the ECYS factor: dizziness; aches and pains; headaches; stomach pains; and vomits often. In addition, the ECYS factor includes nausea and rashes. The ECYS depression/anxious factor contains nine items, of which seven can be found in the ACQ anxious/depressed scale: feels worthless; too guilty; unloved; lonely; nervous and tense; sad and depressed; and worrying. However, the ACQ scale contains six other items that refer to additional anxious feelings. The other two ECYS internal factors—strange ideas/feelings and withdrawn—are much less congruent with the reliable ACQ core patterns of withdrawn or the less reliable pattern of schizoid (not considered as an ACQ core pattern for all age groups).

A comparison of the ECYS mixed delinquency and multiaggression items with the NYS study disclosed that sixteen items were comparable for both samples—even though the NYS study relies on self-reports and the ECYS on parent reports. This overlap indicates that if the self-report researchers had been interested in identifying core behaviors on an empirical rather than an a priori legal basis—they might have also constructed factors that were similar to the ECYS and ACQ results for external behaviors. One study using twenty-six NYS items, found that an adjudicated male delinquent sample yielded a four-factor solution that also distinguished between aggression and other types of illegal behaviors.

Assessing the Overlap Among Core Patterns

Besides identifying distinctive core patterns, and comparing the results with national studies using either parent or self-reports, we also examined the overlap between types of problems. There were indeed significant correlations between all of the three major measures of problems—with the strongest occurring between multiaggression and new internal and mixed delinquent. In order to examine the specific types of overlap more precisely, we constructed a delinquent/aggressive typology by cross-tabulating all mixed delinquent youth who scored above and below the ECYS median score with multiaggression scores above and below the median. Four distinct types of external behavior patterns were created. All youth were classified as one of four distinct types: 1) low delinquency/low aggression; 2) low delinquency/high aggression; 3) high delinquency/low aggression; and 4) high delinquency/high aggression. Because of the moderately strong bivariate relationship between the two measures, there were more youth classified at the low/low and high/high ends of the typology.

The first analysis determined whether there were any differences between the two types of high scoring mixed delinquents—those with low aggression on the four component measures of mixed delinquency (i.e., legal property offenses; truant/runaway; disobey;

and hyperactive). Hypothetically we might expect that no differences would occur between the two delinquent types, since both were categorized by their median scores. However, detailed analysis revealed a difference between the two delinquent types on one of the component measures—hyperactive. The high delinquency/high aggression type had a significantly higher mean score on the hyperactive measure than occurred for the high delinquency/low aggression type. However, the other two types were also significantly lower on the hyperactive measure. We concluded that hyperactive behaviors are more likely to occur with other high delinquent behaviors, but the level increases when high aggression is also present.

A comparison of the two delinquent types on the component measures of aggression (i.e., verbal aggression; fear/perfectionist; legal assault; and unlike/cruelty) revealed that the high delinquent/high aggression type had, as expected, a significantly higher score on all aggression measures, when compared to the high delinquency/low aggression type. On two of the measures—verbal aggression and fearful/perfectionist—the mean scores were the same for two high aggression types. However, the most salient finding was that the high delinquency/high aggression type scored significantly higher than the low delinquency/high aggression type on two of the most physically aggressive measures—legal assault and unliked/cruel.

We can conclude that youths who are highly delinquent and highly aggressive are also highly hyperactive and engage in physically aggressive behaviors. It appears plausible to infer that this type has characteristics that set it apart from the other types. The combined behaviors of this type are similar to Albert Cohen's description of a subcultural delinquent: these are youths who engaged in theft, truancy, malicious mischief, and vandalism in a spirit of spite, contempt, ridicule of conventional authority and adult rules, and with expressive impulsiveness. This inference about the high/high type is buttressed by the fact that a high score on hanging with bad peers is also a correlate of high delinquency. While high delinquency/low aggression is also associated with hanging out with youth who get in trouble, a "pure" delinquent type does not have the highest score on hyperactivity, legal assault, and cruelty.

Assessment of the overlap between new internal scores and the delinquent/aggressive typology discloses that there are no differences between the aggressive types; both aggressive types are clearly higher on new internal scores than the other types. Psychological problems are also linked to high delinquency/low aggression, but it occurs at a lower level of scores than for the aggressive types.

In summary, the analysis of overlap indicates that internal, psychological problems are linked to aggressive behaviors, while bad peers are associated with delinquent behaviors. What appears to be unique about the types is the fact that youth who are high on both core delinquent and core aggressive behaviors (as defined by 1989 ACQ standards) are also the ones who are highest on those external behaviors that expand and elaborate basic patterns. For the ECYS sample, there are no gender differences in the likelihood that high/high youth are either male or female; nor are there age differences. This finding may be unique to this population sample.

Implications

In discussing the specific findings that emerged in this study, we have made references to the fields of child development, criminology, sociology, social psychology, and psychiatry. We believe that there are potential theoretical and/or methodological lessons that can be reasonably inferred from our findings. The field of child development, for example, is a clear leader in the identification of core patterns that can be found among diverse subpopulations of American (and even Dutch) youth—but by including items that are the subject of theoretical debate—such as the influences of like-minded peers and inadequate superego (or conscience) socialization—within any core syndromes, it limits the possibility of examining these variables in greater depth (see the next chapter, for example).

There is one other caution that might be extended to the use of parent reports by child development researchers—paying attention to the representativeness of the clinical samples that provide the "core syndromes." In Achenbach's original studies the sex/age factors that emerged from an analysis of clinical youth were derived from the analysis of parent reports from 42 east coast mental health service organizations. For the national 1989 ACQ study the core syndromes were based on the analysis of parent reports from 18 mental health services distributed across the country. Out of 215 items used by the ACQ researchers only 65 unduplicated items were actually used in the creation of the six consistent core syndromes that are applicable to both males and females, ages 6–16. Missing from the ACQ list of aggressive behaviors are two

Achenbach items that are closest to legal assault—physically attacks people and threatens people (items #57 and 97, respectively). However, both of these items were included in the original Achenbach CBCL aggressive factors for both males and females, ages 12–16. In addition, the ECYS analysis found that these items were also included in a multiaggression factor for both sexes. It is conceivable that the CBCL's 42 east coast mental health sites yield a different problem population than the 18 "national" sites used by the ACQ researchers. Since the escalation of verbal and interpersonal aggression into potential felonious assaults are important behaviors to measure, it could be quite limiting to rely on the ACQ core syndrome of aggression as the best indicator of the behaviors of a mental health sample—much less a court-linked sample.

The fields of criminology and sociology appear to be fearful of including within the construct of "delinquency" any types of behaviors which are not explicitly illegal. As a result, studies of self-reports have not usually included the array of behaviors that can be found in the CBCL or ACQ instruments. Besides this deficiency, there appears to be a reluctance to engage in a factor analysis of the illegal behaviors. Instead, the delinquency indexes were grouped on *a priori* considerations, so that the analysis of empirically derived patterns has been unable to determine whether aggressive-type behaviors would be distinguishable from property-type and drug-type behaviors. The study of adjudicated delinquents, using NYS items, did find that these distinct behaviors emerged as relatively clear factors. If representative studies of adjudicated—or officially designated delinquents—were used as normative groups, then the NYS cohorts could be re-examined to establish national cut-off scores for distinct types of deviant and illegal behaviors. At present, there is an absence of national norms for the self-report studies—but there is no practical reason why the methodology associated with the CBCL and ACQ could not be replicated for this method of describing behaviors.

Unlike criminologists, clinicians are not reluctant to combine legal and illegal behaviors as indicators of a diagnostic categorization of a mental health "disorder." The most widely known (and used) system for classifying mental disorders is the *Diagnostic and Statistical Manual of Mental Disorders* (commonly referred to as DSM-III-R, for the third edition, revised, 1987). If we were to rely on the instructions of the DSM-III-R for classifying and describing antisocial behaviors as "conduct disorder," then a disproportionate number of "normal" children would be declared as exhibiting this type of disorder. According to the DSM-III-R instructions (on page 55), if three out of thirteen antisocial behaviors have occurred over a six month period, then a youth can be classified as having met the "diagnostic criteria" for a conduct disorder. But according to Achenbach's empirical norms for boys 12–16 years of age, a score of at least seven would be required to be classified as a "delinquent" (also using thirteen items of the CBCL). Since the DSM-III-R does not make allowances for frequency of occurrence, the three items could be scored as "somewhat or sometimes true" (a score of 1) or "very true or often true" (a score of 2) for each of the three necessary behaviors—and could be scored anywhere between a score of three and six. In an attempt to pay some attention to empirical correlations, the DSM-III-R authors (a subcommittee of consultants employed by the American Psychiatric Association) have erred on the side of overinclusion—and the labeling of many "false positives." (A similar case could be made with even greater ease if we had used the example of Achenbach's CBCL syndromes, since the CBCL cut-off scores are much higher).

In addition to the problem of overinclusion, the DSM-III-R list continues the original practice of confounding delinquent and aggressive behaviors. Out of the list of thirteen specified behaviors, five are clearly of an aggressive type (e.g., often initiates physical fights, has been physically cruel to people or animals, and used a weapon in more than one fight). The evidence of this study, Achenbach's CBCL studies, and the ACQ study is that aggressive behavior constitutes a distinct syndrome. Rather than creating one list of items that includes two distinct types of behaviors, it would be useful to have two distinct lists—and then create combined types according to precise indicators. If this were done, then the special features of youths who are high on both delinquent and aggressive behaviors could be recognized as presenting the most serious antisocial problems.

The final difficulty of the DSM-III-R approach is the failure to specify the clinical reasons for classifying "bad" behaviors as types of "mad" behaviors. Antisocial, or bad behaviors, can be conceptualized as indicators of immorality, inadequate socialization, cultural deviance, or just plain illegal. Where are the indicators that the list of behaviors are signs of a "mental disorder"—with the implication that the conduct is a symptom of an underlying state of mental ill-health? The behaviors themselves cannot be used, since they are open to other social categorizations in the absence of any specific psychological criteria. Using ECYS data, it appears that an empirical case might be created if more attention were paid to the special correlations between aggressive behaviors and measures of psychological problems. Youths with high aggression—whether low or high in delinquent scores—are much more likely to score high on internal, psychological problems. The DSM-III-R ought to be able to deal with these types of findings and begin to articulate the link between clear mental health problems and external-type behaviors.

4

Explaining the Problems

INTERVIEWER: *Thinking back to when the main problem
first got* started, *why do you think it began?*

*Maybe because I couldn't buy him everything he wanted, so he could go to the store
and steal it. He had plenty of toys.*

Mother of 13-year-old boy

*Because of a reaction to the separation. The separation took the lid off the roof.
When his father left the home, there was no one to control him.*

Mother of a 15-year-old boy

*I think his lack of self-worth and adolescent confusion that he didn't know how to
deal with (made the problem begin). We moved from New York to New Jersey, so he
was probably floundering with that.*

Mother of a 16-year-old boy

This chapter identifies what is responsible for causing delinquency,
aggression and psychological problems of urban youths. As we have
pointed out, most explanatory research relies on information that is
obtained from administrative records or the youths themselves. This
chapter identifies influences that rely on information obtained from
parents. Because we directly ask parents what they think is responsible for causing their adolescent's main problem, we are able to un-

derstand their subjective interpretations of the problems in their child's life. In addition to standard demographic information, we also have other information from the survey that can be used analytically to help explain the behavioral problems of the youths, such as, the youth lacks guilt (a psychopathic item), and hangs out with bad peers (a reference group item), and the youth's problems are similar to those of other members of the family (a family history item). We pay special attention to these items because of their interest from psychodynamic and sociological perspectives. By establishing the nature of the influences, we identify important risk factors in urban youths' lives.

First we conduct bivariate analyses of the influences and the three dependent measures of problems. Then we conduct step-wise multiple regression analyses for each dependent measure. Our aim is to ascertain which combination of risk variables is best able to account for the maximum amount of the variability (or variance) in the occurrence of the problem behaviors. In order to ensure that the regression results are not spurious, further analysis uses demographic and sample variables as statistical controls to determine whether the findings are maintained under a variety of conditions.

We are keenly interested in determining whether the risk variables that emerge in the multivariate analyses also are found in each subsample of boys and girls. Therefore, the findings of the multivariate analysis will be presented for the total sample, and for boys and girls separately. This analytic strategy has proven useful in understanding sex differences in drug problems, as well as adolescent depression (White, 1992; Avison and MacAlpine, 1992).

The analyses that follow are, of course, based on the special characteristics associated with this sample. Analyses from the last chapter provide evidence that the ECYS sample is more similar to clinical samples than to randomly drawn "non-clinical" samples. However, both boys and girls in our urban sample have higher delinquency scores than Achenbach's clinical samples (see chapter 3, Tables 3–1 and 3–2). While Essex County youths are clearly a high delinquency sample in comparison to clinical samples, their aggression scores are similar. Their internal scores vary by sex for a couple of scales. Therefore, it will be extremely important for other researchers to test our predictive models with different samples having different mixtures of problems and different demographic characteristics.

Statistical Assumptions for Prediction

Several considerations guided the statistical analysis, and we present them before discussing the results. First, the survey gave parents an opportunity to say what they felt caused the main problem by direct, open- and closed-ended questions. We are aware, however, that other items in the survey could also be considered causes of the problem. Both direct and indirect influences were used in the analysis. Second, a cross-sectional research design, where measures are secured at one point in time, is a limitation that must be taken into account in a search for influences on behaviors. But it need not stymie efforts at conducting explanatory analyses. In order to engage in a causal line of analysis, three primary conditions must be met: 1) a time order of variables must be constructed that is reasonable and capable of being validated at a further date; 2) there must be an association between the selected independent and dependent variables; and 3) the association must be capable of being maintained even when all reasonable experimental or statistical control variables are employed. These assumptions are met, using the criteria that are explained below.

Three major behavioral problems are the variables to be "explained": delinquency (**mixed delinquency**), aggression (**multiaggression**), and psychological problems (**new internal**). All variables that pertain to the period after the occurrence of the problem behaviors are excluded from explanatory analyses. For instance, there are strong associations between talking to officials in the police department and in court and the measure of mixed delinquency. Since talking to officials is a logical consequence of deviant behaviors, this variable is excluded as an explanatory variable. Similarly, responses to questions about coping with the problem by 1) seeking help, 2) using a social agency, and 3) thinking about preferred types of solutions are excluded. These activities are most likely to occur after problem behaviors are exhibited. Direct and indirect attributions, and demographic or sample characteristics, refer to a time period prior to the reporting of problem behaviors. Further studies could establish if these assumptions about time order are indeed valid; pending a longitudinal study, however, we defend the time order of the explanatory variables on the basis of probability and logic.

For the purpose of assessing influences on the two antisocial behavioral factors of aggression and delinquency, we assume that internal, psychological problems could function as a "cause" of

deviant conduct, even though sociological theorists and many researchers have been reluctant to use psychological measures. We believe it is reasonable to think that psychological problems could
influence deviant behaviors, but that deviant behaviors would be
less likely to give rise to psychological problems. Therefore, we
employ the internal, psychological measure as a risk variable in influencing aggression and/or delinquency, as well as a unique phenomenon to be explained. We explore the variable "bad peers" in a
similar manner, both as an explanatory variable for the two antisocial measures and as a phenomenon to be explained. We are not assuming that aggressive and delinquent behaviors precede
association with bad peers, although some researchers are beginning to explore reciprocal influences (Thornberry, Lizotte, Krohn,
Farnsworth, and Jang, 1991; Thornberry, Krohn, Lizotte, and Chard-
Wierschiem, 1993).

Survey Questions on Causal Responsibility

In the interview parents were asked their ideas about the cause of their
adolescent's main problem, in both open-ended and closed-ended
formats. The open-ended question was: "Looking back to when the
main problem first got *started*, why do you think it began?" Two
closed-ended questions, with four-point Likert-scale categories,
asked parents to rate the degree to which each item was responsible
for causing the main problem to begin or get worse: a lot, some, a little,
or not at all. One closed-ended question refers to individuals: 1) the
adolescent, 2) peers of the adolescent, 3) the respondent, 4) the father
(if not the respondent), 4) a brother or sister, 5) and other relatives inside and outside the house. Interviewers were instructed to find out
the nature of the relationship of other relatives to the adolescent. The
second closed-ended question refers to external causes: 1) bad health,
2) family heredity, 3) TV, movies, newspapers, 4) type of neighborhood, 5) kind of school, 6) not having enough religious faith, 7) family
income insufficient, 8) discrimination, and 9) crowded apartment or
house. These questions measure causes that parents *directly* attribute
to the main problem. They provide us with data on three areas of
causes: 1) the adolescent; 2) the family or other socialization factors;
and 3) the environment.

In addition to questions that determine direct attributions, parents
were also asked to offer ideas about their children's lives *without* di-

rectly discussing how these might relate to the cause of the main problem. For example, parents were asked if the adolescents felt guilty about any of their actions, hung out with youths who got into trouble, or if the adolescents' problems were similar to those of any other members of the family. Responses to these questions could be correlated with delinquency, aggression, or internal, psychological mental health problems, but they could not be classified as *direct* attributions of causality since respondents were not asked whether they believed these responses to be causes. We consider these responses to be *indirect* attributions of causation. All respondents were asked the same questions regardless of the type of problem they identified as the main problem.

Bivariate Relationships for Major Problems

Table 4–1 presents the statistical correlations for five categories of potential explanatory variables and the major dependent measures of behavioral problems, including "hangs around with bad peers." If the associations are significant at a level beyond chance (using .05 as the criterion), then the numerical correlation is shown; if it is not significant, then "NS" is recorded.

Youth Responsibility/Problems as a Risk Factor

The first risk category refers to adolescents' thoughts, feelings, attitudes, or psychological problems that parents directly attribute to causing the main problem. The "youth causes problem" score is based on the closed-ended question regarding how much responsibility the adolescent has in causing the main problem: a lot, some, a little, or not at all. The open-ended question on what caused the main problem ("why main problem") is coded using several categories, including a child-related theme (See Chapter 1, Methods section). A child-related theme refers to feelings, such as sadness, anxiety, or anger, as well as undesirable thoughts or behaviors, developmental problems, and general personality characteristics of the adolescents. In response to the open-ended question, about 17% of the sample spontaneously mentioned that their adolescent was responsible for the main problem getting started.

Our results show that the "youth causes problem score" is significantly associated with mixed delinquency and hanging out with bad peers (.21 and .17, respectively). Youths are not held responsible for

Table 4.1 Bivariate Correlations for Major Dependent Variables, By Risk Categories and Sample Characteristics For Both Sexes

Risk Categories	Major Variables to be Explained			
	New Internal	Multi-Aggression	Mixed Delinquency	Hang With Bad Peers
I. Youth Responsibility/problems				
A. Direct Attributions				
1. Youth Cause Problem Score	NS	NS	.21	.17
2. Why Main Problem? Child Theme	.14	NS	NS	-.16
B. Indirect Attributions				
1. Youth Lacks Guilt	.26	.36	.43	.20
2. New Internal Problems	DNA	.62	.38	.14
II. Socialization Responsibility				
A. Direct Attributions				
1. Family Cause Problem Score	.24	.15	NS	NS
2. Why Main Problem? Missing Family Theme	NS	.14	NS	NS
3. Why Main Problem? Family Theme	NS	NS	NS	NS
4. Why Main Problem? Close Family Theme	.20	.19	NS	-.21

Table 4.1 (Continued)

B. Indirect Attributions				
1. Adult Respondent Had Problem	.16	NS	NS	NS
2. Other Family/Friends Had Prob	.15	NS	.20	.14
3. Ever Heard of Prob	NS	NS	NS	.14
4. All Had Problem	NS	NS	NS	NS
5. Adult Respondent Works	NS	NS	.14	NS
6. Respondent Close Score	-.17	NS	-.18	-.15
7. Mother Figure Closeness Score	-.15	NS	NS	NS
8. Total Mom and Dad Figure Closeness Score	NS	NS	-.14	.15
III. *Perceived Environment Responsibility*				
A. Direct Attributions				
1. Peers Cause Problem Score	NS	NS	.28	.45
2. Why Main Problem? Peer Theme	-.14	NS	.17	.22
3. Why Main Problem? External Theme	-.18	NS	NS	.19
4. Life Disadvantage Responsibility Score	.25	.25	.21	.13
5. Direct Environment Responsibility Score	NS	NS	.18	.30
B. Indirect Attributions				
1. Hangs Out With Bad Peers	.14	.21	.59	DNA
IV. *Onset of Main Problem*				
A. Found Out Year Plus Ago	.17	.22	.25	NS

Table 4.1 (Continued)

Risk Categories	Major Variables to be Explained			
	New Internal	Multi–Aggression	Mixed Delinquency	Hang With Bad Peers
V. Demographic Characteristics				
A. Gender (M/F)	.15	.15	NS	-.16
B. Race/Ethnicity (AO/Black)	NS	NS	NS	NS
C. Adult Respondent Age (30–72)	-.19	-.17	NS	NS
D. Youth Age (12–16)	NS	NS	NS	NS
E. Respondent Ever Married(Nvr/AO)	-.19	NS	NS	NS
F. Welfare (No/Yes)	NS	NS	NS	NS
G. Adult in HH (1–7)	NS	NS	NS	NS
H. Child in HH (1–8)	NS	NS	NS	.13
I. Head of Household (F/M)	Ns	NS	NS	NS
J. Respondent Schooling (0–3 levels)	NS	NS	NS	NS
K. Religion	NS	NS	NS	NS
L. Sample Type (FC/MH)	NS	NS	NS	-.24
M. Zip Code A (Inner Nwk/AO)	NS	NS	NS	NS
N. Zip Code B (All Nwk/Suburb)	NS	NS	NS	NS
O. Zip Code (Newark+suburb/Outsub)	NS	NS	NS	NS

new internal problems and multiaggression; neither correlation is significant. If the question is asked in an open-ended fashion, with the respondent free to choose any cause of the main problems, then the child-related theme is significantly, and positively, associated with new internal problems, and significantly, and negatively associated with bad peers.

The indirect attributions display much stronger associations and are significantly correlated (in varying degree) for each of the problem measures. The "youth lacks guilt" score is based on a single CBCL item, "doesn't seem to feel guilt after misbehaving." Like all Achenbach items, it is scored 0=never or not true, 1=somewhat or sometimes true, or 2=very true or very often true. Only about 41% of the parents answered "never or not true." High scores in lacking guilt are strongly associated with high scores in mixed delinquency and multiaggression (.43 and .36 respectively). While many parents are willing to endorse the judgment that their sons or daughters might be engaged in "psychopathic" behaviors (as identified by Quay, 1965, in a summary of studies conducted in the 1950s and 1960s), it is important to note that this type of attribution is not apt to be made in an open-ended question of why an antisocial behavior got started. Perhaps parents tend to perceive lack of guilt as a characteristic accompanying "misbehaving," whereas social scientists and psychiatrists perceive lack of guilt as potential evidence of an undersocialized conscience or an indication of "super-ego lacunae" (see Empey, 1978, theoretical discussion of "Psychodynamic Version of Control Theory," and Loeber et al., 1991, empirical findings on "untrustworthiness" in a longitudinal sample).

When scores on new internal problems are used as an explanatory variable, it is quite clear that youths reported to be high scorers on new internal problems (i.e., somatic, depression, strange ideas or behavior, and withdrawn) are extremely likely to receive high scores on aggressive behaviors. New internal scores also have a significant correlation with mixed delinquency, but it is evident that the correlations are distinctly different (.62 vs. .38, respectively); the significant correlation of .14 for bad peers is, of course, the lowest of the three associations.

The finding of the first risk factor, that the adolescent causes the problems, provides evidence that variables associated with the "personality system" are probably good candidates for explanations of problem behaviors of youths. This result supports Jessor and Jessor (1977). However, significant bivariate associations that are displayed in Table 4–1 vary by the nature of the problem. Therefore, explanations that refer to a general "deviant proneness" or "comorbidity" will have to pay attention to distinctive types of problems.

Socialization Responsibility as a Risk Factor

The responsibility for socializing children generally is linked to the family and other adults. According to Hirschi's control theory, attachment or commitment to conventional parents and adult norms provide resistance to the attractions of misbehaving. From this theoretical perspective, the associations between socialization variables and antisocial problem measures ought to be particularly strong. In contrast, the multirisk model proposed by Jessor and Jessor (1977) suggests that socialization is only indirectly linked to proneness to engage in deviant behaviors. They contend that the adolescent's personality and perceived environment systems are more likely to provide the immediate contexts for triggering deviant episodes. From Jessor and Jessor's perspective, associations between socialization variables and problem measures ought to be weak or nonexistent. The findings presented in the second part of Table 4–1, in combination with the findings displayed in the first and third parts of the table, tend to support Jessor and Jessor's approach towards understanding multirisk influences on problem behaviors.

Part A of the socialization category refers to direct questions about any responsibility of the respondent or other family members, regardless of whether the relatives lived in the youth's household. The "family cause problem" score refers to direct questions about the degree of responsibility of the respondent/caregiver, father, brother or sister, or other relatives to initiating the main problem or helping it to get worse. A factor analysis of these persons and youth or friend's responsibility disclosed that the family members constituted a single dimension of responsibility whereas youth and peer responsibility responses were each not part of a family factor. Each family member was scored according to whether that individual contributed to the youth's problem a lot, some, a little, or not at all, and the totals add up for a "family cause problem score." The average score was 3.13 out of a maximum score of 10.

According to Table 4–1 a high family cause score is most strongly linked to new internal problems, and then, less strongly to multiaggression (.24 and .15, respectively); associations with mixed delinquency and bad peers are not statistically significant.

The remaining direct items are related to the open-ended question of what caused the main problem to get started. This was coded into the following categories: 1) missing father theme; 2) parent- or family-related theme; 3) child-related theme; 4) peer-related theme; 5) external themes of school, work, or the general environment; and 6) other reasons. Any mention of a theme received a score of 1, and all other responses received a 0; each theme was coded in this "dummy variable" fashion. Section two makes use of the first three themes; section one uses only the child-related theme and section three uses the peer and external themes.

The missing father theme was spontaneously mentioned as a cause (as a first, second, or third mention) by about 6% of the parents. Despite the low rate of occurrence, it proved to be statistically significant with multiaggression scores (.14 vs. not significant for other problems). A family theme was mentioned as a cause by 18% of the respondents, but there were no significant associations with any of the behavior problem measures. When a mention of a child and/or family theme was combined as a dummy variable, about 52% of the parents are coded as employing this causal theme. This dummy variable is significantly and positively associated with new internal problems and multiaggression. This result replicates, and reinforces the findings reported above that the closed-ended family cause problem score is associated with new internal problems and multiaggression. Hanging out with bad peers is negatively correlated with a mention of a child and/or family theme. This finding parallels the negative association of the child-related theme and hanging out with bad peers, the finding reported in section one. At a direct attribution level, high scores on mixed delinquency are consistently not associated with any of the measures of family causal responsibility.

Moving to the indirect measures of socialization responsibility, we investigate a total of eight indicators. The first four indicators ask parents to provide assessments of whether they had ever had a similar main problem while growing up, or whether any other persons in or outside the family had ever had this type of problem. Other questions ask if they had ever heard of this kind of problem on TV, movies, or radio and whether all youth have these kinds of problems while growing up. Taken together, these questions attempt to ascertain whether any imitation or modeling of adult or mass media behaviors are associated with problem measures—even though parents did not note any of these socialization possibilities as a direct cause of a problem.

About 16% of the respondents reported that they had experienced a similar type of problem while growing up. A positive answer was associated only with scores on the new internal measure (.16 vs. not significant). Many more respondents answered that other persons known to them (in or outside the family) had this kind of main problem; about 44% mentioned a family member and 13% noted a person outside the family (primarily a friend of a family member). Knowing others who had this problem while growing up is significantly associated with new internal, mixed delinquency, and hang out with bad peers (.15 vs .20 vs .14, respectively), but not with multiaggression. Having heard about the problem via a mass media outlet is only barely significant for hanging out with bad peers, while the belief that all youths have this type of problem while growing up is not associated with any of the problem measures.

The last three indicators focus more directly on the respondent. If the respondent works outside the home for money, then there is a significant association with mixed delinquency, but not the other measures (.14 vs. not significant). A question about the degree of closeness to the respondent yields significant associations with three of the four problem measures. When respondents were presented with a graphic picture of concentric circles of varying width—like a bullseye target—with the youth in the center of the smallest circle, they were asked to place themselves in one of the circles according to how "close" they were to the youth. Each circle was numbered, with the closest circle receiving a score of three, the next a two, the farthest a one, and outside any of the circles a nil. The respondent closeness score variable received an average score of 1.99 out of a maximum score of 3.00. The lower the respondent closeness score, then the more likely that youth were high scorers on new internal, mixed delinquency, and hanging with bad peers (−.17 vs −.18 vs −.15); however, the aggression measure is not related to the respondent closeness measure. The circle approach to measuring closeness was applied to all mother figures in or outside the home, as well as father figures—but these did not yield as consistent results as the respondent closeness score (see last two lines of the socialization variables).

In general, it is possible to conclude that both direct and indirect attributions are associated with two or more of the problem measures. The direct attribution measures—whether derived from open or closed-ended questions—indicate that parents view the family as responsible for new internal problems and multiaggression. They do not view the family as responsible for mixed delinquency, as might be expected by Hirschi's social control theory.

Measures of indirect attribution of socialization are also linked to new internal scores when indicators of social comparison and respondent closeness are used. Unlike the direct attribution measures, none of the indirect indicators are significantly associated with scores on aggression. Instead, measures of social comparison and respondent closeness are associated with mixed delinquency and hanging out with bad peers. Despite the fact that none of the second type of risk variables yield associations that are as strong as those revealed for youth responsibility or perceived environment, it is important to note that the new internal measure is consistently associated with socialization responsibility measures—regardless of whether they are measured as a direct or indirect attribution, or whether the questions are open or closed-ended. A similar inference cannot be made for the other major problem measures. Both multiaggression and mixed delinquent are sensitive to the content of the socialization attributions. Aggression scores appear to be correlated with direct family attributions (whether open or closed-ended questions are used). Mixed delinquency scores, on the other hand, appear to be correlated with indirect attributions referring to social comparisons (or modeling) and respondent closeness.

Perceived Environment Responsibility as a Risk Factor

The third risk category attempts to assess the role of environmental influences—whether indicated by associations with peers or broader environmental influences such as crowded housing, bad schools or neighborhoods, and lack of money. The first five influences involve parents' judgments of whether any of the environmental circumstances are responsible for the main problem getting started or getting worse. The peer cause problem score is from a single item within the battery of items concerning whether any persons listed were responsible for the problem getting started and becoming worse a lot, some, a little, or not at all. The average peer responsibility score was 1.63 out of a maximum score of 3. This indicator of peer responsibility is correlated with mixed delinquency and, as expected, with hanging with bad peers, but it is not associated with new internal or aggression scores (.28 vs .45 vs not significant, respectively). Besides the appearance of peers in a closed-ended question, the open-ended question of how the main problem got started also evoked a peer-related theme (for about 15% of the respondents). This indicator duplicates the results of the peer cause problem measure, but at weakened levels of association (and a negative association with new internal).

When the open-ended themes are scored by whether the causes are due to environmental reasons (e.g., crowded housing, poverty, bad neighbors, drug neighborhood, or no authority from school), new internal is negatively associated with an external theme, but the aggression and delinquency measures are not associated; only hanging with bad peers reveals a positive association (−.18 vs not significant vs .19, respectively).

The life disadvantage responsibility and direct environment measures each include items that are in a common list of "other things" (besides family and friends) that caused the problems or made them worse. The following items emerged in a factor analysis as consisting of a common factor of "other things" that might be responsible a lot, some, a little, or not at all: bad heredity; crowded housing; family income not enough; discrimination; and not having enough religious faith. We have labeled this factor containing these items as a "life disadvantage" dimension. Each item was scored by the convention of 3 for a lot, 2 for some, 1 for a little, and 0 for not at all. The average score was about 5.87 out of a maximum score of 15. The other set of items emerged as a second factor and included the following items: type of neighborhood; kind of school he/she goes to; and TV, movies, newspapers. These items were scored as a "direct environment" dimension. The average score on this measure was 4.08 out of a maximum score of 9.

The life disadvantage responsibility score is the only measure that behaves as a measure consistently associated with all types of problems (.25 vs .25 vs .21 vs .13). In contrast, the direct environment responsibility score is only correlated with mixed delinquency and hanging out with bad peers. Evidently only quite specific (and perhaps only a limited few) causal measures are associated with all types of youth problems. By way of contrast, direct environmental responsibility measures are positively correlated for all of the possible associations with hanging out with bad peers and 4 of the 5 possible associations with mixed delinquency. Once again aggression associations are dissimilar from mixed delinquency correlations.

Only one indirect attribution of the perceived environment has been identified in the questionnaire—the single question of hanging out with bad peers. While this item is significantly correlated with each of the three major problem measures, it is clear that the association with mixed delinquency is much stronger than for the other two (.59 vs .14 or .21, respectively). This single environmental measure behaves with mixed delinquency in a manner that is similar to the correlation of multiaggression and new internal problems—both are correlated at about .60 (.59 to .62) for the entire sample. However, the causal measures refer to quite distinctly different referents—external environment of bad peers or the personality system of internal problems.

Onset of Main Problem

This category contains only a single item and refers to how long ago the respondent actually found out about the main problem. Any response of more than a year ago was scored as a 1, and a year or less was scored as a 0. About 55% of the respondents found out about the main problem more than a year ago. The evidence is quite clear that the longer the duration of the problem, the higher the score on each of the major problem measures. This measure, like the life disadvantages score, behaves similarly for each of the problem types—and may be another candidate for a limited group of variables that are useful for assessing all types of deviant behaviors.

Sample Characteristics

The final section tests all of the primary demographic characteristics that might be associated with one or more of the problems. In studies of self-reports, the variables of gender and youth's age have emerged as consistent variables in studies of delinquency and mental health problems. Girls usually score lower on delinquency measures and higher on scales measuring depressive systems. For this sample, girls do score higher on the new internal measure, but they also score higher on the measure of aggression. There is no gender difference for mixed delinquency, but girls are less likely to be perceived as hanging out with bad peers. Regarding gender, this sample may have unique characteristics.

Race/ethnicity differences have not been consistent in self-report studies. While Elliott and his colleagues did report a significant difference on assaultive items, this variable did not emerge in consistently explaining any of the variance in the original NYS analyses or any of the more recent studies (Smith, Visher, and Jarjoura, 1991 and Agnew, 1991).

Virtually all of the youth studies use the age of youth as a statistical control variable, but it is difficult to locate any that use the age of parents (particularly the mother). In this sample, there is a negative association for respondent's age and the measure of new internal and multiaggression (–.19 and –.17, respectively). The younger the respondent, the more likely that their children will experience psychological problems and display aggressive behaviors. The use of this variable as a statistical control in the multivariate analyses will be unique, but until other studies disclose the age of the parents there is uncertainty of the uniqueness of this sample.

This sample does not reveal any age of youth associations with the major problem measures. Other studies have revealed that aggressiveness scores diminish with age, and that some types of mixed delinquency increase with age (e.g., truancy, using alcohol and drugs, car theft).

Inspection of the other demographic-sample variables reveals only three other significant associations. Respondents who have never married are likely to have children who score high on new internal problems. Since this variable is also correlated with respondent's age, it will be useful to control for both variables when conducting multivariate analyses with the new internal measure. The number of children in the household has a weak, but significant, association with hanging out with bad peers. The last significant correlation indicates that the cases coming from the family crisis sample are much more likely to yield youth who are more likely to hang out with bad peers. This association may also be related to the gender association with bad peers, and will require a multivariate analysis to indicate whether the uniqueness of the sample contributes to our understanding of who is likely to hang out with bad peers.

Multivariate Analyses of Delinquency

The major purpose in conducting a multivariate analysis of mixed delinquency (as well as the other major problem measures) is to identify the unique contributions that each of the risk categories can make in accounting for the variation (or variance) in the scores. The higher the percent of variance associated with a risk category, then the stronger is the inference that an important influence has been identified. Given the bivariate association of the bad peer variable, we would expect this component of the perceived environment risk category to have a strong share of the variance. However, we do not know how important this variable can be (from a parental perspective) unless we simultaneously control for the existence of other critical variables identified in the bivariate analyses. The analyses that follow are based on step-wise, multiple, regression analyses of the significant variables associated with each risk category and mixed delinquency (see Table 4–1). After the unique variables contributing one or more percent of the variance (that were also statistically significant) were identified, all of the variables were combined and tested for the contribution of any demographic characteristics. These procedures were first used with the total sample, and then with each sex to ascertain whether similar variables accounted for a comparable percent of the variance. The results are displayed in Table 4–2.

Table 4–2 provides strong evidence that the variables that emerged in the multiple regression analyses are capable of explaining an appreciable amount of the variance for the total sample (55.8%). Since many studies of delinquency (like the NYS study) usually reach a maximum variance of 30–35%, the results of this study's findings are striking—and warrant comparison. Focusing only on the total sample, it is clear that bad peers (the only perceived environment variable that proved to be significant) contributes the largest amount of the variance (35.8%). This amount is comparable to the NYS finding reported by Elliott and his colleagues (1989) who found that this index of delinquent peers explained 27%, and male gender explained 4%, for a total of 31%. What distinguishes this study from the NYS study is the inclusion of the risk category of youth responsibility variables—since the related variables account for an appreciable addition to the total variance (16.5%).

It is evident that the finding about the influence of a differential association variable—bad peers—confirms the results of the best self-report studies conducted in the past decade (cited earlier in the chapter). The NYS study might have also increased the total variance explained if they had chosen to include measures of mental health in their statistical analyses. Elliott and his colleagues had asked a national sample of youth in one of the sample years to assess the degree to which youth perceived that parents and peers agreed that the youth had a mental health problem. This measure of perceived mental health "labeling" was highly correlated with a NYS measure of social isolation/loneliness (1989, p.77). A bivariate analysis found

Table 4-2 Comparison of Risk Variables for Mixed Delinquency by Percent of Variance Contribution for the Total Sample and Each Sex

Risk Categories	Percent of Variance (R^2)		
	Total Sample	Boys	Girls
I. *Youth Responsibility/Problems*			
A. Lacks Guilt	9.4%	11.3%	3.9%
B. New Internal Score	5.2	6.5	8.1
C. Child Responsibility Score	1.9	1.4	5.5
Subtotal	(16.5%)	(19.2%)	(17.5%)
II. *Socialization Responsibility*			
A. Others Have Problem	0%	0%	3.8%
III. *Perceived Environment Responsibility*			
A. Bad Peers	35.8%	30.9%	39.6%
IV. *Onset of Main Problem*			
A. Found Out Year Plus Ago	3.5%	3.2%	1.2%
V. *Demographic Characteristics*	0%	0%	0%
Total Variance (R^2)	55.8%	55.3%	62.1%

that NYS youth who were low offending youth were much less likely to score high on a "mental health problems score" (1989, table 3.1, p.55) Evidently they chose not to use their mental health measures because there is no place for distinctly psychological or personality variables in their theoretical model for explaining delinquency. Had they used their mental health measures—as an epidemiological risk variable—Elliott and his colleagues might have added to their total variance, and stimulated other researchers to pay more attention to measures of youth problems and moral responsibility.

The major findings for the total sample are replicated fairly closely for each sex. Even though boys are more likely to hang out with bad peers (see Table 4–1), this variable emerges as the strongest source of influence for both sexes (30.9 to 39.6%). In addition, the amount of variance accounted for by the youth responsibility risk category is quite comparable (19.2 vs 17.5%). While boys have higher mixed delinquency scores if they are perceived to lack guilt, when compared to girls (11.3 to 3.9%), the direct attribution measure of child responsibility has a higher amount of variance associated with girls (5.5 to 1.4%).

Table 4–2 also discloses that the socialization responsibility risk category can be associated as a unique influence on high mixed delinquency scores—but this is only true for the girls of this sample. The onset of the problem contributes a small amount of variance for the total sample, and this is primarily due to a stronger link to the boys. The demographics of the sample do not contribute any significant amount of the variance to an explanation of mixed delinquency scores.

Multivariate Analyses of Aggression

The analyses of the multiaggression measure were conducted with the same procedures as those discussed for mixed delinquency. Table 4–3 displays the results for the total sample and for each sex.

While the amount of the total variance for the entire sample is not as high as that achieved for mixed delinquency, the amount is quite strong (45.7 vs 55.8%). The most striking difference between the two analyses is the complete absence of bad peers as a variable making any variance contribution for multiaggression. As a matter of fact, there is no variance contribution from either the perceived environment or socialization responsibility categories. It is the youth re-

Table 4.3 Comparison of Risk Variables for Multi-aggression, by Percent of Variance Contribution for the Total Sample and Each Sex

Risk Categories	Percent of Variance (R^2)		
	Total Sample	Boys	Girls
I. *Youth Responsibility/Problems*			
A. Lacks Guilt	4.1%	2.3%	6.8%
B. New Internal Score	36.9	36.5	35.7
Subtotal	(41.0%)	(38.8%)	(42.5%)
II. *Socialization Responsibility*	0%	0%	0%
III. *Perceived Environment Responsibility*			
A. Life Disadvantage Responsibility Score	0%	3.6%	0%
IV. *Onset of Main Problem*			
A. Found Out Year Plus Ago	1.7%	0%	2.8%
V. *Demographic Characteristics*			
A. Age: Younger	1.3 %	0%	2.5%
B. Sample type: Mental Health	1.7	0	1.6
Total Variance (R^2)	45.7%	42.4%	49.4%

sponsibility/problem risk category that contributes the lion's share of the total variance (41 out of a total 45.7%). Within this risk category, it is clear that the score on the new internal measure contributes most of the variance. Since the major findings hold for each sex, the evidence is quite strong that high scores on mental health problems are a major source of aggressive types of behaviors in this multiproblem sample of youth.

The likelihood that the strong association between high new internal scores and multiaggression is probably not unique to this sample is buttressed by key findings from Chapter 3, and research results reported by Achenbach. First, it is useful to note that the ECYS scores on multiaggression have a correlation of .93 for boys scored on Achenbach's aggression scales and a .93 for girls scored on the female items; therefore, the ECYS multiaggression items are tapping the same dimension of aggression as Achenbach—but our items are similar for boys and girls. Second, it is also useful to note that when ECYS youth are scored by using only Achenbach scale items, for each sex, their main scores are not significantly different from Achenbach's clinical sample (see Tables 3–1 and 3–2); therefore, the ECYS sample is not unusual in having more aggressive youth than the clinical samples (unlike the higher proportion of high delinquent youth). Third, Achenbach's correlation between the aggression scale and the combined internal scales is also above .60 for each sex (Achenbach and Edelbrock, 1983).

While the high degree of co-morbidity of aggression and mental health problems (as measured by new internal or comparable items and controlled for other correlates of aggression) may not be surprising, the absence of any variance contribution by bad peers or any other peer variable appears, at first glance, to be unusual. After all, even psychiatrists are instructed by the DSM-III-R *Manual* to take into account the subtyping of "conduct disorders" as a "group type" or a "solitary aggressive type" (American Psychiatric Association, 1987). For clinicians following the DSM-III-R *Manual* "conduct disorder" refers to a mixture of delinquent-type and aggressive behaviors. In actual practice, there are many youth scoring high on delinquent measures who also score high on aggressive behaviors—as depicted in the delinquent/aggressive typology tables in chapter 3 (see Table 3–7). But it is the mixed delinquent activities—not the mixed aggression behaviors—that are linked to bad peer associates. The likelihood that high aggression is linked to bad peers primarily when high delinquency is also present is congruent with the findings of Tables 3–7, 4–1, and 4–2.

Indirect support for this inference can also be found in the NYS study. Elliott and his colleagues used two primary measures of delinquency to test their integrated theory of delinquency : general delinquency, a mixture of index and nonindex legal type offenses (22 items); and index only offenses (9 items). The general delinquency measure was able to have about 31% of the variance explained in 1977 and 1978, but the index measure could only produce a R^2 of 14–15% in the same year. The latter measure had six aggressive and three property offenses, whereas the general delinquency measure had twelve nonaggressive and ten aggressive items (Elliott et al., 1989). Since delinquent companions contributed the greatest share of explained variance for both NYS analyses (and a deliberate omission of mental health measures), we are not surprised that the more aggressive measure has a far weaker association with a measure of differential association.

Multivariate Analyses of Bad Peers

Since the bad peer variable has proved to be a unique contributor to understanding mixed delinquency, but a noncontributor to explaining multiaggression, it is important to examine this variable in greater detail. This can be accomplished by displaying the results of regression analyses that are similar to those conducted for the two primary measures of antisocial behaviors. Table 4–4 presents the results for the total sample and each sex.

The risk categories and the demographic characteristics account for a respectable amount of the variance for the total sample. Unlike the two previous analyses, no category is clearly dominant. Further, for the first time demographic characteristics are clearly important, since this category accounts for 13.2% of the variance. Being a male, from a household with an above average amount of children, and being associated with the family crisis subsample are the unique demographic characteristics that are linked to hanging out with bad peers. Many self-report studies have found male gender to account for a comparable amount of the variance with a delinquency measure (e.g., the NYS study); in Table 4–4 gender is indirectly related to mixed delinquency via the peer variable. If we follow the logic of an indirect link to mixed delinquency—via the strong variance con-

Table 4.4   Comparison of Risk Variables for Bad Peers, by Percent of Variance Contribution for the Total Sample and Each Sex

Risk Categories	Percent of Variance (R^2)		
	Total Sample	Boys	Girls
I. *Youth Responsibility/Problems*			
A. Lacks Guilt	3.8 %	0%	17.3 %
B. Child Responsibility Score	2.7	2.4	0
C. New Internal Score	1.6	0	0
Subtotal	(8.1%)	(2.4%)	(17.3%)
II. *Socialization Responsibility*			
A. Why Main Problem? Family Theme Low	2.4%	0%	0%
B. Other Family/Friends Had Problem	0	0	4.3
C. Combined Closeness Score: Low	1.3	2.6	0
D. Adult Respondent Works	0	3.1	0
Subtotal	(3.7%)	(5.7%)	(4.3%)
III. *Perceived Environment Responsibility*			
A. Direct Environment Responsibility Score	10.9 %	10.2 %	0%
IV. *Onset of Main Problem*	0%	0%	0%
V. *Demographic Characteristics*			
A. Gender: Male	3.7%	DNA	DNA
B. No. of Children in Household	2.8	4.4%	0%
C. Sample Type: Family Crisis	6.7	5.7	0
Total Variance (R^2)	35.9%	28.4%	21.6%

tribution of bad peers—then it is evident that for this sample a large household and the family crisis system can contribute to our understanding of one type of antisocial conduct.

The second most important contribution to our understanding of a direct influence on bad peers (and indirect influence on mixed delinquency) is the perceived environment responsibility risk category. The direct environment responsibility score is, as noted earlier, a direct attribution measure—since parents are scored on whether they believe that the type of neighborhood, kind of school, and the mass media bear high degrees of responsibility for causing the "main problem." Parents, functioning as lay sociologists, clearly believe that the immediate social context has an influence on youth associations—and, therefore, on a delinquent-type "main problem." Before the exploration of self-report studies, many academic sociologists held a similar belief (e.g., Shaw and McKay, 1942; Sutherland and Cressey, 1955; and Bell, 1953).

The third category of variance contribution is linked to variables associated with the youth responsibility/problem risk category (8.1%). A direct and indirect attribution of youth responsibility (i.e., child responsibility score and lacks guilt) are the two most important variables in this category, but new internal also makes a slight contribution to the variance subtotal. It is useful to note that the NYS study found that deviant moral beliefs regarding deviance was also an indirect influence on their measures of delinquency.

While socialization responsibility makes a quite moderate contribution (3.7%), it is important to note that this risk category was not involved at all for either mixed delinquency or multiaggression at a total sample level of analysis. The low amount of variance for the socialization category would not surprise Jessor, since he posited that the youth personality and perceived environmental systems were more directly involved in explaining all types of youthful deviance. However, his model would have difficulty in accounting for the fact that demographic characteristics would be of primary importance.

Perhaps the second most striking finding from Table 4–4 is the different routes to hanging out with bad peers for boys and girls. Virtually every variable that makes a significant variance contribution for boys is absent for girls; every variable that makes a significant contribution for girls is absent for boys. For example, lacks guilt contributes 17.3% of the total 21.6% variance for girls—but contributes exactly 0 percent for boys. The indirect attribution of family and friends having similar problems contributes the remaining 4.3% for

girls and nothing for boys. By way of contrast, the boys have contributions from six variables, covering every risk category except onset of the main problem. It appears reasonable to interpret the
divergent findings as indicating two distinct paths for hanging out
with bad peers. From the perspective of parents, girls are more likely
to have bad associates (who can indirectly involve them in mixed delinquent activities) by having a deficiency of guilt feelings, a distinct
aspect of the youth personality system; girls with minimal guilt feelings are responsible for their own choice of friends (and indirectly,
behaviors). In contrast, boys are perceived to have only a slight responsibility for their own associates (and behaviors). Instead, external influences—like the direct environmental attribution (10.2%),
demographic characteristics (10.1%), and respondent working
(3.1%)—are primarily responsible for the bad peers. The responsibility of youth and closeness of parents are only moderate influences on
whether sons will hang out with youth who get in trouble (2.4 and
2.6%, respectively).

The analyses of these divergent paths suggest that even though
boys and girls have virtually the same scores on lack of guilt feelings,
parents indirectly place a greater blame on girls for their deviant
associations. While hanging out with bad peers has the same consequences for boys and girls (as depicted in Table 4–3), parents do not
appear to hold them equally responsible for their actions.

Multivariate Analyses of Internal, Psychological Problems

In the preceding multivariate analyses, we have employed scores on
new internal as a general measure of internal, psychological mental
health problems to predict antisocial behaviors of delinquency and
aggression. In this section, our aim is to treat new internal as a variable
to be explained. Unlike the literature on antisocial behavior, studies of
mental health problems do not usually attempt to explain general
psychological dysfunctioning; instead, the research literature is based
on studies of specific clinical "disorders," psychiatric diagnoses, or
emotional problems (e.g., see the overview in Institute of Medicine,
1989). Even studies that use self-reports of mental health symptoms of
adolescents usually focus on a specific type of problem, such as depression (Avison and MacAlpine, 1992; Gore et al., 1992). In order to
be consistent with the prior analyses, but to also expand our knowledge of mental health problems from the parents' perspective, we

present two types of analyses. One analysis uses new internal as the dependent variable, while a second analysis uses the depression factor as a problem to be accounted for; both analyses use the same risk categories as employed before. However, the depression analysis also interprets the findings within a theoretical orientation that views adolescent developmental stresses as a source for understanding high scores (Avison and MacAlpine, 1992).

Table 4–5 displays the finding that the amount of variance that can be accounted for in explaining new internal scores is much lower than for the other major problem measures—the total variance range from 12.7% for the boys to 22.8% for the girls, with the total sample reaching a figure almost midway. The two largest risk categories for the total sample are the socialization and environmental responsibility risk categories (5.7 and 6.2%, respectively). These are the first times that the direct attributions of family responsibility and the circumstances of a disadvantaged life have proven to be significant influences in accounting for any total sample variance. These findings indicate, therefore, that the specific family and contextual attributions can yield a significant amount of variance (a total of 11.9%). Table 4–5 also indicates that indirect attributions about guilty feelings can also be associated with general mental health problems, as well as mixed delinquency, multiaggression, and bad peers. One demographic characteristic—parent/caregiver age—appears for the first time as a significant variable; the younger the parents, the more likely that their child has internal, psychological mental health problems.

Turning to the difference between the sexes, it is quite clear that the significant variables that yield any amount of variance are completely distinct for each sex. For boys, only two variables yield a significant amount of variance—lacks guilty feelings and a high family responsibility score. From a parental perspective the general mental health problems of boys stem from two sources of influence—youth and parental responsibility.

By way of contrast, parents eschew both of these categories for girls; instead, the direct attribution of a high life disadvantage score accounts for a moderate amount of the total variance (5.1%). But the most interesting finding stems from the demographic category. The combination of a younger mother and an older daughter is capable of accounting for 17.7% of the variance out of a total of 22.8%. This social structural condition for girls appears to be quite important—and may indicate a unique source of adolescent stress for girls.

Table 4.5 Comparison of Risk Variables for New Internal, by Percent of Variance Contribution for Total Sample and Each Sex

Risk Categories	Percent of Variance (R^2)		
	Total Sample	*Boys*	*Girls*
I. *Youth Responsibility/Problems*			
A. Lacks Guilt	4.5%	5.6%	0%
II. *Socialization Responsibility*			
A. Family Responsibility Score	3.6%	7.1%	0%
B. Why Problem? Child in Family Theme	2.1	0	0
Subtotal	(5.7%)	(7.1%)	(0%)
III. *Perceived Environment Responsibility*			
A. Life Disadvantage Responsibility Score	6.2%	0%	5.1%
IV. *Onset of Main Problem*	0%	0%	0%
V. *Demographic Characteristics*			
A. Parent/Caregiver Age: Younger	2.3%	0%	9.1%
B. Youth Age: Older	0	0	8.6
Subtotal	(2.3%)	(0%)	(17.7%)
Total Variance (R^2)	18.7%	12.7%	22.8%

The next section's discussion of depression scores will highlight that this finding can be integrated into a broader stream of studies on adolescent stresses that may be unique for girls.

Multivariate Analyses of Depression

We chose depression as a specific type of mental health problem to be examined in greater detail for several reasons. First, this measurement index is correlated at an extremely high level with the broader new internal measure for the total sample (.84), as well as for each sex (.82 and .85, respectively). Secondly, a detailed analysis of the nine items comprising the depression index of this sample with the national ACQ study (discussed in the last chapter) found that 7 of the 9 ECYS items are exactly similar to the gender-neutral ACQ anxiety/depression scale. Third, there is a growing literature on the problem of depression among adolescents that permits us to compare the results of this study with others. This is particularly useful, since these studies are conducted primarily with white youth, using self-report items, that cover an array of rural and urban samples in the United States and Canada (e.g. see overview by Institute of Medicine, 1989; Wells, Deykiw, and Klerman, 1985; and recent articles by Avison and McAlpine, 1992 and Gore et al., 1992).

In the past two decades, studies have accumulated that provide evidence that adult females consistently report experiencing more depressive symptoms than males. Further, these studies have also found an association between gender, stressful life experiences, and various coping mechanisms or psychological resources (e.g., feelings of personal control and self-esteem, and perceptions of social support from family and friends). Recent studies have confirmed that similar epidemiological risk factors also operate at the adolescent level—particularly for females (Avison and McAlpine, 1992 and Gore et al., 1992). Before presenting our data, it is important to understand the similarities and differences in the measures employed in the recently reported studies and the ECYS study.

The ECYS measure of adolescent depression symptoms is, of course, based on parent reports, whereas the empirical studies used for comparison (i.e., Avison and McAlpine, 1992; and Gore et al., 1992) rely on a self-report measure. In fact, both of the recent studies used a 20-item scale that was first developed for use with adults—the Center for Epidemiological Studies Depression Scale (or

CES–D) developed by Radloff in 1977. This scale attempts to measure only one specific type of mental health symptom—affective depressive feelings—and has been used with a variety of adolescent, as well as adult, samples since its initial use as an epidemiological instrument. Besides exhibiting high degrees of reliability, the measure has correlated strongly with other measures of depressive symptoms. However, it has also been found to be correlated with other measures of "psychological distress" (Weisman and Klerman, 1977; Devins and Orme, 1985).

Achenbach et al. (1989), as reported in the last chapter, have also developed an index (a scale, to use ACQ terminology) that is gender-neutral, but relies on parents' reports about their sons and daughters 6–16 years old. Unlike the CES–D scale, which was guided by the aim of measuring a clinical diagnostic entity, the ACQ had another goal: to discover behaviors that were associated empirically by factor analytic methods. As a result, the ACQ found that a variety of indicators of psychological distress were, in fact, empirically linked to feelings of unhappiness, sadness, and depression. The ACQ researchers labeled their factor "anxious/depressed," and found that the items were statistically reliable for boys and girls, for the age group of 6–11 and 12–16 in American and Dutch clinical samples. The ECYS found that the following ACQ anxious/depressed items emerged in our empirically guided factor analysis: 1) feels worthless, inferior; 2) feels guilty; 3) feels unloved; 4) loneliness; 5) nervous, tense; 6) unhappy, sad, depressed; and 7) worrying; in addition, the ECYS factor included 8) cries a lot; and 9) sudden changes in mood or feelings. It is evident that this list of ECYS items includes such references to "distress" as nervous, tense, moody, too guilty, and worrying. In addition, the ECYS list includes indicators of self-esteem and social support (e.g., worthless, inferior; unloved; and loneliness).

The self-report study conducted by Avison and MacAlpine found that their measure of depression (i.e., the CES–D) had the following significant correlations with their measures of: personal control and mastery (–.43); social support of friends (–.30); self-esteem (–.54); and mother cares and father cares (–.28 and –.40). These significant correlations, based on a sample of white, Canadian adolescents, with an average age of 17.3 years, attending urban and rural high schools, are quite congruent with the ACQ and ECYS items included in a measure of "depression." However, any multivariate analysis that uses the ECYS parent-based measure assumes that the construct to be accounted for, or explained, refers to feelings of low self-esteem and personal mastery, low social support, and feelings of being un-loved by significant others—as well as feelings of sadness, and psy-chological distress symptoms.

While the ECYS analysis cannot include indicators of psychoso-cial resources like self-esteem and feelings of mastery, we can ex-amine the potential influence of stressful events or conditions. The self-report studies have used a check list test of "stressful life events" referring to serious illness or injury, the death of a friend or a family member, financial problems, or troubles with friends. The ECYS study has indicators of family difficulties (e.g., the family responsi-bility score), negative life conditions (e.g., the life disadvantage and direct environment scores), and being the offspring of a teen-aged parent (e.g., the combination of having a younger parent/caregiver and being an older teen). Each of these indicators has already proved to be useful in accounting for significant amounts of variance in the scores of the new internal measure (see table 4–5). Using the theoreti-cal orientation that adolescents who are isolated from peers (deviant or conventional), and experience stressful events are likely to experi-ence feelings of psychological distress, we can now reinterpret the findings pertaining to the analysis of variations in new internal scores—and make predictions about an analysis of the ECYS depres-sion measure. Table 4–5 found that the family responsibility and life disadvantage measures were, in fact, linked to explaining modest amounts of variance—but these indicators of potential stress (or risk) varied sharply by sex. In addition, the second structural condi-tion of having a younger parent (with a minimum age of 30) and an older adolescent (with a maximum age of 16), as an indicator of growing up in a teen-parent household, provided an indicator of family structure stress that was particularly potent in accounting for new internal variance amongst females (17.7 out of a total of 22.5%).

We can hypothesize that similar findings will emerge when the ECYS depression measure is used—but that more variance will be explained because the scale refers to a more limited, focused, range of mental health problems. We expect too, that the analysis of fe-males will be more successful than that of males (as indicated by total variance explained). The self-report studies yield consistent evi-dence that gender is important, but do not provide distinct analysis for each sex. Table 4–6 presents a multivariate analysis for each sex as well as for the total sample.

Table 4.6 Comparison of Risk Variables for Depression, by Percent of Variance Contribution for Total Sample and Each Sex

Risk Categories	Percent of Variance (R^2)		
	Total Sample	Boys	Girls
I. *Youth Responsibility/Problems*			
A. Lacks Guilt	2.4%	3.4%	0%
II. *Socialization Responsibility*			
A. Family Responsibility Score	9.3%	9.4%	4.4%
III. *Perceived Environment Responsibility*			
A. Life Disadvantage Responsibility Score	4.0%	2.6%	12.1%
B. How Responsible Peers? Low Score	3.9	4.5	0
Sub-Total	(7.9%)	(7.1%)	(12.1%)
IV. *Onset of Main Problem*	0%	0%	0%
V. *Demographic Characteristics*			
A. Parent/Caregiver Age: Younger	0%	0%	6.1%
B. Youth Age: Older	0	0	4.0
C. Gender: Female	3.6	DNA	DNA
D. Race/Ethnicity: Non-black	3.0	0	4.3
E. Religion: Non-Protestant and Non-Traditional Protestant	0	4.4	0
Sub-Total	(6.6%)	(4.4%)	(14.4%)
Total Variance (R^2)	26.2%	24.3%	30.9%

Looking first at the total variance explained, it is clear that the amount has increased for each of the columns, when compared to the new internal results—from 18.7 to 26.2% for the total sample, 12.7 to 24.3% for the boys, and 22.8 to 30.9% for the girls. These results justify a more focused inquiry of distinct mental health measures. By way of contrast, separate analyses of the component scales of mixed delinquency and multiaggression yielded opposite results—the separate multivariate analysis of the component scales was less strong than the composite measure constructed by the second-order factor analyses (data not displayed).

The analysis of the total sample reveals that the indicator of family difficulty—the family responsibility score—accounts for 9.3% of the variance. The perceived environment indicator—the life disadvantages responsibility score—accounts for 4.3%, whereas the direct environment score (measuring school and the neighborhood) accounts for no variance (and is absent from the table). The perceived environment risk factor category also reinforces the evidence that youth scoring high on the depression measures are indeed isolated from any peers, since a low score on any peer responsibility for the main problem provides an additional 3.9% of the variance. The indicators of family or life environment stress and social support account for a total of 17.2% of the total variance. These results are congruent with the results from the self-report studies.

In addition to the stress and support indicators, the gender variable—as expected—also contributes a share of the variance (3.6%). A surprising result is the finding that 3% of the variance is accounted for by youth who are nonblack. Separate bivariate analysis of race/ ethnicity indicates that this result may be linked to the fact that black females are more likely than white females to associate with bad peers (.26), whereas black males are equally as likely as white males to associate with bad peers (.08); since any lack of peer association, or isolation, is linked to a high depression score, we interpret the race/ ethnicity relationship to be a result of the variance associated with females.

The remaining variance is associated with the youth responsibility risk category—namely, the youth lacks guilt—(2.4% of the variance). Even this minimal finding seems anomalous, since the depression measures include the item referring to too much guilt feelings. One possible explanation is that this relationship only holds for boys—and on a bivariate basis there is no relationship between lacks guilt and bad peers for males (.08); however, for girls, there is a very strong relationship between bad peers and lacks guilt (.42, and review table 4–4). As noted earlier, any strong association with peers (directly or indirectly) is likely to reduce high scores on depression.

The analysis of each gender reveals, as in the analysis of new internal, that there are strong differences in the variables used to explain a significant amount of variance. However, before examining each sex separately, it is important to note that the primary risk or stress indicators hold up for each sex and the total sample—family responsibility and life disadvantage scores—although the amounts vary for each sex. Males are more closely linked to parents' assumption of family responsibility for youth problems, whereas females are more closely linked to a parental perception that life disadvantages are high (i.e., 9.4 vs. 2.4% for family responsibility, respectively, and 2.6 vs. 12.1% for life disadvantages, respectively). One explanation for this difference which appears plausible is that the family responsibility score for boys is significantly associated (on a bivariate basis) with a combined measure of family closeness (–.23), but this high relation does not hold for females (–.03). Evidently, family responsibility has a link to family closeness for males, but not for females. At this point, we have not figured out why, but must accept this empirical result. Paradoxically, the indicator of life disadvantage is significantly correlated with low combined score for females (–.25), but is not significant for males (–.09). Even though the measure of combined closeness is significantly associated (on a bivariate level) with the depression measure for each sex, the relationships vanish when family responsibility is used in a multivariate analysis for males and life disadvantage for females.

Moving to the demographic category, and the risk condition of a young mother and an older teen, it is evident that this potential source of family stress is operative only for females (and amounts to a total of 10.1% of the variance). The remaining demographic indicators refer to race/ethnicity. Since this variable's link to depression scores has already been discussed (via the indirect association of race/ethnicity and bad peers for females), the only other demographic variable, religion, requires examination. As noted in table 4–1 this variable was coded as referring to traditional Protestant religions vs. AO (and scored 0/1). Because of a high percentage of blacks in the sample, we found that about 60% of the total sample was self-identified by parents as a traditional Protestant (i.e. Baptist, Methodist, Episcopalian, Presbyterian, etc..). The nontraditional referred to Roman Catholic, Protestant Sects, Muslims, and any other

religions. While this indicator of religion is correlated with race/eth-
nicity for both sexes, there is a much stronger bivariate correlation
for males than females in these subsamples (–.44 for males and –.22
for females). Therefore, we interpret the religion variable to function
as a proxy measure for race/ethnicity in the analysis of the male correlation of depression. If we accept this, then the nonblack indicators
account for a similar amount of variance for males as for females (4.4
to 4.3%, respectively).

It is useful to note, before ending this analysis, that the total
amount of variance for the depression measure is quite comparable
to the two recent studies cited earlier. The Avison and MacAlpine
study accounted for 43% of the variance for the total sample, but
this analysis included a variable that is already included in our
measure of depression—namely, self-esteem. When self-esteem is
omitted the total variance is reduced to 23%—quite similar to the
26% figure noted for the total sample column in table 4–6. The Gore
et al. study did not include self-esteem in their analysis; the total
amount of variance reached 25% in this study. The comparability of
our results, using a parent report method for measuring depression
and the risk variables, rather than youth self-reports, are empirically and theoretically significant. The results are even more striking
when we consider that the findings depicted in table 4–6 are based
on a predominantly urban sample, with a composition of 78% black
youth.

Summary and Conclusions

The primary aim of this chapter was to advance our understanding
about major youth problems by using distinct types of information
derived solely from parents. Each type of information was used in a
multivariate analysis that "explained" the variability in scores of delinquency, aggression, and internal problems. Parents were asked
their opinions of what caused problems and to rate the degree of responsibility for the problem getting started or becoming worse from
four different perspectives—youth, family members, friends, and the
impersonal influences of the environment. We categorized these parental opinions about problem initiation, persistence, and responsibility as "direct attributions" because parents made a direct judgment
regarding causation. While we were not in a position to judge the ac-
curacy of a parental claim regarding youth or family responsibility, or

the extent of neighborhood influences, this unique type of information could be assessed empirically. Were enough parents consistent in their attributions so that a statistically significant amount of the variance of a problem score could be "explained"? Would the attributions also be significant for each sex, and would they hold when other types of information were entered in a multivariate analysis? And if the direct attribution mattered (using statistical standards), would it vary by problem type?

The major analytical questions addressed to the variables associated with direct attributions were also asked of less direct assessments about youth attitudes and interaction patterns. We categorized as indirect attributions responses referring to: lacking guilt; hanging out with youth who get in trouble; family members who had similar problems as youths; and the closeness of youth to adult parent/caregivers. These parental judgements were deemed to be "indirect" because the questions that elicited these responses were not couched in a direct causation or responsibility format—but could be presumed to be linked to one or more youth problems.

A third source of information, parental reports of internal problems, was used as a potential explanatory variable for all assessments of antisocial behaviors—delinquency, aggression, and hanging out with bad peers. We reasoned that psychological problems were more likely to precede behavioral problems (and thereby be conceived as a "cause") than *vice versa*. While this assumption appeared reasonable, we subjected this source of information to the same analytical scrutiny as was employed for direct and indirect attributions.

The three sources of information were grouped according to three potential risk categories that might influence the frequent occurrence of youth problems: 1) youth responsibility and problems; 2) perceived environment responsibility; and 3) socialization responsibility. Each risk category could include direct and indirect attributions; in addition, the youth risk category could also include psychological problem scores. Besides these three risk categories, the multivariate analyses also included a control for the length of time the main problem had persisted and an array of demographic variables—for a total of five potential explanatory categories.

All five categories with their associated variables, were used to explain scores for three antisocial measures (i.e., delinquency, aggression, and bad peers) and two psychological measures (i.e., total new internal problems and depression). The findings that emerged can be summarized from three perspectives: 1) an assessment of the relative influence of each risk or control category, regardless of types of attributions; 2) an assessment of the relative influence of direct and indirect attributions for each risk category, as well as for all categories combined; and 3) an assessment of the relative responsibility of youth and external sources of responsibility, regardless of the type of attribution. The findings associated with each perspective will be summarized in sequence, before discussing the potential theoretical implications of all of the findings.

The Relative Influence of Risk Categories

It is possible to conceive of each major risk category—youth, socialization, and environment—as sources of competing influences on the frequent occurrence of youth problems. Some theorists—like Jessor and Jessor—believe that the youth personality and perceived environment systems are relatively equal in influence in explaining all types of youth deviance, and that both are more important than the socialization system or demographic variables. Others, like Hirschi, argue that the socialization variables are primary, and that environmental influences are secondary. The empirical findings of this study indicate that the relative influences of risk categories are not the same for each type of problem, nor do the relative influences function in a similar manner for each sex for comparable problems in all instances.

If we analyze the findings pertaining to the two primary antisocial measures—mixed delinquency and multiaggression—it is quite evident that the most influential risk categories differ by problem type. Mixed delinquency's most salient risk category is the perceived environment, whereas for multiaggression the youth risk category is the most important. These findings are true, regardless of sex. Hanging out with peers who get into trouble accounts for about 31–40% of the variance of mixed delinquency for each sex, whereas attributions of lack of guilt and psychological problems account for about 39–43% of the variance of multiaggression for each sex.

In addition, the two antisocial measures differ in another major respect—mixed delinquency has a second risk category (i.e., youth responsibility) that contributes a large amount of variance, regardless of sex (about 17–19%); however, multiaggression's second risk category is quite modest, regardless of sex (about 3.4%).

While the differences in the importance of risk categories does not vary by gender for delinquency and aggression, a similar inference cannot be made about an analysis of bad peers as the variable to be explained. Given the importance of peers in understanding delinquency (whether using parent or youth reports), hanging out with bad peers was subjected to a multivariate analysis with the same risk categories. For boys, two major categories emerged as comparable in accounting for the variability in bad peers scores—perceived environment and demographic variables (about 10% for each category, respectively). In contrast to these external influences, girls are most likely to hang out with bad peers if youth responsibility for feeling guilt is assessed as low. For boys, parents emphasize influences that are not within the personal control of youth—but this is obviously not the case for girls.

Turning to an analysis of the psychological measures as the variables to be explained, findings again disclose sharp gender differences. Using new internal as the dependent variable, the total amount of variance accounted for by boys is only about 13%, compared to about 23% for girls. For boys the two primary categories are socialization and youth responsibility, whereas for girls, the dominant risk category refers to the ages of parents and youth (i.e., demographic variables).

In an effort to broaden our understanding of psychological problems for ECYS youth, a special analysis was conducted for the single measure of depression. This effort yielded a greater amount of total variance for boys (about 24%) and a modest increase in the total variance for girls (to about 31%). The dominant risk categories for explaining depression in boys are socialization (via family responsibility scores) and the perceived environment (via low peer and life disadvantage scores)—accounting for about 17% of the total variance. For girls, the risk category of perceived environment is also important (via life disadvantage scores), but the demographic variables proved to be even more important (14 to 12%, respectively).

Of the five categories employed in the explanatory analyses of youth problems and hanging out with bad peers, only the length of time of the problems failed to be a dominant risk category. For boys, perceived environment and youth responsibility problems proved to be the major risk categories for antisocial measures, and socialization responsibility emerged as the dominant risk category for either new internal or depression measures. For girls, perceived environ-

ment and youth responsibility also emerged as the major risk categories for antisocial measures, but demographic characteristics
emerged as the dominant risk category for the two psychological
measures. It is clear that gender, as well as type of problem, can be
associated with distinct risk categories.

The Relative Influence of Direct and Indirect Attributions

All of the tables in this chapter were constructed with risk categories
as the major headings—and, as noted, all types of information were
grouped together. In order to understand the use of parental information more fully, it is useful to regroup variables according to
the types of attributions—direct or indirect—and assess their relative influence in understanding antisocial and psychological problems. In this study, direct attributions referred to a parental
judgement that the following persons or conditions were responsible for the main problem getting started or becoming worse: 1) the
youth him/herself; 2) friends of the youth; 3) members of the family,
regardless of their residence; 4) circumstances of disadvantage to the
youth; and 5) the surrounding environment of the neighborhood,
school, and the mass media. These direct attributions consisted of
parental judgments about causation; they were used in the analysis
as indicators of potential influence because it is possible to hypothesize that young people are capable of making choices about their behaviors, that family members/and friends can exert an influence on
behaviors and feelings, and that the external environment can provide negative and positive experiences that are beyond the control of
parents or youth. It is possible to view the direct parental attributions
as types of information that reveal subjective judgments, or as indicators that youth might be responding in an individual manner to
the influence identified by parents. Our analysis of direct attributions views parental responses as both subjective judgments and potential indicators of influences.

Direct, as well as indirect, attributions were subjected to multivariate analyses in order to assess whether the potential influences
were capable of making a unique contribution toward understanding the variability in problem scores. An overview of all the statistical analyses presented in this chapter reveals that two types of direct
attributions can make a significant contribution towards understanding one or more of the three antisocial measures for either the
male or female subsample—youth responsibility and direct envi-

ronment; youth responsibility can contribute up to 5.5% of the variance for mixed delinquency (for girls) and direct environment can contribute up to 10.2% of the variance for hanging out with bad peers (for boys). The other three direct attributions are more clearly associated with making a significant contribution towards understanding the psychological measures of new internal and depression. A low reliance on the influence of friends can contribute up to 4.5% of the variance for depression (among boys); a high score on family responsibility can contribute up to 9.5% of the variance for depression (among boys); and experiencing high scores on life disadvantage can contribute up to 12.1% of the variance for depression (among girls). Depending on the type of problem and gender, the contributions of direct attributions towards a unique amount of variance for a specific analysis can range from 0 to a maximum of about 12%.

An overview of all the statistical analyses of indirect attributions discloses that the unique contributions to the variation in problem scores can be much higher than occurred for direct attributions. Lack of guilt feelings, hanging with bad peers, and references to socialization experience (via close relationships or family members having problems as youths) are most closely linked as influences on antisocial measures. Lack of guilt stands out as an influence that can make a unique contribution in 5 out of 6 antisocial/gender comparisons; it can contribute up to 17.3% of the variance for explaining who is most likely to hang out with bad peers (among girls). The strongest indirect attribution occurs in an explanation of mixed delinquency, where the variable of bad peers can contribute about 31 to 40% of the variance (for boys and girls, respectively).

While direct and indirect attributions can make important contributions to understanding mixed delinquency and association with bad peers, as well as psychological measures, this is not true for our understanding of multiaggression. The most salient variable for understanding mixed aggression is the score on new internal problems. Out of a total variance of 42.4% for male aggression only 5.9% is contributed by a combination of direct and indirect attributions; for female aggression the combined contribution of attributions is only 6.8 out of a total of 49.4%. By contrast, virtually all of the other problem analyses revealed that a majority of the variance is contributed by a combination of direct and/or indirect attributions (with the exception of new internal for girls, where demographic characteristics are of dominant importance).

The Relative Influence of Youth vs. External Responsibility

A third useful way for understanding the influences on the frequency
of youth problems is to combine direct and indirect attributions and
classify them by the location of responsibility—youth vs. external
source of influences. By setting aside the contribution of psychological problems as a separate category, it is possible to gain a sharper understanding of how much parents blame youth for their own
problems, in comparison to external attributions of the family and/or
the environment.

Reviewing the analyses of antisocial measures by gender, it is clear
that attributions of youth responsibility occur for 6 out of 6 comparisons. Youth responsibility ranges from a low of 2.3% of the variance
for male aggression to a high of 17.3% of the variance for female responsibility in associating with bad peers. While parents allocate varying degrees of youth responsibility for antisocial behaviors or
associations, the dominant location of responsibility for the mixed
delinquency of boys and girls is environmental (primarily via bad
peer associates). The sharpest difference between boys and girls occurs in allocating responsibility for associating with bad peers. Parents allocate youth responsibility as the dominant influence on
females associating with bad peers (17.3% out of a total 21.6%). By
way of contrast, boys are held to be responsible in a small way for
their deviant associations (2.4% out of a total of 28.4%).

Parents continue to allocate youth responsibility for males experiencing psychological problems, even though the dominant responsibility occurs with external influences. However, parents do not
allocate any significant youth responsibility for females experiencing psychological problems; the dominant influences are external
and/or demographic. Parents appear to make the sharpest distinctions about youth responsibility for problem types for females. On
the one hand, they hold them most responsible for associating with
bad peers (via a lack of guilt), but fail to allocate any youth responsibility for psychological problems. Boys are allocated some degree of
responsibility for all types of problems, but in none of the comparisons are youth attributions a dominant share of the total variance.

Theoretical Implications

If we take into account all of the findings of this chapter, as well as the
descriptive analyses of the last chapter, then it is quite clear that our

theoretical framework for understanding youth problems needs to be broadened. Currently there is a strong interest in identifying patterns of comorbidity or the coexistence of multiple problems, with the implication that a common theory of deviance proneness can be confidently enunciated. While this study has indeed found that an overlap between problems does exist, we have also found that two problems with a strong correlation—delinquency and aggression—have quite unique sources of causation. Aggressive behaviors have an unusually strong association with high scores on psychological problems—like suspiciousness, feelings of worthlessness and being unloved and tense, sadness or depression, and strange ideas and behaviors—for both males and females. In contrast, delinquent behaviors have an unusually strong association with youth who get in trouble. Youth who are high on both delinquency and aggression require two distinctive causal theories—one to account for the high delinquency and one to account for the high aggression. Empirical studies that fail to make this type of conceptual distinction are apt to obtain confusing findings—as occurred in the NYS finding that a measure of peer association could explain over twice the amount of variance when a broad measure of delinquency was used, in comparison to use of a felony measure that included a high proportion of aggressive behaviors.

Besides the conceptual need to distinguish between types of antisocial behaviors, it is also important to distinguish between types of theoretical assumptions, types of youth variables, types of environmental variables, and types of samples or subsamples. Concerning types of theoretical assumptions regarding antisocial behaviors, it is possible to posit (like Hirschi) that all youth (and adults as well) have an egocentric set of impulses to engage in all types of antisocial behaviors (like stealing, cheating, and hitting)—unless restrained by social control mechanisms. In contrast to this conception of "human nature," it is possible to posit (like Jessor) that there are internal and external influences that can either instigate or restrain deviant types of behaviors. Control theorists, like Hirschi, assume we would all be deviant "if we dared" (p.34), while interactional theorists, like Jessor, assume we are deviant only if the combination of instigations and controls yield a "proneness" to normative transgressions. Elliott's attempt to formulate an "integrated" model of delinquency represents a sociological attempt to restate Hirschi's social control theory so it is in harmony with Jessor's assumption that deviant motivations and restraints can vary separately or together.

The findings of this study support the position that delinquency—one type of deviant activity—is more likely to occur if there exists an "instigation" of bad peers, psychological problems, or hyperactive impulsiveness together with a freeing of "restraint" via a lack of feeling guilt or moral responsibility by youth. In this study, as in many others cited earlier in this chapter, the promotion of delinquent behaviors via association with bad peers is stronger than the restraint variable of a lack of guilt. Therefore, the data reported in table 4–2 is in much greater harmony with the combination of a motivational and restraint assumption, rather than the loosening of the restraint assumption posited by Hirschi.

All of the major theorists of antisocial behaviors rely on variables that refer to the internal states of youth themselves. Hirschi refers to feelings of attachment to adults, commitment to conventional goals and institutions, and moral beliefs about right and wrong behaviors. Elliott and his NYS colleagues incorporate these youth variables as part of their modification of Hirschi's model of delinquency causation. However, these theorists, as well as many other sociologists, do not expand their conception of youth variables to include measures of hyperactivity and psychological problems such as feelings of worthlessness, being unloved, nervous, or moody. While the moral restraint variable of lack of guilt feelings proved to be useful in understanding both delinquency and aggression, it is also evident that measures of psychological problems also proved to be useful—particularly in understanding an important source of aggressive behaviors. Had the NYS study included measures of psychological problems researchers could have undoubtedly increased the amount of explained variance for their measures of general delinquency and felony behaviors.

Most self-report studies of delinquency have also been weak in expanding their measurement of the perceived environment. The variable that has gained the most attention is the bad peer variable. Elliott and his NYS colleagues, for example, measured "deviant peer bonding" by focusing on peer involvement, exposure to delinquent peers, perceived sanctions by peers, peer normlessness, peer isolation, and commitment to delinquent peers. However, they failed to assess whether youth perceived any resources disadvantage or the extent of influences of the neighborhood, school, or the mass media. Had they included these expanded measures of the perceived environment, they might have been able to increase the explained variance for their deviant peer index measure. In this study, the life disadvantage measure also proved useful in understanding one source of the male depression score.

If we combine all of the findings and their links to existing theories, it is possible to summarize the implications of our findings regarding each of the major problems in the following manner. High scores on delinquency are most likely to occur if youth associate with bad peers. Association with bad peers constitutes a "learning environment," where behaviors can be learned via imitating, modeling, direct teaching, or positive reinforcement—according to modern modifications of differential association theory. In addition to these environmental instigations to delinquency, it is also likely that being high on measures of hyperactivity (i.e., impulsiveness, restlessness, and can't concentrate) can also provide a source of motivation for deviant activities, as can the existence of psychological problems. It is likely that the motivation to engage in deviant activities—from internal as well as external sources—is also buttressed by a loosening of moral restraints via a lack of guilt feelings regarding delinquent behaviors. These instigations and the loosening of restraints are more likely to occur if peers provide mutual social support, as well as a learning environment.

This interpretation of our findings regarding delinquency is partially congruent with the theories of social control and differential association. But our findings must also make room for the influence of variable scores on hyperactivity and psychological problems as potential stressors, as well as the possibility that a lack of guilt feeling may be due to faulty socialization, a relative inability to bond to moral values, or a psychopathic temperament. In addition, our understanding of delinquency must also take into account the sources of bad peer associations—as indirect influences on high delinquent activities. Analysis of the bad peers measure indicates that the direct environment and demographic variables are also important. The former variable could provide a learning environment that is more congruent with associations with bad peers, as well as provide another source of social support for delinquent activities. The demographic set of variables—male gender, number of children in the household, and mother working—and the family closeness measure indicate that family structure, roles, and interaction patterns could affect the attention and supervision available for youth, especially males. For girls, association with bad peers may require a stronger loosening of moral restraints (via lack of guilt feelings), when compared to boys.

As for aggressive behaviors, high scores are most likely to occur when psychological problems are also quite strong, regardless of gender or whether scores on delinquency are high or low. Since strange ideas and behaviors provided the strongest link to high aggression (especially when high delinquency was also present), it is reasonable to infer that high degrees of suspiciousness and behaving strangely are likely to trigger physical and verbal aggressive behaviors; the motivations to engage in aggressive behaviors may be partially due to misperceptions of others and aberrant ideas. In addition, the remaining set of new internal measures may refer to a general condition of high "psychological distress"; if this is the case, then future studies might want to focus on the conditions when psychological stress can lead to aggressive or internal responses. As is the case with delinquency, the loosening of moral restraint (via lack of guilt feelings) is also an influence on aggressive behaviors.

Attempts to understand the influences on a general measure of psychological problems were far less satisfactory than the results of a multivariate analysis of the depression measure. The components of the depression measure indicate that feelings of worthlessness, being unloved, and loneliness are potent sources for feeling sad and depressed. For the first time in any of the analyses, family measures proved to be an important influence for explaining a moderate amount of variance, regardless of gender. It is reasonable to infer that a high score on family responsibility is an indicator of intrafamilial stress. For girls, high scores on the depression measure are also likely to occur if families consist of a relatively young mother and an older teen daughter. It is conceivable that being a teenage daughter of a young mother adds a stressful component to the developmental problems of girls. When these stresses are combined with a high life disadvantage score, the results appear to be particularly harmful for girls. Boys appear to be more likely to have high depression score if intrafamilial stress is accompanied by an absence of peer associates and a loosening of moral restraint; it is conceivable that hanging out with peers—even bad ones—can provide a partial antidote to feelings of depression for boys.

The findings of this study are, of course, linked to the special composition of our sample. Besides the uniqueness of the ethnic/racial composition and living in a northern urban center, the sample is also disproportionately representative of a family crisis intervention program (linked to the juvenile court). Because of our awareness of these potential sample influences, we have been careful to consistently compare our results to the findings of the best self-report and parent-report studies. Our finding of the importance of the bad peer variable for understanding delinquency, regardless of gender, is quite congruent with both the NYS national sample and Achenbach's study of clinical samples. Our finding of the strong relationship between aggressive behaviors and internal problems is quite congruent with the correlations reported by Achenbach and Edelbrock, again regardless of gender. It is difficult to directly compare our other major findings, since we were unable to find comparisons that included similar variables and multivariate analyses. However, we would be surprised if the major sources of variance in explaining bad peers—like the direct environment or lack of guilt—did not reoccur in the other studies that pay attention to these types of perceived youth and environmental variables. We would also be surprised if detailed comparisons, by gender, of comparable variables did not continue to yield differential social processes whereby males and females seek out peer associates or respond to family structure and stresses in a distinct manner.

5

Seeking Help

INTERVIEWER: *What kinds of things have you* personally
tried to do to solve or improve the main problem?

*I called the police, and they took him to an agency. . . He was very welcomed there.
He liked to be there. Because when I was called into court, he asked me to tell the
judge to let him stay at that house. He had good care there.*

Grandmother of 16-year-old boy

*I've taken her to some psychiatrists. The school took her to a mental health center. I
tried to keep the home atmosphere calm. I tried to talk to her about becoming a
young lady.*

Mother of 12-year-old girl

*I've tried to provide a little better home—decent clothing—see that she had enough
food. I've tried to instill in her the qualities that would make her more interested in
getting a better education.*

Stepfather of 15-year-old girl

The preceding chapters have provided evidence that the youths display an impressive array of behavioral and psychological problems.
This chapter aims to answer this question: Given this output of problems, how do parents find out about them, cope with them, and be-

gin a process of help-seeking? For the most part, the primary thrust of researchers studying deviance has been in evaluating help-giving policies, programs, and services. Only recently has there emerged a new literature on help-seeking that has begun to match our prior emphasis on help-giving (DePaulo, Nadler, Fisher, 1983, 3 vols.). We use the help-seeking model that was developed by Gross and McMullen (1983), and that builds on the work of Piliavin (1972), to guide the analysis. The model proposes that help is secured as a result of phased decision-making activities composed of: problem awareness; assessment of the problem as normal or not; assessment of the importance of the problem; initiation of efforts at self-help; search for help from intimates, professional contacts, and others; and selection of outside helper.

Models of help-seeking are built on two assumptions. One is that a primary person seeks help from a second person functioning as a potential helper. As we pointed out in Chapter 1, children rarely initiate formal helping efforts. In fact, *none* of the youths in the sample voluntarily initiated an initial appointment at an agency. When asked an open-ended question about whose idea it was to come to the family crisis or mental health service agency, 29% of the parents responded that it was their idea or that of another family member, but not their child. Seventy-one percent responded that it was the idea of someone not related to them. Clearly, the help-seeking process for youths is dominated by third parties, and not by the primary recipients of services.

Another assumption in models of help-seeking is that help is sought voluntarily. In point of fact, many parents may become reluctant or involuntary help-seekers because of external pressures by formal public agencies. In the ECYS sample, for example, only 4% of the parents report that they personally tried to do something about the problem by communicating with police or court officials prior to going to a mental health or family crisis agency. However, 53% of the parents report that they talked to a police or court official prior to visiting the agency. It appears reasonable to infer that most of the 53% of the parents talking to law enforcement officials did not personally choose this type of help. They were forced to become involuntary help-seekers. Models of help-seeking on behalf of youth in trouble must, therefore, be capable of accurately capturing the possibility that the search for assistance may be involuntary as well as voluntary.

The analyses that are presented in this chapter are based on the premise that all or some of the stages of third-party help-seeking pursued by parents can be initiated on a voluntary or involuntary basis. Using this perspective, an attempt is made to understand similarities and differences in the influences that bring parents to a mental health or family crisis agency. Before assessing influences, it is important to specify the operational indicators that could characterize each phase of the proposed help-seeking model. Table 5–1 lists the indicators chosen for each stage of the help-seeking process and then compares any differences between parents associated with the mental health or family crisis system. Presumably, more families became clients of the latter system via an involuntary referral, in order to prevent an appearance in Family Court. Therefore, this comparison should prove useful in describing the help-seeking process.

Help-Seeking in the Two Human Service Systems

Table 5–1 presents the help-seeking indicators and the percent of all parent/caregivers responding for each phase of the proposed ideal model. The table then notes whether any specific variable is associated with a specific human service system.

The first category of help-seeking refers to indicators of initial awareness (Part A). There are two major indicators of problem awareness—who noticed the problem and the time parents found out about the problem. The former group of indicators in Part A refers to who initially noticed one or more of the problems identified in the Achenbach Child Behavior Checklist as a "main problem." The open-ended question was exhaustively coded into one of four types of responses: mother; other intimates of the family; a school person; and police or court officials. The distribution of responses indicates that parents or other intimates notice the bulk of the problems (55 and 22%, respectively), while school personnel are the second-largest group of noticers (26%). Despite the high mixed delinquency scores of the total ECYS sample, only 3 percent of the youth samples were actually noticed by police or court officials. It is clear that the problems presented by youths are unlikely to be a surprise to many parents or family intimates. It is clear, too, that the types of persons noticing the main problems are not associated with either service system. Their knowledge of the problem tends not to be recent, as measured by the time parents found out about its first occurrence.

Table 5.1 Help-Seeking Indicators Associated with One or More Visits to Family Crisis or Mental Health Systems, Total Sample

Help–Seeking Indicators	Percent or Score	Family Crisis System	Mental Health	r Value <.05
A. *Problem Awareness*				
1a. Who Noticed? Mother	55%	–	–	–
b. Who Noticed? Other Intimates	22	–	–	–
c. Who Noticed? School Person	26	–	–	–
d. Who Noticed? Police/Court	03	–	–	–
2. Found Out: 1 year+	55	–	–	–
B. *Assess Problem as Normal*				
1. You Have Problem? Yes	16%	–	–	–
2. Others Have Problem? Yes	59	–	–	–
3. Ever Heard? Yes	72	–	–	–
4. Lot or All Have Problem?	46	–	–	–
C. *Importance of Problem*				
1a. Main Problem: New Internal	16%	Low	High	.22
b. Main Problem: Multiaggression	16	–	–	–
c. Main Problem: Mixed Delinquency	65	High	Low	–.18
2a. Underline Int. Score (14 Max)	2.65[a]	–	–	–
b. Underline Agg. Score (23 Max)	3.28[a]	–	–	–
c. Underline Delinq. Score (13 Max)	4.07[a]	High	Low	–.18
3. Problem Got Worse? Yes	52%	–	–	–
4. Problem Get Better? Definitely	39	–	–	–
5. Time Get Better? Less than 1 year	54	–	–	–
		–		
D. *Prior Personal Efforts*				
1. Go to Agency before? Yes	29%	–	–	–
2a. Personally Try: Talk to child	64	–	–	–
b. Personally Try: Help Self/Family	15	–	–	–
c. Personally Try: Influence Env.	13	–	–	–
d. Personally Try: Go to School	23	–	–	–
e. Personally Try: Human Services	39	–	–	–
f. Personally Try: Reward Punishment	27	–	–	

Table 5.1 (Continued)

Help–Seeking Indicators	Percent or Score	Family Crisis System	Mental Health	r Value <.05
E. *Talk to Others Re Problem*				
1. Talk to 1+ Primary Person	92%	–	–	–
2. Talk to 1+ Formal Org. Person	92	–	–	–
3. Talk to Family Intimates (5 Max)	2.46[a]	High	Low	–.16
4. Talk Other Intimates (2 Max)	0.68[a]	High	Low	–.14
5. Talk to Teachers? Yes	73	–	–	–
6. Talk to Police/Court? Yes	53	High	Low	–.25
7. Talk to DYFS? Yes	38	High	Low	–.18
8. Talk to Family Crisis Worker? Yes	44	High	Low	–.16
9. Talk to Mental Health Worker? Yes	38	–	–	–
10. Talk to Doctor/Minister? Yes	41	–	–	–
F. *Who Suggest This Agency*				
1. Int. Talk to Sugg.	39%	–	–	–
2. Formal Talk to Sugg.	80	–	–	–
3. Teacher Sugg.	36	Low	High	.25
4. Police/Court Sugg.	30	High	Low	–.16
5. DYFS Sugg.	25	High	Low	–.15
6. Family Crisis	25	High	Low	–.15
7. Mental Health Sugg.	12	Low	High	.22
8. Doctor/Minister Sugg.	12	–	–	–
G. *Actual Choice of Agency*				
1. Agency Idea is: Formal Person	71%	High	Low	–.21
2a. Agency Idea is: Police/court	20	High	Low	–.18
b. Agency Idea is: Teacher	16	Low	High	.14
c. Agency Idea is: Human Services	38	–	–	–
3. Why This Agency? Refer/Proximity	60	–	–	–
4. Why This Agency? Positive Reason	28	–	–	–
H. *Willingness To Try Agency*				
1. Agency Can Help? Yes	77%	–	–	–
2. Agency Can Understand? Yes	64	Low	High	.18
3. Why Child Came? Pos. Rsn.	55	Low	High	.17
4. Why Adult Came? Pos. Rsn.	87	–	–	–

[a]Mean Score

More than a majority of parents knew about the main problem over a year earlier (55 percent); again, there are no differences by service system. Based on these indicators, we can conclude that there are no differences between the service systems in how parents become aware of the problems.

Part B provides four indicators of whether the parents perceived the problem as normal for youth. Parents were asked to assess whether they had a similar type of problem while growing up (16 percent answered "yes"); whether they knew anyone else—in or outside the family—who had this kind of problem (59 percent answered "yes"); whether they had ever heard of the problem on TV, in newspapers, books or magazines (72 percent); and whether almost everybody or a lot of people have this kind of problem while growing up (46 percent). The responses indicate that while parents may not be able to identify with the main problem, they are able to perceive that many people personally known to them had this type of problem and that it is widely presented in the mass media. Based on these indicators, we can conclude that there are no assessment differences between the parents associated with each service system.

Part C assesses the importance of the problem to parents by using five types of indicators: 1) the choice of a single problem as most important to the parent; 2) how important each one of the total list of reported problems were of concern to parents and worth underlining by interviewers; 3) whether the main problem got worse since being noticed; 4) whether the main problem is likely to get better; and 5) how long it might take for the main problem to get better.

The first group of indicators in Part C provides evidence that virtually the entire sample was able to define one main problem that could be classified as "most important" to them. Using the three major ECYS behavior factors, the parental choices were coded as new internal, multiaggression, or mixed delinquency. The proportions choosing a specific definition that could be coded as a new internal, multiaggression, or mixed delinquent item are 16, 16, and 65 percent, respectively. Two of the parental definitions are statistically significant. Mental health parents are more likely to define the main problem as a new internal type, while family crisis parents chose a mixed delinquency item. Both groups of parents were equally likely to choose an aggressive item as the most important problem. Responses for the total sample indicate that the mixed delinquency items were most likely to be of concern and underlined by parents, compared to multiaggression and internal items (an average of 4.07

versus 3.28 and 2.65, respectively). Parents in the family crisis system are much more likely to be concerned about mixed delinquency items than parents in the mental health system, but there are no differences for the two other types of underlined problems.

More than one-half the parents believe that the main problem got worse (52%), but there are no differences by sample type. While only 39% of the parents respond that the main problem will "definitely get better," a clear majority believed it would be better within 12 months. Neither optimism or pessimism distinguishes the parents associated with specific sample type. However, the results of Part C provide the first empirical evidence that help-seeking can differ by service system.

Category D attempts to code the personal efforts made by parents to solve the problem prior to attending the human service agency. In response to a direct question about whether they had ever gone to an agency before, 29% answered affirmatively, but there were no differences by sample type. Parents were also asked an open-ended question about what they "personally had tried to do to solve or improve the problem" prior to going to the agency. Their single or multiple responses were coded as follows:

a. *Efforts with the child*—64% of the parents answered that they tried to do one or more of the following: talk to the child; listen to the child; provide additional personal attention; or share interests with the child.

b. *Efforts with self or the family*—15% of the parents answered that they tried to do one or more of the following: talk with members of their family in and outside the home; increase the amount of family activities; attempt to change family relationships; relieve the youth of family responsibilities; attend counseling or an Alcoholics Anonymous meeting; take more personal responsibility; and put a boyfriend out of the house.

c. *Efforts with external environment*—13% of the parents answered they tried to do one or more of the following: talk to neighbors, friends, or a pastor; talk to police or court officials; file a court complaint; and move to a different apartment or neighborhood. As noted earlier, only 4% of the parents voluntarily talked to police or court officials.

d. *Efforts with school*—23% of the parents answered that they tried to do one or more of the following: talk to teachers; work with the school; or change schools.

e. *Efforts with human services*—39% talked to counselors or took the child to counseling, a hospital, a doctor, a psychiatrist, or a place to get help.

f. *Efforts with rewards or punishment*—27% of the parents answered that they tried to do one or more of the following: provide things like clothes or give more spending money; give a special reward for improvement; threaten or administer physical punishment; threaten or administer non-physical sanctions like withdrawing telephone, TV, or friends' access to the house; general threats or punishments; try more discipline or control.

While parents could report more than one type of personal effort, there were no types of prior efforts that were associated with specific sample type. While there were no differences between sample types, the descriptions of prior efforts can be specified further by noting that parents who tried one type of effort were *less* likely to attempt another effort in the following instances (data *not* reported in Table 5–1):

a. Efforts with a child were less likely to be correlated with efforts with self/family (–.14, p<.04);

b. Efforts with the external environment were less likely to be correlated with rewards or punishment efforts (–.17, p<.009); and

c. Efforts with school or human service professionals were much less likely to be correlated with efforts at providing rewards or punishment (–.34, p<.0001).

The results indicate that many parents do not tend to try multiple types of efforts, but rather tend to exhibit a preference for specific modes of self-generated help. Further, the negative associations among some types of help indicate that there are types of self-help that tend to be mutually exclusive for many parents. This is particularly true of parents who voluntarily seek out teachers or helping professionals and those who think and act in the style of administering rewards and punishment. These results are congruent with the finding of child development researchers that parents tend to develop relatively independent styles of parenting (Ingersoll, 1989, pp. 207–212).

Besides reporting on self-generated efforts at dealing with the main problem, parents were directly asked if they talked to a list of specific types of persons about the problem (Part E). When presented with a list of persons they might have talked to, almost all parents reported talking to at least one person from a formal organization or a professional (e.g., mental health or family crisis worker, teacher, counselor, policeman, doctor, minister). Among formal persons talked to, it is evident that there is a rank order to the types of persons talked to: teachers (73%); police/court (59%); family crisis workers (44%); doctors or ministers (41%); and mental health or New Jersey Division of Youth and Family Services (DYFS) (38% each).

It is instructive to contrast the responses of the persons talked to with prior personal efforts, since there are two specific categories that yield distinct discrepancies: teachers/school personnel and police/court officials. While only 23% of the parents report voluntarily communicating with school personnel prior to attending an agency (see D2d), 73% of the parents report talking to teachers (see E5). It appears likely that a significant portion of parents may have been involuntary communicators with school personnel. As noted earlier, only 4% of the parents report seeking police/court officials as a "prior effort," but 53% talk to these types of formal persons. It appears likely that schools, as well as police, are sources of involuntary stimuli to help-seeking parents. However, unlike police, teachers actually notice an appreciable number of problems (see A1, "who noticed").

Section E of Table 5–1 also provides cogent evidence that who parents talk to is clearly associated with sample types. Family crisis parents are more likely to talk to family and other intimates, as well as police/court officials, youth and family workers, and family crisis workers. Mental health parents are not as active in soliciting the advice of informal or formal persons. There exist clear differences for this phase of the help-seeking process for specific types of persons, as well as similarities for talking to teachers and mental health workers prior to going to an agency.

Section F is related to persons talked to, since parents were directly asked if any of the persons on the "talked to" list suggested going to a specific agency. The responses provide strong support that formal types of persons are much more likely to suggest an agency than family or intimate persons (80 to 39% of F2 and F1 respectively). The detailed listing in Section F provides evidence that the suggestions of specific formal persons range from 12 to 36%. The data also provide strong support for the inferences that specific sources of suggestions are associated with sample types. Mental health parents are more likely to be associated with both teacher and mental health suggestions, while family crisis parents are linked to suggestions from police/court, youth and family service workers (DYFS), and family crisis workers. It appears that each system tends to be linked to specific referral sources.

In addition to the data presented in Table 5–1, a separate correlation analysis was conducted between types of persons talked to and types of persons making suggestions to go to an agency. The correlations between similar persons talked to and making suggestions tended to be positive as expected, but the associations vary by type as indicated by the following associations:

1. talk to teachers and teacher making a suggestion (r=.29)

2. talk to police/court officials and police/court suggestions (r=.53)

3. talk to youth/family worker (DYFS) and youth/family suggestions (r=.64)

4. talk to family crisis workers and family crisis suggestions (r=.49)

5. talk to mental health worker and mental health suggestions (r=.34)

6. talk to doctors/ministers and doctors/ministers suggestions (r=.38)

All of the correlations are statistically significant at p<.05, but it is clear that talking to youth/family worker (DYFS) or police/court officials is most likely to be associated with a "suggestion" to go to a specific agency. Evidently talks with teachers are least likely to result in a specific agency suggestion. Analyses by each sex resulted in comparable findings.

Section G provides three types of indicators referring to the actual choice of an agency. Parents were asked an open-ended question about whose idea it was to go to a specific agency. One overall code grouped family intimate versus professional or organizational persons, and found that 71 percent of the parents chose a formal type as the major source for the idea. Coding more specifically, human service workers were chosen most frequently (38%), followed by police/court officials and teachers (20 and 16%, respectively). The "agency idea" variable is also linked to sample type. Mental health parents are more likely to report family members and teachers as idea sources for going to the agency, while family crisis parents report formal organizational personnel and police/court officials as idea sources.

The last category refers to parental willingness to utilize agency services. A clear majority of parents report that they believe the agency can help with the problem (77%) and that the agency is a place where their problems as parents can be understood (64%). When asked if youth came because they wanted to, 55% of parental responses were coded as offering a positive reason. Evidently, parents are unable to offer a positive reason for the other 45% of the youth sample. Parents are much more likely to report that they came because they wanted to (87%). Parent responses to whether agencies understand their parenting problems and whether children came voluntarily are linked to sample types; mental health parents report that they are clearly more likely to feel understood and report that youths go to agencies for positive reasons compared to family crisis parents.

A review of the significant associations between sample types and the indicators of the proposed model of help-seeking provides evidence that the latter phases are most clearly linked to one of the human service systems. The most consistent results are linked to types of persons talked to, and the suggestions and agency ideas associated with informal and formal persons (Sections E, F, and G, respectively). This primary finding is congruent, to a degree, with other studies in the help-seeking literature. Wills, for example, reviewing studies of help-seeking in general population samples, concludes that "when people seek help, it is predominantly from friends, family members, ministers, or physicians" (1982, p. 117). Seeking help on their own behalf, adults tend to rely predominantly on informal social networks and, if that fails, to seek out professionals that are known to them—doctors or ministers. This study provides evidence that as third-party help-seekers, parents probably begin in a similar fashion—but then rely more on professionals specializing in working with youth (i.e., teachers, youth/family workers, mental health and family crisis social workers). In addition, they may also come into contact with officials who offer suggestions and ideas that outside help with youth problems may be necessary in order to prevent more serious consequences in the future. However, there are distinct gender differences in the patterns of help-seeking, and these, too, must be noted.

Help-Seeking for Boys and Girls in the Two Service Systems

Table 5–2 provides a systematic comparison of service system differences by gender for critical indicators of help-seeking: the types of formal persons talked to, formal suggestions, and the choice of a specific agency. In addition, comparisons are made between associations of service system samples and ECYS scores on the three major measures of presenting problems: new internal, multiaggression, and mixed delinquency. Although problem scores are not part of the help-seeking process, they are presented as an objective indicator of potential system differences.

If parent reports of problems are correlated with sample type for each sex, then it is clear that there are no significant associations for boys (Part A). Boys who score high on new internal, mixed aggression, or mixed delinquency are equally likely to be found associated with either human service system. This is a surprising finding, since it might be expected that service systems would differ on this measure. Girls also exhibit no differences for new internal and multiaggression scores, but this is not the case for mixed delinquency scores. For girls, high scores on mixed delinquency are distinctly associated with the family crisis system (–.23).

If parents are asked which problems they view to be main problems, then there is gender agreement that the mental health system is associated with the choice of new internal items (.22 and .20, respectively). However, parents of girls are much more likely to choose mixed delinquency as a main problem if they are linked to the family crisis system. Both sets of parents who underlined more delinquency items are associated with the family crisis systems. Perceptions and evaluations of problems appear to be stronger indications of system differences than the actual indicators of problems.

Section C provides strong evidence that the parents of family crisis boys are much more likely to talk to police/court officials (–.37); this is not the case for girls. Girls are more likely to be associated with parents who talk to family crisis workers prior to attending an agency (–.25), but this is not true for boys. Both sets of parents are especially likely to talk to DYFS workers if they are associated with the family crisis system.

Table 5.2 Critical Help–Seeking Indicators Associated with Service Systems, by Sex

	Service System Type Associations (FC/MH)[a]		
	Boys	Girls	r Value <.05
A. *ECYS Problem Score*			
1. New Internal Score	–	–	–
2. Mixed Aggression	–	–	–
3. Mixed Delinquency	–	FC	–.23
B. *Importance of Problem*			
1. Main Problem: New Internal	MH	MH	$.22^B$, $.20^G$
2. Main Problem: Mixed Delinquency	–	FC	–.25
3. Und. Mixed Delinquency	FC	FC	$-.17^B$, $-.20^G$
C. *Talk to Others Re: Problem*			
1. Talk to Police/Court	FC	–	–.37
2. Talk to DYFS	FC	FC	$-.19^B$, $-.21^G$
3. Talk to Family Crisis Worker	–	FC	–.25
D. *Suggest This Agency*			
1. Teacher Suggest	MH	–	.32
2. Police/Court Suggest	FC	–	–.26
3. DYFS Suggest	FC	–	–.21
4. MH Suggest	–	MH	.38
E. *Actual Choice of Agency*			
1. Agency Idea Is: Police/Court	FC	–	–.21
2. Agency Idea Is: Teacher	MH	–	.27
3. Agency Idea Is: Family	MH	MH	$.18^B$, $.24^G$

[a] FC/MH refers to the coding of service systems as family crisis/mental health, with a score of 0/1
[B] r value for boys
[G] r value for girls

Moving to organizational persons making suggestions, it is clear that the parents of boys have a distinct pattern. Teacher suggestions are linked to the mental health system (.32), while police/court and DYFS suggestions are associated with the family crisis system (–.26 and –.21, respectively). These types of associations between formal suggestions and service system do not hold for girls. The only suggestion type linked to girls and service system is for mental health (.38).

The final section (E) provides additional corroboration that the parents of boys who talk to police also offer agency ideas that are associated with the family crisis systems (–.21). Again, this is not the case for girls. Getting ideas from teachers is associated with the mental health system, but only for boys (–.27). Family ideas about an agency, however, are linked to the mental health system for both sexes.

In general, it appears that the parents of boys are linked to the family crisis system if they talk to and receive suggestions and ideas from police/court officials—even though the actual behavior of boys does not vary by service system. This pattern does not hold for girls. Both sexes are linked to the family crisis system if DYFS workers are talked to, but the parents of boys are apt to receive more DYFS suggestions about an agency choice. The school system is, by contrast, linked to the mental health system—but this is primarily the case for boys. Girls are clearly linked to the mental health system if parents talk to and receive suggestions from another mental health person. It appears that critical help-seeking variables are differentially linked to service systems for each sex.

Besides sex, it is likely that each source of help is potentially capable of being influenced by other variables. The purpose of the analyses that follow is to examine for the total sample, and by sex, the significant influences for each major type of formal help-seeking advisor. First, each type of person talked to will be examined separately, and then a comparison of influences will be set forth and discussed.

Influences on Seeking Help:
Talking to Mental Health Workers

Table 5–1 revealed that 38 percent of the total sample talked to psychologists or mental health counselors prior to going to a family crisis or mental health agency. If the ideal model for help-seeking has empirical relevance, then it can be hypothesized that indications of earlier help-seeking efforts should prove useful in understanding the influence on parents who talk to mental health workers in their search for help. Besides using help-seeking variables associated with the ideal model, it is possible that other variables are also potentially influential. The step-wise, multivariate, regression analyses that were conducted used the following categories of variables as additional potential influences on talking to mental health workers:

1. *Problem Scores*—It could be expected that objective scores on measures of youth problems could account for some of the variance in talking to mental health workers.

2. *Causal Attribution*—The way in which parents think about the causes of the problems could have an impact on who might be sought as a source of help. Responses to open and closed-ended questions were used as indicators of causal attribution.

3. *Causal Theory Variables*—Independent of how parents think about problem causes, analyses of mixed delinquency and multiaggression in earlier chapters disclosed that specific variables were excellent explanatory variables, especially hanging out with bad peers and lack of guilt feelings. These two items, plus indications of family closeness, were used.

4. *Solution Responsibility*—Attitudes regarding the degree of responsibility parents projected for relatives, professionals, and officials in solving youth problems could be presumed to be associated with seeking sources of advice.

5. *Solution types* —Besides being directly asked about degree of responsibility of the list of persons, parents were also asked about their preferences for specific types of help. Parents seeking specific types of help—like living away from home— could be influenced to seek specific helping sources.

6. *Demographic Variables* —As in earlier analyses, a range of background variables were used to ascertain whether specific demographic characteristics were influential in accounting for any variance of a dependent variable.

Table 5–3 presents the final results of a sequence of multi-variate regression analyses, beginning with categories of the help-seeking process variables (listed in Table 5–1), and then proceeding to enter groups of other potential influences. The final results are presented in the percent of variance accounted for, by the types of variables. Findings are presented for the total sample and for each sex, in order to systematically assess whether influences on help-seeking are common to both sexes.

Table 5.3 Comparisons of Mental Health Persons Talked to, by Percent Variance Contribution for Total Sample and Each Sex

	Percent of Variance (R^2)		
	Total	Boys	Girls
I. *Help-Seeking Variables*			
A. Problem Awareness	0%	0%	0%
B. Problem Assessment	0	0	2.8
C. Problem Importance	4.3	2.7	0
D. Prior Efforts	8.8	11.3	0
E. Persons Talked to:			
1. Intimates	4.9	3.4	0
2. Doctor/Minister	0	7.3	0
3. Teachers	0	0	8.9
4. Police/Court	0	0	16.0
5. Another	0	0	0
F. Willing to Try Agency	0	0	9.0
Subtotals	(18.0%)	(24.7%)	(27.7%)
II. *Problem Score*	0	0	0
III. *Causal Attribution*	0	0	0
IV. *Causal Theory*	0	0	0
V. *Solution Responsibility*	0	0	0
VI. *Solution Types*	0	0	9.0
VII. *Demographic*	0	0	0
Total Variance	18.0%	24.7%	36.7%

Table 5–3 provides strong support for the reasoning underlying the ideal model—since all of the variance associated with talking to mental health professionals is linked to the help-seeking variables for the total sample and each sex. However, there are striking distinctions that emerge in a more detailed comparison of the regression analyses. While all of the help-seeking variables, except for problem awareness, are utilized as a potential source of influence, there is a lack of consistency between boys and girls for each group of indica-

tors of the help-seeking process. In addition, there are striking differences in the total variance accounted for—both sexes are appreciably higher than the total sample.

The specific sources of influence are so strikingly different for each sex that it appears that the results for the total sample could be misleading—particularly for the smaller number of girls in the sample. The primary influence for boys is prior efforts with human service persons (11.3%), whereas the primary influence for girls is talking to police/court officials (16.9%). While it could be expected that there is some overlap between persons talked to, it is quite striking that police/court contact influences mental health interaction for girls, but not boys. It appears reasonable to infer that both police/court officials and teachers are major sources of direct or indirect influence in talking to mental health workers for girls—but this is not the case for boys. Instead the parents of boys talking to mental health workers are influenced by intimate networks and professionals known to them (i.e., doctors/ministers).

Influences on Seeking Help: Talking to Family Crisis Workers

The finding that the parents of girls are influenced to seek help differently from the parents of boys is also evident in a regression analysis of talking to family crisis workers. Table 5–4 presents the final results of regression analyses that began with significant help-seeking variables, and then entered indications of other potential types of influences. Again, findings are reported for the total samples and for each sex.

Table 5–4 reveals that the only variable in common for both sexes is prior efforts. As in the analysis for talking to mental health workers, the dominant sources of influence are associated with the help-seeking variables—but the sub-totals are strikingly different for each sex (13.4% for boys and 36.2% for girls). The major source of influence for parents of girls is talking to family members and other intimates (21.4%), whereas for boys talking to doctors/ministers is the major source of variance (10.3%).

Three types of variables not directly associated with the ideal help-seeking model—causal attribution, causal theory, and demographics—also contribute degrees of influence on talking to family crisis workers for each sex. For boys 5.2% of the variance is accounted for by parents attributing cause to a child characteristic. For

Table 5.4 Comparisons of Family Crisis Persons Talked to, by Percent Variance
Contribution for Total Sample and Each Sex

	Percent of Variance (R^2)		
	Total	Boys	Girls
I. *Help-Seeking Variables*			
A. Problem Awareness	3.1%	0%	0%
B. Problem Assessment	0	0	0
C. Problem Importance	1.6	0	0
D. Prior Efforts	8.1	3.1	12.0
E. Persons Talked to:			
1. Intimates	6.0	0	21.4
2. Doctor/Minister	0	10.3	0
3. Teachers	0	0	0
4. Mental Health	0	0	2.8
5. Another	0	0	0
F. Willing to Try Agency	0	0	0
Subtotals	(18.8%)	(13.4%)	(36.2%)
II. *Problem Score*	0	0	0
III. *Causal Attribution*	2.3	5.2	0
IV. *Causal Theory*	0	0	6.8
V. *Solution Responsibility*	0	0	0
VI. *Solution Types*	0	0	0
VII. *Demographic*	0	0	3.3
Total Variance	21.1%	18.6%	46.2%

girls 6.8% of the variance is associated with high scores on lack of
guilt and 3.3% with sample type.

Influences on Seeking Help: Talking to Police/Court Officials

Unlike talking to mental health or family crisis workers, parents who
talk with police or court officials are hypothesized to be doing so involuntarily. Therefore, it is instructive to see whether help-seeking

Table 5.5   Comparisons of Police/Court Officials Talked to, by Percent Variance Contribution for Total Sample and Each Sex

	Percent of Variance (R2)		
	Total	Boys	Girls
I. *Help-Seeking Variables*			
A. Problem Awareness	0%	0%	0%
B. Problem Assessment	0	0	0
C. Problem Importance	0	0	0
D. Prior Efforts	2.8	0	0
E. Persons Talked to:			
1. Intimates	2.5	0	0
2. Doctor/Minister	0	0	0
3. Teachers	0	0	0
4. Mental Health	0	0	8.5
5. DYFS	0	0	0
F. Willing to Try Agency	0	0	0
Subtotals	(7.2%)	(0%)	(8.5%)
II. *Problem Score*	0	0	20.3
III. *Causal Attribution*	0	4.2	0
IV. *Causal Theory*	15.8	22.4	0
V. *Solution Responsibility*	5.6	0	0
VI. *Solution Types*	0	0	3.5
VII. *Demographic*	7.6	10.7	3.8
Total Variance	36.2%	37.3%	36.1%

variables associated with an ideal voluntary model contribute any influence, and whether there exist sharp differences between the sexes.

Table 5–5 reveals that the ideal model variables function quite differently for talking to police or court officials, as compared to talking to mental health or family crisis workers prior to attending a specific agency. For boys none of the variance is associated with help-seeking variables, whereas for girls only 8.5% out of a total of 36.1% is associated with the ideal model. Instead two distinct non-help variables dominate. For boys 22.4% of the variance is associated with hanging out with bad peers (i.e., causal theory). For girls 20.3% of the variance is accounted for by a high score on the mixed delinquency items.

While there exist differences between the sexes in the primary influence and the degree of the help-seeking influence, there is similarity in some reliance on demographic variables. For boys 10.7% of the variance is accounted for by older boys and sample type, whereas for girls living in a male-headed household is associated with talking to police/court officials.

The possible reasons for the dominant influences for each sex are worth noting. While hanging out with youth who get in trouble is, indeed, associated with a high mixed delinquency score, it is quite possible that police/court officials are responding to boys as members of a deviant social network—and not just as individual youths presenting problems. In contrast, the high problem scores of girls are associated with police/court officials, but without the influence of peers. It is possible that the individual deviance of girls, rather than their peer associations, provides the critical cue for initiating a parental contact by police/court officials. This line of reasoning would be congruent with the earlier finding that hanging out with bad peers has a strong ecological context for boys, whereas the associations of girls with deviant peers is likely to be influenced by individual, psychological variables (see Chapter Four).

Influences on Seeking Help: Talking to Teachers

An earlier analysis disclosed that teachers were the only major professional group that actually noticed a substantial amount of youth problems (see Table 5–1, Part A). Given this fact, it would be reasonable to expect that problem awareness might be an important influence on whether parents talk to teachers as a source of help with youth problems. Table 5–6 indicates that problem awareness is a slight influence for the total sample, but that this is primarily due to the association with boys. About 6.6% of the total variance for boys is associations with teachers noticing the problem, but accounts for none of the variance for the girls. The parents of boys are also more likely to be influenced by intimates compared to girls (9.5% to 0). While a large share of the total variance for boys is accounted for by help-seeking variables, causal attribution (via low ranking of peer responsibility,

Table 5.6 Comparisons of Teachers Talked to, by Percent Variance Contribution for Total Sample and Each Sex

	Percent of Variance (R2)		
	Total	Boys	Girls
I. *Help-Seeking Variables*			
A. Problem Awareness	2.7%	6.6%	0%
B. Problem Assessment	0	0	0
C. Problem Importance	0	0	0
D. Prior Efforts	5.3	3.4	15.7
E. Persons Talked to:			
1. Intimates	2.7	9.5	0
2. Doctor/Minister	0	0	0
3. Mental Health	0	0	6.7
4. Police/Court	0	0	0
5. All Others	0	0	0
F. Willing to Try Agency	0	0	0
Subtotals	(10.7%)	(19.5%)	(22.4%)
II. *Problem Score*	0	0	3.6
III. *Causal Attribution*	0	4.9	0
IV. *Causal Theory*	0	0	0
V. *Solution Responsibility*	0	0	0
VI. *Solution Types*	5.8	4.1	0
VII. *Demographic*	0	0	0
Total Variance	16.4%	28.5%	26.0%

4.9%) and solution type (via high score on living away from home index, 4.1%) also contribute to the total variance.

In contrast to the boys, the major source of variance for girls is the parent report that they tried to communicate with professionals prior to going to the agency (15.7%). The parents of boys also report a prior effort, but it is much smaller and refers to an effort with the child. The parents of girls also yield a strong influence of talking to mental health workers. It is unknown whether mental health workers advised parents to talk to teachers, whether talking to mental health workers stimulated a desire to seek out teachers, or whether talking to mental health workers followed a contact with teachers. We lack a means for unraveling the time order of the multiple communications. Another possibility for interpreting the talking to mental health workers might be the higher scores on mixed delinquency (3.6%). A glance back at Table 5–3 reveals that police/court contact for girls is strongly associated with talking to mental health workers. Presumably this stimulus to mental health contact is linked to higher mixed delinquency scores.

Influences on Seeking Help: Talking to Child Welfare Workers

In New Jersey, workers for the Division of Youth and Family Services (DYFS) are linked to the protective custody, social control functions of child welfare. Parents could seek these persons out for services. Table 5–7 provides the final results of regression analyses that examine influences on talking to DYFS workers prior to visiting the agency. The amount of variance for the total sample is quite small, but this changes when the results for each sex are compared. Again, there are striking differences recorded between boys and girls.

The major influence for boys is parents' choice of multiaggression as the main problem and a high score on concern about mixed delinquency (15.7 and 2.6%, respectively). These two variables, grouped as "problem importance," account for all of the help-seeking variance, and offer the major contribution to the total variance for boys. Adults desiring to discuss the problem as a solution type and type of sample also contributed to the total variance for boys (5 and 4.2%, respectively).

In contrast to the boys, the variance for the girls is located primarily in the non-help-seeking variables via problem score and demographics (12.9 and 4.4%, respectively). However, the high problem score refers to mixed delinquency and the demographic variables refer to race/ethnicity (i.e., more blacks). The problem importance indicator also has a referent different from the boys—namely, the problem got worse (4.5%).

Influences on Seeking Help: Analysis of Patterns

An examination of influences on help-seeking by parents—using five types of persons talked to as the dependent variable—revealed that there were distinct gender differences. In order to assess these differ-

Table 5.7 Comparisons of Youth and Family Service (DYFS) Workers Talked to, by Percent Variance Contribution for Total Sample and Each Sex

	Percent of Variance (R2)		
	Total	Boys	Girls
I. *Help-Seeking Variables*			
A. Problem Awareness	0%	0%	0%
B. Problem Assessment	0	0	0
C. Problem Importance	3.3	18.3	4.5
D. Prior Efforts	0	0	0
E. Persons Talked to:			
1. Intimates	0	0	0
2. Doctor/Minister	0	0	0
3. Teachers	0	0	0
4. Mental Health	0	0	0
5. Police/Court	0	0	0
F. Willing to Try Agency	4.5	0	0
Subtotals	(7.8%)	(18.3%)	(4.5%)
II. *Problem Score*	0	0	12.9
III. *Causal Attribution*	2.0	4.9	0
IV. *Causal Theory*	0	0	0
V. *Solution Responsibility*	0	0	0
VI. *Solution Types*	0	5.0	0
VII. *Demographic*	3.2	4.2	4.4
Total Variance	13.0%	27.5%	21.8%

ences more fully, it is useful to compare the five patterns of help-seeking simultaneously for each sex, respectively, and then to compare the findings. Table 5–8 presents the data contained in Tables 5–3 to 5–7 by the sources of influences, for each sex. Sources of influence are reclassified as being either parent-related or externally influenced. For the purpose of this analysis, parent-related refers to five sources of influence that are linked to ideas, beliefs, attributions, efforts, and interactions that are directly or indirectly controlled to some degree, by parents. External influences refers to four sources of influence that are not under the control of parents, and can occur regardless of what parents think or do. More specifically, the five parent-related sources of influence used in Table 5–8 refer to:

A. *Direct Attitudes/Attributions*—Variables coded in Table 5–1 as problem awareness (except teacher notice), assess problem as normal, and willingness to try agency; in addition variables coded in Tables 5–3 through 5–7 as parental choice of direct causal attribution, perception of solution responsibility, and preference for solution type are also included.

B. *Prior Efforts*—Variables coded in Table 5–1 as prior personal efforts.

C. *Problem Importance*—All variables coded in Table 5–1 as importance of problem.

D. *Network Contacts*—All variables coded in Table 5–1 as talked to others if the persons were family or other intimates and doctors/ministers.

E. *Formal Organization Contacts*—All variables coded in Table 5–1 as "talked to others" if the persons were associated with mental health or family crisis agencies, schools, or Division of Youth and Family Services (DYFS).

The four categories of external events and influences refer to the following:

A. *Police/Court Talk or Teacher Notice*—Variables coded in Table 5–1 as school or police notice, and talk to police or court officials.

B. *Problem Scores*—Scores on the indexes of new internal, multiaggression, and mixed delinquency.

C. *Causal Theory*—Variables used in the explanation of mixed delinquency and multiaggression in Chapter Four, particularly association with bad peers, lacks guilt, and measures of closeness to mother and father figures.

D. *Demographics*—Variables used as control variables in Tables 5–3 through 5–7.

The reason for re-categorizing the variables for the analysis of gender patterns is rather straightforward: we want to reduce the total number of variable categories in order to discern distinctive differences. It appeared feasible to group categories by whether the influence was directly or indirectly linked to pro-active parental help-seeking efforts. The noticing of behaviors by teachers and talking to police were usually not due to parental efforts and were, therefore, classified as external. Total scores on problems are related to youth, and the occurrence of lack of guilt and hanging out with bad peers are independent of parents believing these are influences on help-seeking. However, if a parent gave his own reasons for causation as a child-centered theme or due to the influence of bad peers, these influences were coded as parent-related. Talking to mental health, family crisis agencies, schools, or DYFS were classified as parent-related because it was not possible to clearly judge whether contacts were initiated by parents or organizational personnel (with the noted exceptions of talking to police and court officials and being noticed by teachers). However, contacts with doctors/ministers were included with family and other intimates as part of network contacts because of the findings summarized by Wills (1982, p. 100).

Part A of Table 5–8 provides a clear image that the parents of boys are likely to be most clearly influenced by parent-related variables for all persons talked to, except the police/court officials. The subtotals of variance accounted for by each of the two categories of influences indicate that mental health and family crisis have no external influence for boys, while teacher and DYFS have a small amount of external influence.

Part B of Table 5–8 provides strong evidence that the parents of girls are also more likely to be influenced by parent-related variables for three of the four types that were found for boys (i.e., mental health, family crisis, and teacher). However, moderate degrees of external influence exist for mental health and family crisis—16 and 10% of the variance, respectively—unlike the absence of external influence for males for these helping types. The pattern for DYFS is clearly different for boys and girls, and results in variances explained that are almost mirror opposites (i.e., 23.3 and 4.2% for boys vs. 4.5 and 17.3% for girls).

An examination of specific sources of influence discloses that the number of similarities and range of variances are roughly similar for the two sexes on the following five variables:

1. *Attitudes/Attributions*—Variables coded with this category account for 4.2 to 9% of the variance in 4 out of 5 comparisons for

Table 5.8 Summary of Regression Findings for Persons Talked to, by Percent Variance Contribution for Each Sex

Part A   Percent Variance for Each Type Talked to, Boys Only

	MH	FC	Tch	DYFS	Pol/Ct
I. *Parent–Related Variables*					
A. Attitudes/Attributions	0%	5.2%	9.0%	5.0%	4.2%
B. Prior Efforts	11.3	3.1	3.4	0	0
C. Problem Importance	2.7	0	0	18.3	0
D. Network Contacts	10.7	10.3	9.5	0	0
E. Formal Org. Contacts	0	0	0	0	0
Subtotals	(24.7%)	(18.6%)	(21.9%)	(23.3%)	(4.2%)
II. *External Events/Influences*					
A. Pol/Ct Talk or Teacher Notice	0	0	6.6	0	0
B. Problem Scores	0	0	0	0	0
C. Causal Theory	0	0	0	0	22.4
D. Demographics	0	0	0	4.2	10.7
Subtotals	(0%)	(0%)	(6.6%)	(4.2%)	(33.1%)
Total Variance	24.7%	18.6%	28.5%	27.5%	37.3%

Table 5.8 (Continued)

Part B. Percent Variance for Each Type Talked to, Girls Only

	MH	FC	Tch	DYFS	Pol/Ct
I. *Parent-Related Variables*					
A. Attitudes/Attributions	11.8%	0%	0%	4.5%	3.5%
B. Prior Efforts	0	12.0	15.7	0	0
C. Problem Importance	0	0	0	0	0
D. Network Contacts	0	21.4	0	0	0
E. Formal Org. Contacts	8.9	2.8	6.7	0	8.5
Subtotals	(20.7%)	(36.2%)	(22.4%)	(4.5%)	(12.0%)
II. *External Events/Influences*					
A. Pol/Ct Talk or Teacher Notice	16.0	0	0	0	0
B. Problem Scores	0	0	3.6	12.9	20.3
C. Causal Theory	0	6.8	0	0	0
D. Demographics	0	3.3	0	4.4	3.8
Subtotals	(16.0%)	(10.1%)	(3.6%)	(17.3%)	(24.1%)
Total Variance	36.7%	46.3%	26.0%	21.8%	36.1%

boys and 3 out of 5 comparisons for girls (with variances ranging from 3.5 to 11.8%).

2. *Prior Efforts*—Variables coded within this category account for 3.1 to 11.3% of the variance in 3 out of 5 comparisons for boys and 2 out of 5 comparisons for girls (with variances ranging from 12 to 15.7%).

3. *Police/Court Talk or Teacher Notice*—Variables coded within this category account for 6.6% of the variances in 1 out of 5 comparisons for boys and 1 out of 5 comparisons for girls (with variance of 16%).

4. *Causal Theory*—Variables coded within this category account for 22.4% of the variance in 1 out of 5 comparisons for boys and in 1 out of 5 comparisons for girls (with a variance of 6.8%).

5. *Demographics*—Variables coded within this category account for 4.2 to 10.7% of the variance in 2 out of 5 comparisons for boys and in 3 out of 5 comparisons for girls (with variances ranging from 3.3 to 4.4%).

In contrast to these general similarities for five specific variables, there are distinctive differences for four of the following specific variables:

1. *Problem Importance*—Variables coded within this category account for 2.7 to 18.3% of the variance in 2 out of 5 comparisons for boys and 0 out of 5 comparisons for girls.

2. *Network Contacts*—Variables coded within this category account for 9.5 to 10.7% of the variance in 3 out of 5 comparisons for boys and in 1 out of 5 comparisons for girls (with 21.4% of the variance).

3. *Formal Organization Contacts*—Variables coded within this category account for none of the variance in 5 comparisons for boys and 4 out of 5 comparisons for girls (with variances ranging from 2.8 to 8.9%).

4. *Problem Scores*—Variables coded within this category account for none of the variances in 5 comparisons for boys and 3 out of 5 comparisons for girls (with variances ranging from 3.6 to 20.3%).

These comparisons of variable patterns and general categories support the inference that parents are likely to be more proactively help-seeking on behalf of boys, as compared to girls. More variance tends to be accounted for by external variables for girls in help-seeking contexts other than police/court officials. In addition, the comparisons of problem importance and problem scores indicate that parental problem concern is likely to trigger more help-seeking on behalf of boys, whereas parents of girls are associated with problems *per se* evoking external responses by others.

The pairing of network contacts and formal organization contacts also indicates a difference in proactive behaviors by parents. Talking to family, intimates, and personal doctors and ministers are much more closely linked to voluntary communications, whereas formal contacts have a mixture of voluntary and involuntary communications linked to talking to teacher and DYFS workers. A separate analysis of the inter-correlation of formal persons talked to conducted for each sex (but not shown), revealed that the inter-correlations are quite low for boys but quite high and numerous for girls. The parents of girls who tend to talk to one type of formal person are much more likely to talk to another type, whereas this is not the case for boys. Evidently, the parents of girls are more likely to rely on the advice of formal persons, whereas the parents of boys rely more on family, intimates, and known professionals.

Summary and Conclusions

Most studies of services for delinquent and deviant youths have tended to focus on an evaluation of the impact of programs. While these types of studies are useful, particularly if the evaluations are targeted towards assessing new strategies or techniques of change, there is a critical need to understand the cultural, social, psychological, and organizational processes associated with the delivery of human services for youths. Without better knowledge of help-seeking and the processes of service delivery, efforts to improve effectiveness are hindered and theories about changing youths are likely to be incomplete.

The analysis of help-seeking for urban youths in trouble was initially guided by an attempt to operationalize and assess the usefulness of an ideal model provided by the field of social psychology. According to a quasi-rational model of help-seeking, people in trouble are likely to follow a sequence of problem-solving efforts be-

ginning with awareness, assessment, and a rating of problem importance, and ending with efforts at self-help and the advice of others to
find new sources of help. The model is modified to take note of three
empirical facts: 1) parents, not children, act on behalf of the youth's
problems; 2) parents share the noticing of problems with other
adults; 3) help-seeking can occur on an involuntary, as well as a voluntary basis.

The operationalization of a modified help-seeking model provided evidence that the process categories offered by the social
psychology literature were quite useful in organizing and assessing
important aspects of parental help-seeking. Parents of urban youths,
together with family friends and intimates, are the primary noticers
of youth problems. Only schools tend to share screening and noticing functions with parents and intimates. Parents—primarily mothers—also provide evidence that they can readily assess the
normality of problems, rate their importance, initiate self-help efforts on behalf of their sons and daughters, and seek the advice of
family, intimates, doctors and ministers, and representatives of formal organizations. A comparison of service system differences discloses that the most significant associations are linked to the later
stages of the help-seeking process—either voluntarily talking to and
receiving suggestions and agency ideas from known professionals
and formal organizations, or being involuntarily stimulated by the
actions of police and human service personnel. While comparisons
of service system differences, by gender, reveal distinct patterns of
voluntary and involuntary help-seeking, the critical importance of
relying on the advice of intimates and formal persons remains for
both sexes.

The finding that seeking the advice and counsel of family, intimates, and professionals constitutes a critical component in the
help-seeking process is congruent with the findings of other studies.
Using this insight, multivariate analyses of five formal persons
talked to were conducted in order to discern the kinds of influences
associated with seeking advice. While the variables associated with
an ideal help-seeking model were found to be quite useful in understanding influences associated with talking to sources of advice,
there were distinct differences between the sexes in the types of influences that proved to be significant.

Comparisons of regression analyses, by gender, disclose that each
sex tends to be influenced by five types of variables to a roughly similar degree, although not for the same types of persons talked to for

advice. The five variables that are shared as sources of influence are:
1) attitudes of awareness, problem assessment, and willingness to
try an agency, as well as attributions of cause and solution responsibility; 2) prior efforts in dealing with the problem; 3) noticing by
teacher or talking to police or court officials; 4) theoretical causal
variables, like bad peers or lack of guilt; and 5) an assortment of demographic characteristics. In contrast, there were four types of variables that exhibited strong gender differences. Problem importance
is an influence for parents of boys, but not for the parents of girls; by
contrast, actual problem score is an influence for the parents of girls.
Parents of boys tend to be influenced by the network contacts of their
doctors and ministers, as well as family members and intimates; by
contrast, parents of girls are more likely to be influenced by formal
organization contacts.

   In an effort to expand our understanding of the difference between
the help-seeking efforts of parents on behalf of sons and daughters,
the more detailed findings associated with each type of variable are
combined into fewer categories. This broader analysis reveals that it
is quite useful to classify the categories of influence as either parent
related or externally related. Using this analytic perspective, it is
found that parents are much more likely to be proactive on behalf of
boys for four types of potential helping contexts—talking to mental
health and family crisis workers, teachers, and youth and family service workers. The parents of girls are proactive for the first three
types of helping contexts, but not for youth and family service workers. Instead, external variables account for the bulk of the variance.
In addition, even where parents of girls are more likely to be proactive, a higher proportion of total variance is associated with external
influences for girls than for boys. Parents of girls talking to mental
health workers, for example, are quite strongly influenced by discussions with police and court officials, but this was not true for boys.

   The findings of these analyses indicate that the dichotomy of voluntary and involuntary help-seeking may be too rigid, since it does
not take into account degrees of self-help and externally induced
help-seeking efforts. The decision to assess findings according to the
degree of parent-related and external influences disclosed, as expected, that police/court contacts were initiated primarily by external events for both sexes. But in addition, the analysis of the Division
of Youth and Family Service context (i.e., DYFS) yields clear evidence that parents of girls are primarily influenced by external
events; this is not true for boys.

The finding that parents of girls are less likely to be associated with parent-related help-seeking efforts, as compared to boys, is a surprising one. The literature on help-seeking is quite clear that women—acting on their own behalf—are much more likely to seek help from others, in comparison to men (Gross & McMullen, 1983; and McMullen and Gross, 1983). As McMullen and Gross note: "That large sex-differences in help-seeking exist in our culture can no longer be questioned" (1983, p. 235). But this study reveals that when women function as third-party help-seekers, they may not perform their roles as might be expected—with similar parent-related efforts for both sons and daughters.

It is quite possible that mothers, as third-party help-seekers, might be more proactive on behalf of their children (regardless of sex), in comparison to fathers. We lack a sufficient sample of fathers to test this reasonable hypothesis. But this projected, hypothetical, difference between mothers and fathers could coexist with the finding that mothers act differently on behalf of their sons, in contrast to their efforts for daughters.

It is conceivable that gender findings could be explained by the composition of the sample (i.e., 78% black); this view would hypothesize that black mothers have distinctive gender preferences on behalf of boys. But it is also plausible, and more parsimonious, to suggest that the findings are related to the overall cultural biases of American society. Since there are biases in American society that favor males in dominant social, political, financial, and religious institutions, it is not unreasonable to hypothesize that these biases are reproduced in both white and black American families. Perhaps mothers are more likely to be proactive on behalf of sons who are in trouble because they tend to blame boys less for hanging out with bad peers and favor boys over girls, as does the dominant culture.

The finding that mothers are more likely to be proactive on behalf of sons may not be unique to the type of problem associated with help-seeking. In a recent study of parents caring for developmentally disabled children of all ages, Lerman and Camasso (1992) found that parents of boys were much more likely to report that relatives helped them with various care activities; in addition, the same study found that parents of boys were also more likely to utilize services of local non-profit organizations. These proactive behaviors on behalf of males were not influenced by the age of parents or children, years of education, or other demographic variables. The study of disabled families hypothesized that parents might favor males because of a number of possible reasons: 1) parents feared that boys might get into trouble and needed more outside help; 2) boys might be thought to be more active and required more outside support services; 3) boys were more dependent and required greater amounts of assistance; or 4) parents and family members clearly favored boys over girls. The study lacked the data to test any of the hypotheses, but the pro-male bias in help-seeking (and perhaps help-giving) was unmistakable.

It is conceivable that the gender preferences found in this study and the care of developmentally disabled children do, in fact, reflect the general gender biases of the dominant culture. Since mothers tend to be the primary third-party help-seekers for their children—regardless of type of problem—the issue of gender preference is an important one. We look forward to other studies that attempt to replicate our findings with different samples and a variety of problems. Had one of the authors not been sensitized by the findings reported in this chapter, the gender preference in helping developmentally disabled males might not have been investigated.

6

Becoming a Client

INTERVIEWER: *Why was this agency picked, rather than someplace else?*

I like the agency and it is close to my home. I had therapy there and liked the help I got.

Mother of 16-year-old girl

It was close to the neighborhood, the officer suggested it and my friend came down to investigate this place and spoke to someone.

Mother of 15-year-old boy

It was the only one in our area.

Mother of 16-year-old girl

The previous chapter examined the help-seeking process primarily from the perspectives of those parents who attended an agency at least one time. However, not all parents who are referred or seek services actually utilize them. Individuals who do not attend an agency for even one intake interview are often ignored in reports of an agency's activities because it usually takes one face-to-face contact to be considered a "client." The purpose of this chapter is to identify and assess the influences associated with becoming a client in the two human service systems of mental health and family crisis. The study of potential clients is just as important as the study of actual

169

clients if we are to improve our understanding of service delivery problems and practices.

One way to study the influences on becoming a client is to compare parents who went to an agency at least one time with those who did not attend. We have two sources of data that are capable of furnishing information about clients and non-clients. The first source is collected on the sample of agency-based parents and the second source is collected on the Rutgers-Newark sample (see Chapter 1 for details about each sample).

An interview schedule form (ISF) was filled out for the agency-based sample to obtain basic information about the referral. Since agencies vary enormously in how much is recorded about referrals prior to a formal intake, the information is limited. However, we were able to find out information in three areas: 1) organizational; 2) demographic; and 3) problems of youth. Characteristics of the organization, the youth, and the problems have been found to help distinguish between individuals who are high and low utilizers of services in a variety of helping contexts (Benjamin-Bauman, 1984; Lerman, 1984; Fulkins, 1983; and Leveson and Pope, 1981).

The agency-based sample can provide important data on how youths become clients, but information on the perceptions and attitudes of parents who are non-attenders at agencies is absent. But based on our knowledge from the help-seeking literature (cited in the last chapter), as well as the findings of this study, we expect that one or more of the indicators of help-seeking could also influence whether parents and children show up at an agency. These kinds of variables have not been used to study the problems of becoming a client, to the best of our knowledge. To assess the influences of help-seeking attitudes on becoming a client, the retrospective responses of the Rutgers-Newark sample can be analyzed. Parents who went to the agency for help were asked identical questions as parents who did not show up for their clinical intakes. The questions included indicators of help-seeking, such as problem awareness, assessment, problem importance, prior efforts, and person talked to.

Shows and No-Shows in the Agency-Based Sample

All human service organizations experience difficulty in attracting and holding clients, but some have more problems than others. In the agency-based study, intake "no-shows" proved to be a major problem for both human service systems (see Chapter 1). One mental health organization (MH/A) experienced a first intake no-show rate of 57% compared to 32% for the other mental health organizations and 34% for the family crisis system. The first analysis provides information that distinguishes MH/A characteristics from the other mental health organizations and the family crisis system. MH/A is an important agency to single out for two reasons: 1) it was the most cooperative agency, so we are quite confident that all cases were completely reported; and 2) it furnished over one-half of the total potential mental health system cases (86 out of 168).

Table 6–1 indicates that the family crisis system and the mental health organizations differ on three important levels: organizational, demographic, and the perceived presenting problem. On an organizational level, agencies that offer intakes at one restricted time (8:00-10:00 a.m.), or on one primary day (Monday), provide parents with fewer opportunities for their children and themselves to become clients. In addition, organizations differ on the number of days that elapse between a request and a scheduled intake. MH/A, for example, had 47% of their cases wait at least 15 days before granting an intake appointment, and only tried one time to obtain the appointment in 81% of the referred cases. Other data (not shown) reveal that family crisis organizations scheduled 90% of their intake dates within 7 days, compared to 71% for the other mental health organizations and 25% for MH/A.

The available demographic characteristics of potential intake youth indicate that the systems also vary in types of referred clients. The organization with the highest rate of no shows (MH/A) had fewer boys, but a higher proportion of blacks, when compared to other mental health organizations and the family crisis system. Both MH/A and the family crisis system recruited their clientele primarily from Newark, while one-third of the other mental health organizations lived in the suburbs.

As might be expected, the family crisis system is much more likely to be presented with behaviors that are designated as delinquent and aggressive-external behaviors like truancy, runaway, assaultive, stealing, and disobedience at home and school (76 to 36%). The family crisis system workers are also less likely to report that the referral sources are family members, as compared to MH/A and other mental health organizations (53 to 21 to 9%, respectively). Non-family referral sources include schools, police, courts, and social agencies.

Table 6.1 Characteristics of Total Eligible Agency-Based Sample, by Delivery System

| | In Percent | | | | | |
Variable Type	MH: Org A (N=86)	MH: All Other (N=82)	All FCIU (N=240)	Total N	DF	Probability Level
A. *Organizational*						
1. First Intake: No Show	57%	32%	34%	408	2	.0001
2. Hr First Intake: 8–10 a.m.	75	21	20	348	8	.0001
3. # of Days to Intake: 15+	47	05	01	302	4	.0001
4. Intake Day: Monday	51	35	19	397	8	.0001
5. Total Agency Efforts: 1 Only	81	71	69	406	4	.0007
B. *Demographics*						
1. Sex: Boys	45	56	59	398	2	.05
2. Age: 14–15	48	51	60	397	4	.18
3. Race: Black	92	31	77	311	2	.0001
4. Zip Code: Outer Suburbs	06	33	08	379	6	.0001
C. *Problem of Youth*						
1. Intake Def: External	36	36	76	408	1	.0001
2. Number Problems Noted: 3+	05	42	42	304	6	.0001
3. Referral Source: Family	53	21	09	338	2	.0001

Presumably, the reports of family and formal organizational referral sources provide the basis of the initial perceptions of the presenting problem, since the ISF is based on pre-intake knowledge about youth behaviors.

Mental health organization MH/A had differences in three areas that could influence the relative ease of becoming a client. In order to determine which characteristics are most salient in distinguishing it from the other MH and FCIU agencies, a step-wise multiple regression analysis was performed. The regressions were conducted in several stages, in order to maintain a maximum number of cases; the best variables of each category were combined (table not shown). Unfortunately, because of ISF data deficiencies the number of usable cases was reduced from a maximum of 408 to 244; therefore, the results should be treated as suggestive of differences.

The bivariate analysis disclosed that MH/A was clearly distinguishable from all other organizations on 11 of the 12 variables depicted in Table 6–1. However, the multivariate analysis discloses that only four variables are required to describe 56.8% of the total variance between MH/A and all other agency types. Organizational characteristics of intake scheduling is clearly the most salient variable. Date differences, an indicator of delay in response-time, plus the other organizational characteristic—intake time—accounts for over 40% of the total variance. Type of presenting problem is also quite important—accounting for 15% of the variance—but it is clearly not the most distinguishing characteristic. It is important to note that none of the demographic variables accounts for any of the variance. Instead, an additional 1.3% is associated with being a voluntary family referral. We can readily conclude that the manner in which MH/A organizes its intake activities is more important than the presenting problem, referral type, or demographics in distinguishing it from all other agencies in the sample.

If we shift the analysis to determine whether the family crisis system can be characterized by a similar set of variables—by combining MH/A with the other mental health organizations—then a similar result emerges. Only three variables account for 43.8% of the variance (data not shown). The date difference in scheduling (in an opposite direction from MH/A) accounts for 30.8% of the variance, presenting problem for 11.1%, and referral source for 2.0%. Intake time is not included in the regression model, nor were any of the demographic variables.

In order to ascertain whether the type of organizational characteristics associated with MH/A actually influence the likelihood of
an intake occurring for the entire eligible agency-based sample, a
separate multiple regression analysis was conducted. With the first
intake appearance as the event to be "explained," the significant
variables listed in Table 6–1 were entered into the model in a step-
wise fashion; sex, age, race, and MH/A were used as control variables. Using all of these variables unfortunately reduced the N from
a maximum of 408 to 191; therefore, the results should again be
treated with caution. The model that emerged from this analysis accounted for 16.1% of the variance. Date difference between request
and intake appointment again proved to be the best variable (6.3%
of the variance), followed by two demographic variables (race and
age totaled 5.3%). Being referred by non-family sources and the existence of an internal problem also increases the chances of a show
at first intake (2.2 and 2.3%, respectively).

The agency-based study did not initially set forth any explicit hypotheses regarding system differences in intake appearances.
However, there existed an implicit assumption that presenting
problem, population characteristics, and referral routes might be
the prime candidates as the critical variables that could distinguish
service systems. Older black males with external problems, referred by authorities, were the types of expected variables that
might be associated with higher rates of no-show, based on customary agency reports about "resistant" clients. While race, age, and
type of problem proved to be influential as expected, referral source
yielded the surprising fact that non-family referrals were more
likely to show up at first intake appointments. These variables are
not directly under the control of any agency. However, the response-time in scheduling intake is under agency control. This
variable is the most important one influencing the likelihood of appearing at the first scheduled intake. This finding is important
theoretically, but is even more important at a policy level. Population characteristics and presenting problems are not readily ame-
nable to planned change efforts, whereas administrators and their
staffs can learn to organize the delivery of services in a more responsive manner.

Shows and No-Shows in the Rutgers-Newark Sample

The sample interviewed at Rutgers-Newark consisted of 63 intake shows and 37 no-shows. As noted, this sample includes parent attitudes and perceptions to use in analyzing the processes of becoming a client. In this analysis 9 of the 37 no-show respondents were associated with the mental health system; all other respondents were from the family crisis system. Table 6–2 provides a listing of significant correlations obtained from responses to similarly worded questions for the total Rutgers-Newark sample, and each gender. The result yielded 18 significant correlations for one or more of the sample groupings, categorized into four groups as follows: Section A refers to ideal help-seeking variables identified in Chapter 5; Section B refers to attitudes towards solution responsibility and types of preferred solutions; Section C refers to problem scores; and Section D refers to demographic variables. All noted correlations are statistically significant at the .05 level, unless specifically noted otherwise in the table.

All of the associations depicted in Table 6–2 are in the direction of a family showing up at an FCIU designated agency (and are therefore positive). Of the ten help-seeking variables that yielded significant correlations, six occurred for the total sample, four for boys, and three for girls. Besides these discrepancies, there are no variables that are significant for both boys and girls. Because there are more boys than girls (61 to 39), the significant correlations revealed for the total sample tend to be more congruent with boys than with girls. For the total Rutgers-Newark sample, parents who attend at least one intake are more likely to report that they did or thought the following: 1) personally tried to contact human services prior to being referred to an agency; 2) talked to family and intimates, as well as family crisis and mental health workers, prior to an agency referral; 3) talked to a doctor/minister who suggested attending an agency; and 4) believed an agency person could understand the problem from a parent's perspective. The parents of boys concur with the total sample in trying human services, talking to mental health, and receiving suggestions from doctors or ministers; those of girls concur with the total sample only in talking to family crisis workers.

Attitudes toward solutions of the main problems disclose a sharper disparity between the parents of boys and girls. Of the four identi-

Table 6.2 Significant Correlations of Variables Associated with Showing Up at an Agency, Rutgers-Newark Sample Only

Variable Types	Significant Correlations (p<.05)		
	Total (N=100)	Boys (N=61)	Girls (N=39)
A. *Help–Seeking Model*			
1. Personally Try; Human Services	.24	.27	—
2. Personally Try: Teacher	—	.28	—
3. Talk to Intimates	.21	—	—
4. Talk to Others	—	—	.33
5. Talk to Family Crisis Workers	.23	—	.42
6. Talk to Mental Health	.23	.31	—
7. Agency Idea: Formal Org.	—	—	.34
8. Doctor/Minister Sugg. Agency	.23	.31	—
9. Agency Understood Parent	.21	—	—
10. Agency Can Help	—	—	.42
B. *Parent Attitudes Re: Solutions*			
1. Adult Needs Help with Own Will	—	—	.33
2. Adult Needs to Discuss	.25	—	.46
3. Adult Needs Most: Will or Discuss	—	—	.32
4. Family/School Solve Responsibility	—	—	.32
C. *Problem Scores*			
1. Multiaggression	.22	.29	—
D. *Demographics*			
1. Respondent Schooling Years	.29	.23[a]	.37
2. Zip Code; Live in Suburbs	.30	.30	.29[a]
3. Household Head: Female Type	—	.26	—

[a] Significant Correlations (p<.07)

fied significant correlations, parents of interviewed girls are distinctly in favor of obtaining assistance with improving their own will-power, discussing the problem, and believing that solving the main problem is a family or school responsibility. By contrast, none of the correlations are significant for boys, and only one is significant for the total sample—the need of adults to discuss the problem.

Only one problem score distinguished shows and no-shows in the Rutgers-Newark sample. High scores on multiaggression items were more likely to be reported by the total sample and the parents of boys.

Three demographic characteristics were identified as providing a significant correlation with one of the sample sub-groups. Two items—years of respondent schooling and residence in a suburb outside of Newark—tended to be significant for both sexes, as well as the total sample. These are the only 2 variables out of the 18 significant variables that tended to behave in this manner. Association with a household headed by a female was significant only for the parents of boys.

To identify the most salient variables that differentiate show and no-show respondents, it would have been useful to conduct multiple regression analyses for each sex, as well as the total sample—as was done in the chapter on the help-seeking process. Unfortunately, the small number of female no-shows makes it difficult to conduct multiple regression analyses with great confidence. Rather than present potentially incomplete or misleading findings, only the results of the regression analyses for the total sample are discussed (table not shown).

In the initial step-wise regression analyses for the total sample the significant ideal help-seeking variables were entered first as a group. After the critical help-seeking variables were identified, the remaining variables identified in Table 6–2 were examined. The best of both analyses were then combined for a final analysis. The final results of the regression analyses disclosed that for the total Rutgers-Newark sample the variable with the strongest bivariate relationship—zip code area of residence—accounted for the greatest amount of variance (9.5 out of a total variance of 21.4%). Parents living outside the city of Newark, regardless of race or ethnicity, are much more likely to attend an agency at least one time. In addition, three help-seeking variables can influence parent attendance at an agency: 1) desire to discuss problems; 2) being personally understood by agency personnel; and 3) receiving a suggestion to attend the agency by a doctor or minister. The three help-seeking variables account for 11.9% of the total variance, slightly more than the demographic characteristic.

Summary and Conclusions

Participants and observers of the field of human services have known for some time that many persons referred to an agency do not show up even for an intake session. The customary response, as we learned in our agency-based effort, is to blame the problem on the "resistance" offered by those referred. The empirical data, in corroboration with other studies, discloses that the issue of client no-shows is more complicated. There are multiple reasons why parents and children do not become clients of an agency. The analysis of agency-based potential clients and the responses of interviewed no-shows provides empirical evidence concerning some of the influences that bear on the issue of whether parents, as third-party help-seekers, will become an agency client.

One mental health organization associated with the highest rate of no-shows, presented families with an unusual set of restrictions to entering the system as clients: 1) intakes could not occur, on the average, for at least 15 days from the date of request or referral; 2) intakes would only take place on Mondays; and 3) the primary time for an intake could only occur between the hours of 8:00-10:00 a.m. These restrictions, particularly the delay in response-time and the limited hours, proved to be important organizational variables that distinguished the highest no-show agency from all other agencies. An analysis of the likelihood of showing up at intake in the entire agency-based sample supported the inference that delay in response-time—an organizational variable—is indeed an important influence on becoming a client. These findings for a sample of deviant youth are congruent with past studies with other samples.

Using the survey responses of Rutgers-Newark parents, it is evident that help-seeking variables are also important. Whether parents perceive worker empathy (i.e., feel understood), desire discussions as parents, and have access to the suggestions of doctors or ministers can also influence the likelihood of becoming a client. When combined, the influences for no-shows can be categorized as follows:

1. *Organizational Variables* as indicated by delay in response-time and the hours of scheduling intakes;

2. *Help-Seeking Variables* as indicated by desiring to be understood and suggestions from known professionals;

3. *Demographic* characteristics as indicated by area of residence, ethnicity/race, and age;

4. *Presenting Problems* as indicated by definition of problem as psychological or external.

Help-givers charging fees have recognized for some time that without a written or phone reminder, potential clients are likely to forget an appointment scheduled more than seven days ahead of time. Non-profit help-givers, without fees to lose, may not be as sensitive to the consequences of a lengthy response time or providing potential clients with a choice of agency hours. Funding sources do not customarily request this type of organizational information, so there are few incentives for agencies to improve response time, provide scheduling choices, or provide an appointment reminder within 24 to 48 hours of an intake. In the absence of fiscal incentives or penalties for influencing the rates of showing up at initial appointments, it is possible that the dissemination of empirical findings could stimulate concern about reducing the rate of no-shows by responsible agency leaders.

While the identified organizational variables are clearly under control of agency leaders, it may appear at first glance that the other categories of variables are the responsibility of non-agency sources. While organizations cannot readily change the demographic composition or the mix of presenting problems, without changing agency location or boundaries of service, they may be able to partially influence help-seeking behavior by parents. The desire to be understood by parents is a social psychological phenomenon that could be influenced by stimulating special efforts by initial agency contact persons. Agency persons can be trained to communicate the ideal triad of help-giving services: warmth, empathy, and genuineness (Truax, 1973). The help-giving literature has identified these characteristics as targets of education and training for successful engagement with clients. These kinds of efforts can also be directed at improving the responses and organization of intake services—so parents can more readily perceive an empathic readiness in a phone conversation, a letter, or face-to-face contact.

7

Utilizing Services

INTERVIEWER: *Why do you feel the agency was not able to help?*

Because he didn't show changes in his behavior while he was with that agency. I don't think the counselor was experienced enough or strong enough to cope with his manipulative behavior.

Mother of 16-year-old boy

First of all, psychological therapy is long term and he only went for two months. It was too short a time.

Mother of 15-year-old boy

We went at least a month, every week. We'd sit there and he'd talk to me and he'd talk to my son. My son needs mental help. Need someone with more experience.... There was not a change in him from going there. The teacher said he'd gotten worse.

Mother of 13-year-old boy

The last chapter focused on understanding the influences bearing on whether parents and children would visit an agency for at least one contact. Neither the mental health nor family crisis agencies deemed that one visit was sufficient to accomplish an agency's goal of stabilizing or remediating a problem. The family crisis agencies were funded by the county to provide services for a treatment period of 90 days; the number of visits was not specified, but weekly contact for about 3 months could result in 12 sessions paid for by the county. The mental health agencies were funded on a different basis, but there, too, there was a staff expectation that those families who have the greater number of contacts with an agency have a greater chance of receiving and experiencing help.

Many families did not return for a second visit, while others not only returned for a second time—they came a third, fourth, or more times. The average number of family visits—for those who came at least once—was about 5.7 times per case. Despite the difference in funding and treatment philosophy regarding the existence and duration of a crisis, there were virtually no statistical differences between the family crisis and mental health systems regarding the average number of youth or adult visits. Instead, there were wide differences in the utilization of services within each service system. The goals of this chapter are to identify, analyze, and interpret the influences that help account for the variations in the utilization of agency services.

The number of potential influences on service utilization are quite varied according to the existing literature. However, very few studies refer to adolescent populations, particularly youth in trouble. According to published reports, based primarily on adult mental health populations, the following types of variables have been found to increase the risk that clients will not fully utilize agency services: ethnicity/race (blacks are less likely to receive treatment); institutional, rather than private referral; low socio-economic status; parental denial of a problem; large families; previous experience; and a history of truancy (Backeland and Lundwall, 1975; Benjamin-Bauman, 1984; Turner and Vernon, 1986; and Viale-Val, Rosenthal, Curtiss, and Marohn (1984). Virtually all of the studies rely on agency records or staff perceptions as a basis for identifying potential influences on agency utilization.

This study differs from others on service utilization by relying primarily on parent reports of help-seeking activities and perceptions, and parent attributions about causes and solutions. In addition, this study permits us to study service utilization patterns from two time perspectives: prospective and retrospective. The agency-based sample design included telephone interviews with human service workers six or more months after the initial post-intake interview with parents. Therefore, for the agency-based sample, we possess data on the number of agency visits by adults or children that were gathered independently six months *after* parents provided answers to questions about help-seeking and attributions about causes and solutions. Neither the human service workers nor the interviewers were aware of the responses parents had provided six months earlier.

A similar design could not be employed with the Rutgers-Newark sample. Instead, retrospective analysis was conducted for the Rutgers-Newark sample. It will be recalled that this sample was drawn primarily from closed family crisis cases (see Chapter 1). Interviewed parents who attended an agency were asked to recall how many times they and their children, respectively, actually visited a family crisis agency. Questions were asked about youth and parent visits separately. Unfortunately, this was not done for the prospective study—so the two methods of gathering information are difficult to compare directly. However, both methods of studying utilization employ the same variables that have already been found to be so useful in understanding the processes of help-seeking and becoming a client. We would expect that the utilization of services can also be influenced by the way parents approach a search for help.

Prospective Analysis of Utilization: Agency-Based Samples

A total of 126 parents were interviewed at either a mental health or family crisis agency. We were able to interview six months later, by telephone, the human service workers most knowledgeable about 116 of the cases, in order to determine the number of times a parent or child visited an agency after the initial intake. Although there are no statistically significant differences in the average number of post-intake contacts between service systems, it is important to note that the analyses that follow are disproportionately influenced by the number of cases associated with the family crisis system (83), compared to those associated with the mental health system (33).

Using the number of post-intake visits of parents or youth to either system as the critical indicator of agency utilization, bivariate correlations were conducted for all of the help-seeking variables discussed in Chapter 5. It was hypothesized that parent or youth utilization could be influenced by the manner in which help was sought for problems. Influences might occur because parents made social comparisons that their children's problems were not "normal" and/or were quite serious (as indicated by variables referring to problem assessment or importance), and therefore required ongoing services. Influences might also occur because parents engaged in coping behaviors or possessed attitudes that were congruent with further modes of seeking help (as indicated by prior efforts and a willingness to try formal agencies of help). Or influences might occur because of responsiveness to social influences associated with prior contacts with family and friends, known professionals, or formal agency referrals (as indicated by persons talked to and offering suggestions and ideas). These three theoretical perspectives—social comparisons, coping behaviors, and social influences—are associated with social psychological writings on help-seeking and service utilization (DePaulo et al., 1983).

In addition to pursuing the theoretical implications of the variables associated with the help-seeking process, it was deemed useful to also test whether parental attributions of causal and solution responsibility, or types of preferred solutions, influenced service utilization. According to attribution theorists, the manner in which persons allocate blame or responsibility for causing and/or solving problems can influence the types of preferred solutions and how persons accept help (Ames, 1983; Brickman, Rabinowitz, Karuza, Coates, Cohn, and Kidder, 1982). Individuals who blame external events for problems, for example, are thought to be less likely to seek or use formal help than those who blame themselves or their children.

Table 7–1 presents the significant bivariate correlations that occurred for either the total agency-based sample or for one of the gender groups. Besides the major categories of help-seeking and parent attributions, significant external influences are also listed in a third category. As noted earlier, all parent responses and external variables were collected at least six months prior to securing information about the number of adult or youth post-intake visits. To the best of our knowledge, the type of detailed data reported in Table 7–1 has never been reported in the help-seeking or deviance literatures on youth in trouble.

The help-seeking category refers to eight types of variables (A–H) that could be associated with the number of visits by parents or youth. Of the eight variable types only two do not have any significant correlations with the number of post-intake visits—talking to others (E) and willingness to try (H). The remaining six variable types have at least one significant correlation with the total agency-based sample. Besides noting the correlational values for each variable, Table 7–1 also notes how many associations could have occurred for each variable type. For example, the "assess problem" category (B) has two significant correlations out of a roster of four

Table 7.1 Significant Correlates of High Agency Utilization of Agency-Based Sample, by Total Sample and Each Sex

| | Correlations of Visits by Parents of Youth | | |
| | | (p<.05) | |
Potential Influences	Total Agency Sample (Max N=116)	Boys (Max N=69)	Girls (Max N=47)
I. *Help–Seeking*			
A. *Awareness* (5 Vars.)			
1. Who Noticed? Intimates	−.26	−.31	—
B. *Assess Problem* (4 Vars.)			
1. Ever Heard of Problem? Yes	−.23	−.25	—
2. Others Have Problem? Yes	−.20	—	—
C. *Importance of Problem* (9 Vars.)			
1. Main Problem: Aggressive	.20	—	—
2. Underline Mix Delinq Score	−.20	—	—
3. Problem Get Better Score	.25	.—	.32
D. *Prior Efforts* (7 Vars.)			
1. Personally Try: Ext. Env.	−.20	—	−.31
2. Personally Try: Hum. Serv.	—	—	.30
3. Personally Try: Reward/Punishment	−.29	−.27	−.32
E. *Talk to Others* (10 Vars.)	—	—	—
F. *Suggest This Agency* (8 Vars.)			
1. Doctor/Min Suggest	—	.24	—
2. Police/Court Suggest	−.19	.—	−.19
3. Mental Health Suggest	—	−.24	.24
4. Family Crisis Suggest	.22	.24	.22
G. *Actual Choice of Agency* (6 Vars.)			
1. Agency Idea: Hum. Serv.	.18	—	—
2. Agency Idea: Teacher	—	.24	—
H. *Willingness to Try* (4 Vars.)	—	—	—
II. *Parent Attributions Re: Cause/Solution*			
A. *Cause Attribution* (11 Vars.)			
1. Why Problem? Child Theme	.25	.37	—
2. Why Problem? Child/Family Theme	.19	.30	—
B. *Solution Attributions/Types* (21 Vars.)			
1. Child need most: Teach or Discuss	—	.35	—
III. *External Influences*			
A. *Problem Score* (3 Vars.)			
1. Mixed Delinquency	−.23	—	−.29
B. *Causal Theory* (7 Vars.)			
1. Bad Peers	−.19	—	—
C. *Demographics* (14 Vars.)			
1. Race/Ethnicity: Black	−.19	—	—
2. Respondent Schooling Years			
3. Father Figure in Home	−.19	—	−.40
4. Zip Code: Inner Newark/All Other	—	—	−.33
5. Other Adults in House Work	—	—	−.29

variables used as indicators of "awareness"; in contrast, talk to others had none out of a roster of ten variables, and "suggest this agency" category (F) had two out of a roster of eight variables. If we just examine the strength of each correlation, then personally trying reward or punishments had the highest value (–.29), but if we assess the proportion of variables that proved to be significant, then assessing problems could be deemed of greater importance—since two out of four variables proved to be significant for the total sample.

The total sample provides 11 significant correlations associated with help-seeking variables. Since there are a total of 53 variables that were used, by chance we might have expected about 3 to have been significant (at .05 level). Since the number of significant correlations are well beyond a chance occurrence, we can be fairly confident that the number of visits are, indeed, potentially influenced by how parents seek help on behalf of their children. There is also evidence for the total sample that attributions of causes (but not solutions), as well as external variables, could also influence the number of post-intake visits.

A review of the associations of help-seeking variables with each gender discloses that there are fewer significant associations than is the case for the total sample (i.e., 11 versus 8 and 6, respectively). However, some of the reduction is probably due to the disparity in the size of the total sample, as compared to each gender group. The smaller the number, the greater the difficulty in establishing a correlation that is beyond chance. Therefore, it is important to note when the total sample and each gender group is in agreement—as occurs for personally try reward or punishment and family crisis suggest an agency. There are no similarities between the gender groups and the total samples for any of the potential external influences.

While a number of the bivariate relationships are congruent with the findings occurring in the literature—like type of problem, and ethnicity/race—some are distinctly at odds with potential expectations. For example, the presence of a father figure in the home is negatively associated with number of contacts for the total sample, and is particularly relevant for girls. Lack of a father figure in the home is more likely to be associated with low socio-economic status and being on welfare—and this is true for the ECYS sample. Prior studies of attendance of adults at mental health agencies, noted earlier, indicate that low socio-economic status variables are related to low utilization rates; in the ECYS sample, by contrast, girls living at home

Table 7.2 Results of Regression Analyses of Variables Associated with Number of Post-Intake Contacts of Agency-Based Sample, by Total Sample and Each Sex

| | Percent of Variance Accounting for Contacts | | |
Potential Influences	Total Sample	Boys	Girls
I. *Help–Seeking*			
A. *Awareness*	0%	0%	0%
B. *Assess Problem*			
1. Ever Heard of Problem? (–)	8.5	11.7	0
C. *Importance of Problem*			
1. Problem Get Better	8.8	0	0
D. *Prior Efforts*			
1. Personally Try: Ext. Env. (–)	0	0	8.4
2. Personally Try:			
Reward/Punishment (–)	10.5	0	0
E. *Suggest This Agency*			
1. Family Crisis Suggest	5.9	0	0
2. Doc/Min Suggest	0	6.8	0
Subtotal	(33.7%)	(18.5%)	(8.4%)
II. *Parent Attributions Re: Cause/Solution*			
A. *Cause Attribution*			
1. Why Problem? Child Theme	2.7	12.5	0
III. *External Influences*			
C. *Demographics*			
1. Father Figure in Home (–)	0	0	15.9
2. Respondent Schooling Years (–)	0	8.4	0
3. Zip Code: Inner Newark	0	0	5.9
Subtotal	(0%)	(8.4%)	(21.8%)
Total	(36.4%)	(39.4%)	(30.2%)

Letters for variable types are the same as those used for categories in Table 7.1.

without a father and residing in an inner city neighborhood are associated with a higher rate of utilization.

In order to clarify which types of variables are more influential in accounting for higher rates of agency utilization, a multivariate analysis of significant variables was undertaken for the total sample and each gender group. The results of the step-wise, regression analyses are reported in Table 7–2. As in earlier analyses, the results are reported by the percent of variance accounting for the dependent variable (i.e., number of agency contacts by parents or youth).

Before examining the contribution of variable types and specific indicators, it is important to take note of the total amount of variance that is accounted for in Table 7–2. Accounting for 30–39% of the variances for a specific outcome is a very respectable figure. The fact that the total variance is based on longitudinal data, collected independently of the outcome variable, provides a measure of confidence that the identified influences are substantively important in understanding the utilization of services by parents and youth.

For the total sample, the amount of variance contributed by help-seeking variables is quite large—33.7 out of a total of 36.4%. The social comparison categories—assess the problem and problem importance—contribute 17.3% of the variance. Parents who tend not to have heard about the problem in the mass media and those who are the most optimistic about the problem getting better contribute the critical social comparison indicators. In addition, parents who avoid mentioning rewards or punishment for handling youth problems contribute 10.5%, while those who pay heed to family crisis suggestions contribute 5.9%. Evidently, prior parental coping efforts and social influences, as well as social comparison judgments, can be useful in understanding the utilization variability in the total sample. Parent attributions about cause add an additional small amount of variance (2.7%).

It is important to note, too, that four help-seeking variable types do not make any contributions to explaining the variance of the total sample: Awareness (Category A); Talk to Other (Category E); Actual Choice of Agency (Category G); and Willingness to Try (Category H). This finding suggests that from a longitudinal perspective, only limited parts of the help-seeking process are likely to function as ongoing influences on how parents actually utilize agency services. For the total sample, the four variable types referred to in Table 7–2 are capable of accounting for the bulk of the variance without any contribution from external influences.

Analysis of gender findings provides strong support for the inference that explanations pertaining to utilization of services are likely to vary by sex. For boys, help-seeking variables contribute 18.5% of the variance, whereas for girls the amount is 8.4%. The utilization of agency services by parents and boys is also influenced a substantial amount by causal attributions, compared to parents of girls (12.5 to 0%, respectively). For girls, the most critical influences center around demographic variables, compared to boys (21.8 to 8.4%, respectively). These findings are congruent with the earlier analyses of how parents sought help (see Chapter 5).

For boys, the primary help-seeking variables pertain to social comparisons (i.e., "ever heard") and the social influences of known professionals (i.e., "doctor/minister suggested"). For girls, the primary help-seeking variables refer to prior efforts of coping via an avoidance of influencing the external environment. But for girls, the single strongest influence on utilization is the absence of father figures in the household. It is a matter for speculation to understand why the absence of a father figure should have such a beneficial impact on the utilization of services by girls and their parents, compared to boys and their parents. It may be related to specific social psychological consequences pertaining to missing fathers *per se* for girls, or to the relationships of missing-father households with other influential variables. It is also possible that the relationship between missing fathers and higher utilization is unique to the ECYS agency-based sample of primarily black female youth in trouble.

Retrospective Analysis of Utilization: Rutgers-Newark Sample

Out of the 100 adults interviewed away from the human service agencies, at offices on the Rutgers-Newark campus, 63 parents participated in at least one intake interview. This group of persons was asked to report how many times, if any, they visited an agency other than an intake session; a similar question was asked about their children as potential clients. A total of 59 respondents furnished usable answers about adult and children agency contacts, respectively. Since all 59 respondents attended family crisis agencies, the analysis is limited to only one agency type. Because of size restrictions, all analyses are for the total eligible Newark sample only.

Rutgers-Newark parents reported that they visited an agency an average of 2.6 times, and that their children went an average of 3.2 times. It will be recalled that the prospective analysis reported that the post-intake contacts of the agency-based sample were an average of 5.7 contacts of "youth or adult" visits. The Rutgers-Newark combined visits of 2.6 and 3.2 add up to a similar number of adults or youth visits—5.8 contacts.

Table 7–3 presents the significant bivariate correlations that occurred for the number of adult and child contacts, respectively. As in the prospective analysis, it is hypothesized that variables referring to help-seeking, parental attributions, and external influences could be associated with the number of adults and/or children contacts. As Table 7–3 discloses (Part IV), there was a very high correlation between the number of agency visits of Rutgers-Newark adults and youth. Since parents are more likely to influence youth, rather than vice versa, we used adult agency contacts as another potential influence on the number of child contacts. For the purpose of analyzing child contacts, these adult visits are categorized as a current effort—since they are quite analogous to the prior efforts of parents in the help-seeking process, but occur during the period of potential agency services.

Four categories of potential help-seeking influences produced significant correlations with the number of adult contacts: Importance of Problem (C); Prior Efforts (D); Talk to Other (E); and Suggest this Agency (F). It will be recalled that the prospective method yielded associations with six categories for the total sample. In addition, the prospective method had eleven significant bivariate associations between number of contacts and help-seeking variables; the retrospective sample yielded eight significant correlations. However, if the number of child contacts is included, then the number of significant categories and specific correlations are quite comparable.

There is no *priori* reason why the number of adult contacts should yield more significant associations with help-seeking variables, in comparison to child contacts (8 versus 4). As third-party help-seekers it might be expected that there might be similar influences bearing on adult or child contacts. But the data suggest that the fewer associations between the help-seeking variables and child contacts is also spread among fewer theoretical categories (i.e., Assess Problem and Importance of Problem), yield significant associations for adult contact and none for child contact. Both adult and child contacts are associated with coping categories (i.e., Prior Efforts and Willingness) and social influences (i.e., Talk to Others and Suggest Agency).

The number of adult contacts is also associated with indicators of causal and solution attributions and each of the external influence categories. Leaving aside current parent efforts (Category III), child contact is only associated with one non-help-seeking variable (i.e., parent causal attribution). In general, we can conclude that the analysis of bivariate associations reveals fewer sources of influence that are linked to child contacts, as compared to adult contacts.

Table 7.3 Significant Correlates of High Agency Utilization of Rutgers-Newark Contact Sample Only, by number of Adult and Child Contacts

	Correlations of Visits by Adults or Child	
	Adult Contact Number (Max N=59)	*Child Contact Number (Max N=59)*
I. *Help–Seeking*		
A. *Awareness*	—	—
B. *Assess Problem*	—	—
C. *Importance of Problem*		
1. Underline New Int.	.28	—
2. Underline Mul. Agg.	.26	—
3. Problem Got Better Score	−.29	—
4. Time to Get Better	−.30	—
D. *Prior Efforts*		
1. Personally Try: Self/Family	−.29	—
2. Personally Try: Reward/Punishment	—	−.31
E. *Talk to Others*		
1. Fam. Crisis Talk	—	.25
2. Mental Health Talk	.29	—
F. *Suggest This Agency*		
1. Mental Health Suggest	.30	—
2. Family/Int. Suggest	.39	—
G. *Willingness To Try*		
1. Agency Can Help	—	.31
II. *Parent Attributions Re: Cause/Solution*		
A. *Causal*		
1. Why Problem? Child Theme	−.28	—
2. Direct Environment	—	−.24
B. *Solution Attributions/Types*		
1. Child Needs to Be Taught	.31	—
III. *External Influences*		
A. *Problem Score*		
1. Total Score: All ECYS Items	.29	—
B. *Causal Theory*		
1. Lack of Guilt	.27	—
2. Closeness to Absent Father	−.33	—
C. *Demographics*		
1. Respondent Schooling Years	.31	—
2. Zip Code: Inner Newark/All Other	.33	—
IV. *Current Parent Efforts*		
1. Number of Adult Contacts	.NA	.53

Table 7.4 Comparisons of Variables Associated with Number of Post-Intake Contacts of Rutgers-Newark Samples by Percent of Variance Contribution for Adult and Child Contacts

Potential Influences	Percent of Variance (R2)	
	Adult Contact Number	Child Contact Number
I. *Help-Seeking*		
D. *Prior Efforts*		
1. Personally Try: Self/Family	5.3%	0%
2. Personally Try: Reward/Punishment	0	4.3
F. *Suggest This Agency*		
1. Family/Int. Suggest	8.5	0
G. *Willingness To Try*		
1. Agency Can Help	0	12.6
Subtotals	(13.8%)	(16.9%)
II. *Attributions*		
A. *Causal*		
1. Direct Environment Score (–)	—	4.3
III. *External Influences*		
C. *Demographics*		
1. Zip Code: Inner Newark/All Other	15.6	—
IV. *Current Efforts*		
1. Number of Adult Contacts	NA	28.0
Total Variance	29.4%	49.2%

Letters for Variable Types are the same as those used for the categories in Table 7.1.

In order to further the analyses of potential influences on agency utilization, two distinct multiple regression analyses were conducted for each type of contact. Table 7–4 indicates that each indicator of agency utilization accounts for a respectable amount of total variance, with a limited set of variables (29.4 and 49.2%, respectively).

Although child contacts had fewer bivariate help-seeking relationships, the amount of variance accounted for by help-seeking variables is slightly higher as compared to adult contacts. A subtotal of 16.9% is accounted for by these prior coping variables of avoiding the reward and punishment of youth and an attitude of willingness to try, as compared to a subtotal of 13.8% for coping and social influence indicators. The two types of contacts differ more sharply in their use of causal attributions and demographics as sources of influence. Child contacts are more likely to occur if parents do not attribute blame to school or neighborhoods for child behavior. Adult contacts are strongly influenced by whether families live away from the City of Newark and nearby suburbs.

The greatest amount of variance for child contacts is clearly linked to the attendance of parents at family crisis agencies. If parent utilization is high, then fully 28% of the variance of child contacts can be "explained." When this critical influence of current effort is added to the influence of past efforts and attitudes the amount of total variance is quite substantial. The data clearly support the inference that agency attendance by youth is unlikely to occur unless parents also participate in utilizing the services.

If the results of both analyses are read together, then it is evident that youth were high utilizers of agency services if their parent's high rate of utilization was associated with prior efforts and supported by the suggestions of families and intimates. In addition, the potential support of neighborhood context may accompany high adult contacts. The current efforts of parents contribute 28 of the total 49.2% of the variance for child contacts, but over 21% is contributed by other sources. The influence of other sources indicates that a substantial amount of variance can occur independent of the direct influence of adult contacts. For children to be high utilizers, parents must also have a coping style that avoids undue reliance on rewards and punishments and exhibit an attitude of believing that an agency can help their child.

Comparing Prospective and Retrospective Methods

The results of both modes of analyses have yielded findings that indicate areas of similarities and differences. In order to highlight the major similarities and differences, and offer a parsimonious interpretation of the regression findings, a special comparison table has been prepared. Table 7–5 collapses the eight ideal phases of help-seeking into three major categories that refer to social-psychological indicators of social comparison, coping skills and social influences. According to the help-seeking literature, efforts at securing help can be influenced as follows: 1) by how parents compare their problems by assessing the degree of normality and seriousness; 2) by how parents engage in self-directed efforts with receptive attitudes and coping skills, and 3) by how parents are open to positive suggestions and ideas from friends, intimates, professionals, and others (DePaulo et al., 1983). Each theoretical tradition is distinctively linked to efforts at explaining help-seeking behaviors, but it is rare to find studies that can compare their relative utility in a multivariate analysis—so that each set of theoretical variables has an opportunity to test their relative efficacy in competition with each other.

In Table 7–5 the category of social comparison refers to indicators of awareness and problem importance (see Tables 7–1 and 7–3). Prior coping efforts/attitudes refers to indicators of prior personal efforts and willingness to try agency; and social influences refers to indicators of talking to others and the suggestions and ideas of persons talked to. The second major category is also referred to in the help-seeking literature, but since it was not included in the original ideal model (discussed in Chapter 6), it has been categorized separately. Only causal attributions are referred to, since solution responsibility or type failed to yield any significant variance in any of the multivariate analyses. The third category, demographics, is self-explanatory. The fourth category, current coping efforts, as noted earlier, refers only to the number of ongoing adult contacts, and is used only with child contacts. The percent of variance accounted for is taken from Tables 7–2 and 7–4.

Focusing first on the help-seeking categories, it is clear that each one can contribute to our understanding of the utilization of human services. However, if we had been unable to conduct a prospective analysis, it appears unlikely that we would have understood the potential influence of social comparison variables. The retrospective analyses do not have any variance associated with social comparison indicators. While the prospective method is methodically stronger as an analytical design, it suffered from an inability to construct separate analyses of child and adult contacts. The retrospective analyses indicate that different results can emerge, depending on whether adult or youth contacts are used as the variable to be explained. Adult contacts exhibited influences of prior coping and social influences, but youth contacts omitted any contribution of social influence.

The analysis of gender differences among help-seeking categories (in the prospective analysis) provides strong support for conducting distinct analyses whenever possible. The contacts of all parents and boys are primarily influenced by social comparison and social influence variables, whereas the contacts of parents and girls are primari-

Table 7.5 Comparison of Regression Findings of Post-Intake Contacts, by Prospective and Retrospective Methods and Sample Type

Potential Influences	Agency-Based Sample Prospective Method			Rutgers-Newark Sample Retrospective Method	
	Total Sample	Boys	Girls	Adult No.	Child No.
I. Help-Seeking Categories					
A. Social Comparison	17.3%	11.7%	0%	0%	0%
B. Prior Coping Attitudes/Efforts	10.5	0	8.4	5.3	16.9
C. Social Influences	5.9	6.8	0	8.5	0
Subtotals	(33.7%)	(18.5%)	(8.4%)	(13.8%)	(16.9%)
II. Attributions					
A. Causal	2.7	12.5	0	0	4.3
III. External Variables					
A. Demographics	0	8.4	21.8	15.6	0
IV. Current Coping Efforts					
A. No. of Adult Contacts	NA	NA	NA	NA	28.0
Total Variance	36.4 %	39.4 %	30.2 %	29.4 %	49.2 %

See text for Variable Types included in help-seeking categories.

ly influenced by the prior coping attitudes and efforts of parents. In addition, the contacts of parents and boys are influenced by attributions that the child's problems are due to characteristics associated with the child (and not the external environment). In contrast, the contacts of parents and girls are most seriously influenced by demographic variables.

Aside from the influences that bear on a parental search for help, the data strongly support the ongoing coping efforts of parents. If they fail to maintain high rates of contacts with the agency, then it is less likely that children will continue to go to agencies. In fact, a retrospective analysis of child contacts indicates that virtually all of the variance is accounted for by the past and current coping efforts and attitudes (16.9 plus 28% or 44.9 out of 49.2% of the total variance). Fortunately, the prospective analyses help to remind us that there are other potential influences.

The influences linked to social-psychological theories are easiest to comprehend and link to prior studies of service utilization. However, this is not the case with demographic variables. While the retrospective sample provides variables that are congruent with the studies reported in the literature—as it pertains to social class or area of residence—this is not the case for the prospective sample. Here the demographic variables refer to inner city areas and absent father figures, particularly for girls. Only an array of further studies with diverse samples can assist in unraveling whether the utilization of services is so variable in relation to demographic influences.

In summary, it is clear that different methods of studying the utilization of services can yield distinctive findings. Differences in findings can also occur in the separate measurement of agency contacts by parents and youth. And, finally, it is clear that the utilization of services can vary by gender.

8

Whose Responsibility?

INTERVIEWER: *What kinds of help were they able to offer or arrange for another agency to give?*

Maybe get a job for him. He does not want to go to school anymore. And because he likes to sleep during the day, maybe they could get him a night job.

Grandmother of 16-year-old boy

Hopefully, something to get her less angry. She has a lot of rage in her that she doesn't know how to control. I have a lot of rage too, but I control it.

Mother of 12-year-old girl

As we told them our problem, the counselor suggested—in fact, he raised her problems directly to her and helped her realize that she had to help herself. (interviewer emphasis)

Mother of 16-year-old girl

In this chapter, the focus of analysis shifts from examining causes of youths' problems to examining how parents think about who is responsible for solving them. Here we explore whether they favor particular types of help depending on the nature of the problems. We ask the question: What are the influences on parents' preferences for help? In answering the question, we test the model of help-seeking developed by Brickman and his colleagues (1982). The model describes how people attempt to help others or how they themselves cope with problems. As described in chapter 2, it posits that if we know how actors attribute responsibility for causing a problem *plus* how they attribute responsibility for solving a problem, then it is possible to predict the specific types of help that would be preferred to solve the problem. Depending on how high or low actors attribute responsibility for causing a problem, and how high or low actors attribute responsibility for solving a problem, four distinct types of helping are posed: 1) moral, 2) compensatory, 3) enlightenment, and 4) medical. In the moral type, the "actor" (or help-seeker) considers him or herself to be highly responsible for causing and solving the problem. In the compensatory type, the actor considers him or herself to be highly responsible for solving the problem, but not for causing it. Actors preferring the enlightenment type feel highly responsible for causing the problem, but not for solving it. And, in the medical type, actors do not feel themselves to be much responsible for causing or solving the problem. As will be described in more detail shortly, we operationalize the four types of help as preferences to: 1) use *will* to try harder to solve the problem (moral model); 2) be *taught* new ways of acting to overcome the problem (compensatory model); 3) be provided *discipline* to overcome the main problem (enlightenment model); and 4) be *told* what to do to overcome the main problem (medical model). We also add an additional preference of *discuss* the problem in order to examine it as a non-theoretical but plausible helping type.

First, we conduct bivariate correlates of the five specific types of helping with: 1) kind of problem; 2) prior coping efforts by parents; 3) causal attributions; 4) solution attributions; and 5) demographics (e.g., gender, age, and race/ethnicity). Then, we use indices of causal and solution responsibility from the survey to construct several typologies of causal and solution responsibility attributions. The typologies take account of the fact that parents are third-party help-seekers and may hold themselves and/or their child responsible for the problems and solutions. We directly test the predictions of Brickman et al. (1982): does knowing causal and solution attributions improve the likelihood of predicting the type of help that is preferred to solve the problem?

Not only do we use the four helping types that Brickman poses together with the non-theoretical additional one, we also use a question from the survey about whether parents would want their child to live away from home to help solve or improve the problem. We analyze the reasons why parents might prefer that their child live away from home to help solve the problem. We are interested in whether parents are more likely to favor a drastic solution of "living away from home," when they hold the youth highly responsible for solving the problem. Or is their preference for the child living away from home due to their prior efforts and relative success in coping with youth problems?

Correlates of Helping Types

The model of helping and coping presented by Brickman and his colleagues is based on the assumption that the variables concerning causation and solution responsibility attributions combine to yield helping types. On a bivariate level of association, we might expect that the number of significant correlations between helping types and causation attributions should be about equal to the number of significant correlations between helping types and solution responsibility attributions. If this did not occur, then we could expect that either the causation or responsibility attributions were likely to be more important when the two variables are combined in a typology. Further, we should not expect the correlations between helping types and causation attributions to be appreciably stronger than those found between helping types and solution responsibility attributions (or vice versa). Again, if this finding did not occur, then we might expect that the two critical variables were not functioning in an even manner.

In addition to the assumption of equal importance between the two attribution variables, the Brickman reasoning assumes that the models of helping and coping will occur regardless of problem. On a bivariate basis we should not expect one specific type of problem (or a concern about the problem) to be more strongly related to a specific helping type than any other type of problem. However, delinquency, for example, might have a stronger association with a preference for "enlightenment" help than the aggression or internal, psychological measures do. If that were the case, then we might think that helping preferences are influenced by the type of problem, as well as attributions of causation and solution responsibility. As currently proposed by Brickman, there is no hypothetical reason for the model outcomes to vary if the types of problems are different.

The Brickman models are presented as if the actors are experiencing the problems for the first time and making judgments that will influence preferences for specific solution types. But many actors, including the parents in this sample, have attempted a variety of prior efforts over time. Presumably, if parents are unsuccessful in these prior efforts, they might be prepared to think differently about either causation and/or solution responsibility. On a bivariate basis, we would expect significant correlations to occur if there were a link between prior efforts and specific helping types.

Each of these questions is tested with the data presented in Table 8–1. The types of influences that could be significantly associated with the helping types are presented in the left-hand column. Of the six types of helping (found at the top) that are used in the analysis, five were obtained from asking parents to respond to single questions (worded in a similar fashion) about working with a "counselor" who might do any of the following with their child: 1) "tell him/her exactly what to do to overcome the main problem" (as an indicator of the medical model); 2) encourage the child "to use his/her own will to try harder to overcome the main problem by him/herself" (as an indicator of the moral model); 3) "provide him/her with a disciplined program that he/she can follow to overcome the main problem" (as an indicator of the enlightenment model); 4) "offer to teach him/her new ways of acting so he/she can learn to use the new ways to overcome the main problem" (as an indicator of the compensatory model); and 5) "discuss with him/her what could be done to overcome the main problem" (as an indicator of a neutral, non-theoretical, type of solution). Parents were asked to respond to each "kind of help" as "definitely yes" (scored as 2), "maybe" (scored as 1), and "definitely not" (scored as 0). Average scores for each solution type ranged from 1.62 (for "discipline") to 1.75 (for "discuss") for the total sample.

The sixth solution type—"live away"—is derived from a question about how parents would "feel about *(name)* living away from home for a short time in order to help overcome the main problem" (as an indicator of a strong example of the enlightenment model). Parents were asked to respond "definitely yes," "maybe," or "definitely not" for seven "outside places": 1) youth shelter; 2) foster home; 3) detention center; 4) group home; 5) psychiatric hospital; 6) residential treatment center; and 7) residential school. A factor analysis of all outside places yielded one single factor and, thereby, indicated that the list constituted a single dimension (or concept) referring to "living away from home." Each outside place was scored as 2 (definitely), 1 (maybe), 0 (definitely not). The average live-away score was 2.78 (out of a maximum score of 14) for the total sample.

Table 8.1 Correlates of Solution Types, by Hypothetical Influences for the Total Sample

Types of Influence	Tell	Will	Discipline	Teach	Discuss	Live away
			Types of Preferred Solution Types for Youth			
I. *Type of Problem*						
A. *Problem Score*						
1. New Internal	—	—	—	—	—	.14
2. Multi-Aggressive	—	—	.16	—	—	.23
3. Mixed Delinquency	—	—	.27	.21	.15	.51
B. *Problem Concern*						
1. Underline Internal	.14	—	.16	—	.17	.17
2. Underline Aggressive	—	—	.19	.15	.15	.17
3. Underline Delinquency	—	—	.26	.21	.19	.37
4. Problem Worse	—	—	—	—	.14	.21
C. *Problem Onset*	—	—	.15	—	—	.18
II. *Prior Coping Efforts*						
A. *Personally Try*						
1. Child/Family	—	—	—	—	—	—
2. Self/Family	—	—	—	—	—	—
3. External	—	—	—	—	—	.19
4. School	—	—	—	—	—	.23
5. Human Service	—	—	—	—	.13	.24
6. Reward/Punishment	—	—	—	-.18	—	—

Table 8.1 (Continued)

Types of Influence	Tell	Will	Discipline	Teach	Discuss	Live away
			Types of Preferred Solution Types for Youth			
III. *Causal Attributions*						
A. *Responsible Sources*						
1. Child	—	—	—	—	—	—
2. Peers	—	—	.15	—	—	.22
3. Family	—	—	—	—	—	—
4. Life Disadvantage	.14	—	—	—	—	.14
5. Direct Environment	—	—	—	—	—	.15
IV. *Solution Attribution*						
A. *Responsible Sources*						
1. Child	—	—	.22	—	—	—
2. Family/School	—	.14	—	—	—	—
3. Professionals	—	—	.18	—	.21	.23
4. Others	—	—	.23	.18	.14	.42
V. *Demographics*						
A. Age	—	—	—	—	—	—
B. Sex (m/f)	—	—	—	—	—	—
C. Sample Type	—	.17	—	—	—	-.17
D. Race	—	—	.29	—	—	—

Each of the potential "influence" variables in Table 8–1 have been used in one or more of the earlier analyses. Looking at each of the five variable categories separately, it is clear that each category has one or more statistically significant correlation with at least one of the proposed solution types. For type of problem, knowing the score of the major problem measures yields six significant associations. It is clear that knowing the delinquency score will result in more significant associations than either the aggression or internal, psychological scores. The only solution type that yields a significant association for all three of the problem measures is "live away"; however, the association between mixed delinquency and "live away" is far stronger than any of the associations with the other measures (i.e., .51 to .23 to .14, respectively). The Brickman assumption that the type of problem is not a salient variable in influencing parental preferences is not supported by the data. In Table 8–1 the solution types referring to two of the helping and coping models—"discipline" and "live away" as indicators of the enlightenment model, and "teach" as an indicator of the compensatory model are related to type of problem. The "discuss" association is not linked to any of the Brickman models; however, an inter-correlation matrix of solution-types indicates that the "discuss" option is strongly associated to the "tell" type solution (data not contained in the table).

Problem concern in Table 8–1 refers to questions about whether parents were concerned about any of the problems included in the CBCL, and whether the main problem got worse. Each of the problems, measured by concern items that were underlined (and scored as 0 or 1), is related to at least three of the solution types. Only the solution type "will" does not have at least one significant association with a problem concern score. Concern about delinquency yields the strongest association (.37 for live away). Using a question of whether the main problem got worse, there are two significant associations; a similar result occurs for knowing how long ago the problem got started (i.e., onset). The Brickman assumption that the type of problem concern or onset is not a salient variable in influencing parental preference is not supported by the data in Table 8–1.

The second category of variables refers to those coping efforts that parents "personally have tried to do" in order to "solve or improve the main problem." Parents provided open-ended replies, and these were coded into the following "prior coping effort" variables as a 1 for being mentioned and 0 for no mention: a) child/family; b) self/family; c) external environment; d) school; e) human services

agency; f) rewards or punishments. Four of the six prior coping efforts have at least one significant association with a solution type.
However, prior coping efforts do not yield as many significant
associations as type of problem across solution types, nor does any
association exceed a correlation of .24. While the Brickman assumption that prior efforts do not constitute a salient variable is not sub-
stantiated, it is also evident that this variable category may not be as
important as problem concern or problem scores.

Moving to the third category, causal attribution, three of the five
attributions yield at least one significant association with a solution
type (i.e., peers, life disadvantage, and direct environment). However, this category is weaker than the other two that were considered—since only two solution types have an association (discipline
and live away, as indicators of the enlightenment model), and the
strongest association is .22.

The solution attribution category provides at least one association
for each of the four types of responsibility variables. Unlike causal
attribution, every solution type has at least one significant association with each solution type. It is also clear that one solution attribution—others solve (referring to probation officers, court officials, or
other non-household relatives)—yields one association that is far
stronger than any of the causal attributions (.42 with live away versus .22 for peers responsibility and live away). The Brickman assumption that attributions concerning cause and solution
responsibility are of equal importance in predicting solution types is
not supported by the data reported in Table 8–1.

The fifth category, referring to demographic variables, produced
two variables that are associated with at least one solution
type—sample type and race/ethnicity. It is evident that at a minimum at least two demographic variables will have to be used as statistical controls in any multivariate assessment of the Brickman
models.

In summary, the bivariate analysis depicted in Table 8–1 discloses
that influences other than attributions of cause and solution responsibility may be operative in opting for one or more solution types.
Type of problem and problem concern appear to be potent candidates for inclusion in a multivariate analysis of all types of influences. In addition to these general findings, it is important to note
that two of the solution types have minimal associations with any
source of influence. Having a child told what to do or using his/her
own will are solution types that are hardly correlated with any influ-

ence. We would expect that the medical and moral models of helping are less likely to appear in subsequent analyses than the projected models of compensation and enlightenment.

Testing Brickman et al. Model of Help-Seeking

Concentrating solely on the direct attribution variables of causation and solution responsibility as measured in the survey, it is possible to construct several combinations that can test the underlying reasoning set forth by Brickman and his associates. In Table 8–2 five combinations of cause and solution responsibility are assessed for their ability to predict the outcomes that the Brickman models would project. For the casual parts of the typologies, four causal attributions that were used in Chapter 4 are used again here: 1) the child, 2) the family, 3) peers, or 4) the environment (i.e., school, neighborhood or mass media). Types of solution responsibility are based on the results of a factor analysis of persons that might have a role "in solving or improving the main problem—a lot, some, a little, or not at all." Family members and school personnel emerged as one distinct responsibility source, professionals as a second group, and others (primarily probation and court officials) as a third. Child responsibility remained as a unique fourth source.

In Part I attributions of child cause and child solution responsibility were scored, divided at the median of each respective score, and then cross-tabulated to yield the four types of combinations depicted in Table 8–2. Following the logic of Brickman and his associates, we have set forth the logical prediction associated with each combination. The only significant solution type that was statistically significant referred to the child needing to learn more discipline—a solution type associated with the enlightenment model of high causal responsibility and low responsibility for undertaking a solution. The same analysis of variance test used in the analysis of the delinquent/aggressive typology (in Chapter 3) is used here. Any letters that are the same are not statistically different from each other; only different letters indicate any significant difference. In Part I, it is evident that a preference for discipline is highest for three combinations, and lowest for the low cause/low solution responsibility combination. About 6.2% of the variance between the types is associated with the discipline score. The Brickman model is only partially supported, since the combinations that are expected to be associated

Table 8.2 Testing of Attributions of Cause and Solution Responsibility Combinations, by Solution Type Scores for Five Combinations[a]

I. Child Cause and Child Responsible for Solution Combinations

I. Predictions and Significant Solution Types	Lo Cause/Lo Sol. Type	Lo Cause/Hi Sol. Type	Hi Cause/Lo Sol. Type	Hi Cause/Hi Sol. Type	R^2
A. Brickman et al. Predicts:	Tell	Teach	Discipline	Will	
B. Significant Solution Types					
1. Discipline Score	B	A	A	A	6.2%

II. Family Cause and Family/School Responsible for Solution Combinations

II. Predictions and Significant Solution Types	Lo/Lo	Lo/Hi	Hi/Lo	Hi/Hi	R^2
A. Brickman et al. Predicts	Tell	Teach	Discipline	Will	
B. All Solution Types	A	A	A	A	NS

III. Family Cause and Profession Responsibility for Solution Combinations

III. Predictions and Significant Solution Types	Lo/Lo	Lo/Hi	Hi/Lo	Hi/Hi	R^2
A. Brickman et al. Predicts	Will	Discipline	Teach	Tell	
B. Solution Types					
1. Discuss	B	A	A/B	A	3.9%
2. Live Away	B	A	A/B	A	3.3%

Table 8.2 (Continued)

IV. Peers Cause and Others Responsible For Solution Combinations

Predictions and Significant Solution Types	Lo/Lo	Lo/Hi	Hi/Lo	Hi/Hi	R^2
A. Brickman et al. Predicts	Will	Discipline	Teach	Tell	
B. Solution Types					
1. Discipline	B	A/B	A/B	A	4.0 %
2. Live Away	B	A	B	A	7.7 %

V. Direct Environment Cause and Others Responsible for Solution

Predictions and Significant Solution Types	Lo/Lo	Lo/Hi	Hi/Lo	Hi/Hi	R^2
A. Brickman et al. Predicts	Will	Discipline	Teach	Tell	
B. Solution Types					
1. Discipline	B	A/B	A/B	A	4.3 %
2. Live Away	B	A	B	A	10.5 %

[a] The combinations are tested by using the Waller–Duncan K-ratio analysis of variance tests. Only letters that are different are statistically significant from each other, using .05 as a probability level. A represents the highest means, while B represents the lowest means.

with "teach" or "will" behave in the same fashion as the discipline prediction of high cause and low solution.

In Part II the cause and solution combinations change to family cause and family/school solution responsibility. None of the types yielded a significant difference on their mean scores—so each type is recorded as an A. Part III maintains family as the cause of the problem, but combines low and high scores with professionals as a source of solution responsibility. Part III types yield two solution types that have a distinct association with a cause/solution combination. Both solution types are clearly associated with high professional responsibility, regardless of the cause (i.e., lo/high and high/high). Knowledge about the attribution of the family as the cause does not appear to contribute to an understanding of which solution type will be preferred. This conclusion is at odds with the assumptions underlying the Brickman models.

Part IV uses peers as the cause and others as responsible for a solution. Two solution types—discipline and live away—yield clear differences between the types. For discipline, the only clear differences are between high/high and low/low; the predicted combination of low/high does not yield a clear difference in mean score. For live away, the predicted combination of low/high does yield a significantly higher score—but this is also the case for the medical combination of high/high. Again, it is knowledge about solution responsibility that provides the clearest understanding regarding preference about living away from home. The last combinations, depicted in Part V, yield results that are quite similar to Part IV—the strongest difference for live away (10.5% of the variance) and high solution responsibility, and a significant difference between high/high and low/low.

In none of the combinations is there any clear example of support for the models proposed by Brickman and his colleagues. High causal attribution is important only when high solution responsibility is also present—but the results are not supportive of Brickman predictions regarding preference for specific solution types. In addition, in three combinations that yielded differences regarding living away from home, the critical variable was high solution responsibility—regardless of causal attributions.

It is possible that the failure to find any clear support for the models is due to our inability to formulate solution types that could adequately capture each model's preferred mode of coping. This criticism might be levelled at the single statements referring to tell, will, teach, and discipline—but does not appear as reasonable for the measure of live away. The measure of live away is composed of seven distinct places that emerged as a single dimension; the construct appears to be quite reliable. In addition, it has the strongest bivariate correlation with discipline (.32), a logical consequence of being forced to live away from home. Since the strongest results in the test of the typologies are linked to live away, we feel fairly confident that any preferences for the enlightenment model are adequately measured in our survey questions. At a minimum, the results of Table 8–2 disclose that there is an inability of the causal attribution variables to play a significant role in determining when live away will be a preferred solution type.

The Brickman Model: Multivariate Combinations

The results of Tables 8–1 and 8–2 clearly indicate that the solution type that yields the strongest statistical associations involves "living away from home." On a bivariate level, three of the four significant associations for causal attributions include live away scores. As a final test of the Brickman model, and to further our understanding of multiple influences, we conducted stepwise regression analysis of live away—using five variable categories: a) prior coping efforts; b) type of problems; c) direct causal attribution; d) solution attributions; and e) demographics.

The percent of the total variance for the total sample, as well as for each sex, is quite respectable (38.7 versus 34.1 versus 50.9%, respectively). Each variable category—except any causal attribution (direct or indirect)—makes a significant contribution towards the total variance for each of the sample groups. If the Brickman enlightenment model was operative (as might be predicted by using live away as the variable to be explained), then some type of causal attribution should have made a contribution towards explaining part of the variance for at least one of the sample groups. In contrast, attributing high solution responsibility to probation and court officials (i.e., "others solve") contributes 6.8% or more to the total variance for each of the sample groups. In addition, being favorable to living away from home is also congruent with adults believing that they, too, need to learn more about how to discipline the child.

Table 8–3 also reveals that the type of problem is the most salient variable category for understanding a drastic solution preference.

Table 8.3 Comparisons of Influence on Live Away Scores, for Total Sample and Each Sex (in Percent of Variance)

| | Sample Groups | | |
	Total Sample	Boys	Girls
Types of Influence			
A. *Prior Coping Efforts*			
1. Try Human Service	2.0%	0%	2.3%
2. Try Change Environment	1.3	0	5.9
Subtotal	(3.3%)	(0%)	(8.2%)
B. *Type of Problem*			
1. Mixed Delinquency	23.4%	19.2%	29.9%
2. Main Problem: Delinquency	1.8	2.8	0
Subtotal	(25.2%)	(22.0%)	(29.9%)
C. *Any Causal Attribution*	0	0	0
D. *Solution Attribution*			
1. Others Solve Responsibility	7.7%	6.8%	9.5%
2. Adult Needs Learn Discipline	2.5	3.2	3.3
Subtotal	(10.2%)	(10.0%)	(12.8%)
E. *Demographics*			
Age : Older	0	2.1	0
Total Variance	38.7%	34.1%	50.9%

Knowing the score on mixed delinquency can explain 19.2 to 29.9% of the variance for each of the sample groups.

The two remaining variable categories do not affect each sex in the same fashion. Knowing about prior coping efforts—via trying to secure help from a human service agency or changing the environment prior to attending family crisis or mental health agency—is important for the total sample, but especially for the girls. For girls, if prior efforts have failed to produce changes, then parents are willing to consider living away from home; this is not the case for boys. The other sex difference involves age; younger boys are not as likely to be considered as candidates for living away from home.

Summary and Conclusions

This chapter attempted to provide information that would expand our understanding of the role of parent/caregivers as third-party help-seekers for youth problems. In the process of securing information that is rarely found in the literature, we were also able to test the assumptions and reasoning about the types of problem solutions that are likely to be preferred by help-seekers—as formulated by Brickman and his colleagues at the University of Michigan about a decade ago. According to the Brickman theory about helping or coping with problems, the manner in which actors think about the causes of problems and the responsibility for solving problems influence the types of solutions that are preferred. Other variables—like types of problems or prior coping efforts—are not included as important influences on solution preferences.

A bivariate analysis of the correlates of specific solution types reveals that variables other than causal and solution attributions are significantly associated with more than one type of solution. Prior coping efforts that were personally attempted by parents are associated with three solution types—teach, discuss, and live away from home. Even more associations were found between problem scores or concerns. The drastic solution type—live away from home—yields an unusually strong relationship with mixed delinquency scores.

An attempt to create the Brickman models was operationalized by combining distinct types of causal attributions and solution responsibility combinations. Causal attributions referred to child, peers, family, and the direct environment. Solution responsibility attributions referred to the child, family/school, professionals, and others (i.e., probation and court officials). There was a lack of support for any of the projected combinations predicted by the Brickman assumptions and mode of reasoning. Instead, the strongest support for a solution type involves the importance of attributions of solution responsibility, regardless of the causal attribution. This result is particularly strong for the solution type associated with the projected enlightenment model—live away from home. Since this measure has the strongest methodological underpinnings of any of the solution types used to test the Brickman ideas, the greatest degree of confidence can be placed in the findings concerning live away.

A multivariate analysis of live away confirms that causal attributions are unimportant for explaining any of the variability in live away scores. While allocation of solution responsibility proves to be an important variable for the total sample and each gender, the most important variable for explaining the maximum amount of variance is the kind of problem—particularly scores on mixed delinquency. Evidently, when delinquency is high, parents begin to consider the possibility of solving or improving the problem by having living away organizations and/or officials deal with the delinquent-type behaviors. Transferring responsibility for solving the problem to probation and court officials constitutes a secondary source of influence on types of solution preferences. To believe in the usefulness of residential placements is congruent with the corollary idea of diminishing personal or family responsibility for solving the problem. In addition, believing that prior personal efforts have been tried and have failed to improve the problem—particularly for girls—increases the likelihood that parents will accept living away from home as a viable solution.

The finding that causal attributions do not play an equal part with solution responsibility in explaining solution preferences constitutes an important reason for questioning a key assumption of the Brickman model of help-seeking by others. Since these models do not include problem type, prior coping efforts, and age as significant influences on solution preferences, it is evident that these variables—as well as attributions of solution responsibility—must be included in any theorizing about how parents cope with problems.

9

Implications for Policy and Services

This concluding chapter presents a summary of the major findings as it discusses the implications for social policy and delivery of services in inner-city areas. First, we present the three major behavior patterns and potential policy targets. Second, we discuss proposals that could improve the organization and delivery of services to youths and their families. Finally, we recommend developing a pro-social youth policy, and discuss in detail its assumptions and ingredients. We also identify potential objections to it, and make specific recommendations to research it.

The Delinquency Pattern

The core activities that are included in the mixed delinquency pattern for 12–16-year-old males and females refer to five types of relatively non-aggressive, undesirable behaviors: 1) disobedience and disaffection from home; 2) disobedience in, and disaffection from, school; 3) disobedience of property rules; 4) dishonesty in dealing with others; and 5) precocious use of alcohol and drugs. These core activities are not unique to this sample in Newark; they are found in diverse locations and other samples in the United States (and perhaps other Western societies). What makes this sample different is the disproportionate number of youths who display this delinquency pattern compared to clinical samples of youths. It is distinguished also by the impulsive and hyperactive behaviors which expand the core pattern.

The core and expanded mixed delinquency pattern is not likely to be conducted as a solo activity by individual youths. Instead, the activities are engaged in with the support of, and active participation with, like-minded peers. Like national youth self-report research studies, our study finds that the single most powerful explanatory variable for delinquency is differential association with "bad peers" or other youths who get into trouble with adult authorities. Unless a social policy for youths addresses the subcultural and interpersonal support for core and expanded delinquent behaviors, it is unlikely to make an appreciable dent in the "delinquency problem." This is particularly true for inner-city areas, where official statistics have documented the disproportionate occurrence of elements of the core pattern like truancy, theft, incorrigibility, and vandalism since the turn of the century (Breckenridge and Abbott, 1912).

Besides focusing on bad peers, a viable delinquency reduction strategy also would have to deal with internal, psychological problems, such as the lack of guilt, impulsiveness, and hyperactivity. The challenge for an overall youth policy would be to pay attention to promoting individual ethics and relieving the sources of psychological problems within a broad strategy to deal with the cultural and social context of deviant behaviors. We believe this can occur within a major policy emphasis on reinforcing and expanding pro-social behaviors, attitudes, and norms in targeted neighborhoods. The specific suggestions that could form the basis of a pro-social youth policy will be discussed in later sections.

The Aggression Pattern

The core activities of the pattern of multiaggression refer to three types of hostile behaviors: 1) verbal; 2) interpersonal; and 3) physical assault. Verbal and interpersonal types of aggression can be found in a variety of locations and samples in the United States, according to a national study of parent reports. However, physical assault behaviors are added to the core aggression pattern in these inner-city youths. The physical assault behaviors of the core pattern are the activities most likely to be defined and processed as examples of illegal violence.

A moderately strong relationship exists between mixed delinquency and multiaggression pattern scores. While the two anti-social patterns are empirically distinct, it is important to highlight that the highest rates of cruel and assaultive behaviors occur when youths are classified as exhibiting high scores on the core patterns of both mixed delinquency and aggression. Highly aggressive youth do not require the association of bad peers to be violent, but their level of cruelty and assaults are likely to increase in a high delinquent context that includes the support of bad peers. A social policy strategy that could reduce the rates of high delinquency and the support of bad peers could have a significant, indirect impact on the levels of assaultive behaviors in a community. While a reduction in the high delinquency pattern could have an impact on the level of assaultive behavior, it is important to note that the primary instigation to all types of youthful aggressive behaviors occurs at an individual level of explanation. Very high rates of internal problems co-exist with the occurrence of high levels of aggressive behaviors. Any strategy to reduce levels of youthful violence in a community would have to address the sources of psychological stress of youth, in addition to the cultural and social context to promote pro-social attitudes and behaviors.

Internal, Psychological Problems

The measure of psychological problems includes beliefs and feelings referring to: 1) strange ideas and behaviors; 2) depressive and anxious feelings; 3) somatic complaints; and 4) symptoms of withdrawal behaviors. Unlike the two anti-social patterns, only two types of internal problems in this sample are congruent with those found in national clinic samples—the somatic and depressed/anxious problems.

A detailed analysis of the depressed pattern revealed that besides feelings of moodiness and anxiety, sad and depressed feelings were also accompanied by reports of low self-esteem, worthlessness, being unloved, and loneliness. This combined pattern of psychological problems is most likely to occur among females. A high score on the depressed/anxious pattern is most likely to occur among girls if they are teenage daughters of young mothers, and if they are personally responsive to a disadvantaged environment. These sources of psychological stress are not likely to be operative for boys. Instead, for boys, parents report that direct family conflict, peer isolation, and a lack of guilt are more influential on depression.

These results indicate that any programs that are designed to help youths and their families must pay attention to gender, as well as individual differences.

Improving Individual-Level Services

The results of our study demonstrate that policies to help inner-city adolescents with delinquent, aggressive, and internal, psychological problems would need to include services that attend to the processes of third-party help-seeking. Using the analysis of parents' experiences in seeking help, reported in the second half of the book, we suggest focusing on six areas: 1) improving the responsiveness of agency systems; 2) improving the ability of parents to become more effective help-seekers; 3) improving the utilization of services; 4) providing multi-services for multi-problems; 5) expanding sensitivity to gender differences; and 6) encouraging youths to be their own help-seekers.

Improving System Responsiveness

It is difficult to receive timely help with youth problems if agencies construct their offers of assistance in a rigid or inflexible time-frame. Agencies that waited 15 days for an intake about urgent problems, and then demanded that working parents receive an initial work-up only on Mondays, between the hours of 8:00-10:00 a.m., can hardly be classified as responsive agencies. Besides finding this type of inflexible mental health agency, we also determined that a second mental health agency forced worried parents to attend two intakes before offering any hope of professional help—one for a record intake to document the problem and a second for a clinical intake to diagnose the problem; only after a third visit could a parent begin actual counseling sessions.

It does not seem unreasonable to expect that agencies would present families with dates and times that were of convenience to clients, even if it required evening and weekend appointments. Emergency rooms of hospitals are equipped to provide services for health problems at irregular times and hours. Mental health services might be expected to also be available on an as-needed basis. A few of the family crisis agencies were organized to provide services on an emergency basis, but these were exceptions.

In addition to being available at a time of interpersonal or psychological crisis, human services funded with public funds should be expected to remind clients of appointments. In the private sector, where missed appointments are synonymous with lost revenues, many doctors have instituted appointment reminders by phone (or a postcard), so that "no-shows" will be held at a minimum. The publicly funded agencies in our sample did not receive any financial or reputational penalties if appointments did not show up. Not surprisingly, it was difficult to identify any agency that routinely communicated an appointment reminder. If middle- or upper-income clients can benefit from a reminder, so, too, can low-income households.

Besides re-organizing internal scheduling arrangements and instituting reminder procedures on a regular, systematic basis for all client sessions, human services agencies need to pay attention to the friendliness of each client contact. Whether clients and their families speak to telephone receptionists, intake workers, or clinical professionals, they should feel as though the service organization is a place where they can be helped and understood. Organizations can train all persons who come into contact with youth and their parents to provide warmth, empathy, and a sense of genuine concern about their problems. While these appear to be interpersonal variables, there is evidence that organizations can regulate the types of communications being provided to clients. The ECYS parents offer evidence that becoming a client can be influenced by paying attention to how well personnel communicate with prospective clients.

Improving the Ability of Parents to Become Better Help-Seekers

Before most parents become clients of a human services agency, they engage in a variety of efforts to deal with the problems presented by their sons or daughters. ECYS parents do not appear to differ from middle-class persons in seeking help for family problems. Either they or other intimates of the family are likely to be the primary people who notice the problems. In fact, a majority of ECYS parents knew about the main problem more than a year prior to seeking help. In an effort to solve the problem, they engaged in social comparisons to decide whether the problem was a normal part of growing up, assessed whether it was worth talking about to family members and intimates, and tried an array of coping efforts—like talking to the

child, providing punishments or promising rewards for better behavior, or talking to a school teacher, doctor or minister. Only after
these coping efforts failed to resolve the problem were they able to
become voluntary help-seekers or be responsive to the involuntary
suggestions of police or child welfare workers.

An unexplored area of human service agencies, or other formal
organizations, is whether the help-seeking efforts of parents can be
improved—rather than relying on the existing help-seeking process to continue in a traditional fashion. For example, over 90% of
ECYS parents talked to a family member or intimate about the problem prior to going to an agency (or being referred and not going). A
well-conceived public education campaign could attempt to influence how this informal system of communication defined problems, promoted coping techniques, and advertised available
services. Perhaps parents might not wait as long to deal with problems that were getting worse, rather than better. Or, to use another
example, what if local doctors and ministers—traditional sources
of help from professionals—were exposed to a similar education
campaign? Could they become more useful in helping parents to
choose among available services in a shorter period of time? We do
not know the outcome of such efforts to influence the help-seeking
process because we doubt that it has been tried on a large scale in
low-income communities.

Besides exploring how we might aid the help-seeking process to
assist parents in finding quicker help with problems, it is also useful to think about educating two critical official agencies—schools
and the police. Next to family members and friends, teachers are the
most likely to notice the problems. On the basis of ECYS parent reports, they tend to refer primarily to local mental health agencies—even though a number of the family crisis agencies were
clearly more responsive to youthful problems and crises. While police noticed few deviant behaviors directly, they were involved in
over half of the cases represented in the sample—and even made
suggestions about an agency for about 30% of the families. Their referrals also tended to be stereotypically similar; the police tended to
rely primarily on family crisis agencies, even though mental health
agencies may have been more appropriate for specific cases. Special youth officers in particular could make better referral suggestions if they were more fully informed about all available
community resources.

Improving the Utilization of Services

There are very few studies on the utilization of services by youth and their families, assuming they are successful in their help-seeking efforts and actually become an agency client. Virtually all of the studies that exist rely on agency records or staff perceptions as the primary data source for studying agency utilization. By using parent reports about their own help-seeking activities and perceptions, as well as their attributions about the main problem, we were able to learn about service utilization patterns on a prospective as well as retrospective basis.

The retrospective analysis provided quite cogent evidence that when adults or formal agencies initiate referrals, there is a reduced likelihood that youth will attend any sessions if they are not accompanied by parents. Agency personnel unable to persuade parents that their services are potentially helpful would have extreme difficulty in retaining their youthful clients. Even if an agency's philosophy is to focus solely on youth, they would have to pay attention to the parent (primarily mothers) in order to assure an actual visit. Once again, the issue of organizational responsiveness to parent's time and day preference would become important, assuming that agency personnel were interested in achieving maximum utilization of available services.

The prospective analysis provided evidence that clients usually deemed to be "resistant"—residents of the inner city, without father figures in the household—would utilize available services. High utilization could occur if specific attention were paid to how clients engaged in the help-seeking process. Parents who engaged in a social comparison about ever having heard about the problem, and made a negative judgment, were much more likely to be high utilizers than those who treated the problem as a normal occurrence. Agency personnel who take the time to understand how parents evaluated the problem prior to attending the agency, and who inquired about the parent's reasons for being optimistic or pessimistic, might be able to influence a caregiver's willingness to expand their utilization pattern.

The prospective analysis also revealed that some referral sources have a good chance of producing a high utilization rate, while some do not. If doctors or ministers made a suggestion about seeking out a human service agency, then there was a greater likelihood of high utilization. Paying heed to a family crisis intake worker also in-

creased the attendance rate. Surprisingly, police or teacher suggestions did not have any noticeable impact on the number of visits.
Agency personnel who are particularly attentive to police or teacher
suggestions might be able to openly discuss the issue of becoming an
involuntary client.

Finally, understanding how parents attribute responsibility for
causing the problem can also influence the rate of utilization. Parents
who think that children are primarily responsible for causing the
problem are likely to be responsive to continue attending the agency.
Attributions about other causes of the problem—like peers or the
neighborhood—may signal reduced willingness to believe that the
agency can be of continued assistance.

Providing Multi-Services for Multi-Problems

Most of the youth referred to ECYS agencies had multiple problems.
The problems were multiple within a pattern of activities, and there
also tended to be an overlap among the patterns. However, each system organized their services as if there were a single problem to address. The family crisis agencies were reimbursed by the counties to
provide 90 days of counseling services for a "crisis," because it was
assumed that a single family conflict could be subsumed within a
"crisis definition" of the presenting problem. The mental health
agencies, in order to justify specialized funding, sought to attach a
DSM-III-R diagnosis to the presenting problem. Both systems primarily provided traditional counseling or therapeutic services to
deal with the "crisis" of the "diagnosis."

Recent conceptions of human services for youths have projected a
much broader approach towards the presenting problems and the
types of services to be provided. The general philosophy of the new
look in mental health service system design, for example, is best captured in a paper disseminated by the Child and Adolescent Service
System Program (CASSP) of the National Institute of Mental Health
(Stroul and Friedman, 1988). The most important "guiding principles" of a responsive care system state the following:

1) children and youth with emotional problems (including "conduct disorders") should have access to a comprehensive array
   of services that address the child's physical, emotional, social,
   and educational needs;

2) children and youth with emotional problems should receive individualized services in accord with the unique needs and potentials of each child and be guided by an individualized service plan.

A demonstration project, conducted at Fort Bragg, North Carolina, by the state Division of Mental Health and Developmental Disabilities, has attempted to implement this services philosophy by providing the following continuum of community-based services, coordinated by case managers:

1. *Outpatient Services*

    a. Emergency crisis available 24 hours per day throughout the year

    b. Intake and assessment services

    c. Preparation of individualized treatment plans within a limited time period

    d. Youth and family treatment provided in offices or at home

    e. In-school support

2. *Family Prevention Services*

    a. In-home crisis stability services on call around the clock for up to 6–8 weeks

    b. Short-term crisis-emergency services within the home

    c. Day parenting

3. *Day Treatment*

    a. Therapeutic pre-school

    b. Moderate management with public school for half-day

    c. Moderate management with public school for full-day

    d. High management for full-day

    e. Therapeutic vocational placement

    f. Afterschool or work in evening for half-day equivalent

4. *Out-Of-Home Residence Nearby Community*

    a. Therapeutic foster-care for emergencies and lengthier stays

    b. Therapeutic group homes for emergencies and lengthier stays

                                                        (Behar, 1991)

While the Fort Bragg demonstration project uses DSM-III-R criteria in their assessment process, it is clear that the array of services is designed to deal with multiple problems. The individualized service plans and the functioning of youths are reviewed every 45 days subsequent to the initial screening and planning. At this time, team members—in or outside the mental health clinics—assess whether the planned services have reinforced "adaptive competencies" of youth and their families. If necessary, service plans are modified for another 45-day period of targeted services. The Fort Bragg demonstration is fortunate in also being able to subsidize, on an as-needed basis, therapeutic camping, crisis stabilization in a hospital setting, supervised independent living, or as a last resort, residential treatment.

The Fort Bragg demonstration, as well as other redesigned service systems, attempts to provide a package of the most recent non-residential, innovative services—like family preservation, therapeutic foster care, and day parenting—and allocate them in a planned, coordinated manner. Case managers help to monitor the quality, as well as the delivery and intensity of the individualized package of services at Fort Bragg and elsewhere (Burchard and Clarke, 1990).

None of the human service agencies in our study came near to approaching the philosophy or actual administration of an individualized continuum of services. While lack of funding may inhibit the implementation of a full individualized package of services, it is evident that a shift in conceptualizing problems, services, and management would also have to occur. Organizations serving inner-city residents, similar to those found in our study, appear to be far behind in conceiving and implementing a multiple-service system for multiple problems.

Expanding Sensitivity to Gender Differences

In conceptualizing a more responsive system of mental health services for youth, Stroul and Friedman (1988) stress the importance of paying particular attention to a diversity of individual needs. They also argue that a responsive system should be culturally appropriate. Building on their efforts, Isaacs and Benjamin (1991) have written a monograph on designing a system of effective services for minority children. While we support the efforts of systems of care to design "culturally competent," individualized services, we believe a special effort should be made to expand our sensitivity to gender differences and become "gender competent" as well. There are four types of gender differences that emerged in the ECYS analysis that are worthwhile paying attention to: 1) female aggression; 2) parental attributions of higher personal responsibility for peer associations; 3) the risks of being a teen-age daughter of a young mother; and 4) pro-active maternal help-seeking in favor of boys.

Most studies of anti-social behavior emphasize males. Given the historical differences in the rate of serious delinquency and crime between males and females, this research emphasis is not surprising. However, there are neighborhoods and agency samples where the gender differences may not be as sharp. In our study there were no gender differences in the delinquency pattern when the behavior checklist items were held constant for each sex. Even using Achenbach's gender specific measures of delinquency on our sample, the percent scoring above the cut-off scores were quite comparable. However, when males and females were compared on the aggression pattern, the ECYS girls scored significantly higher. Analysis of the typologies revealed that girls were more likely to be located in the high aggression/low delinquency type than the boys. In contrast, boys were more likely to be high delinquent/low aggression or "peer delinquent" types. There were no gender differences for the other two types. These empirical facts indicate that the usual gender differences on aggression—usually thought of as a masculine trait—may not be true for service systems used by inner-city youths. We would urge that service systems become "gender competent" to recognize gender similarities, as well as differences, and respond accordingly.

The second difference emerged in the analysis of influences on associating with bad peers. It will be recalled that this differential association measure emerged as the most salient explanatory variable in this study—similar in statistical strength to the findings of a national youth study using self-reports. In our study, when variables were assessed to determine which ones survived a multivariate analysis for explaining bad peer scores, sharp gender differences emerged. Parents held their daughters themselves much more responsible for their peer associates than boys. In contrast, parents emphasized direct environment influences like schools and neighborhood for their boys. In addition, parental closeness and holding a job were also important for boys. Understanding how parents might place differential attributions of causal responsibility for their daughters, in comparison to their sons, is also an important element in achieving "gender competence." Girls may be expected to feel guilty for their peer associates to a degree that is not true for boys—and service personnel should become sensitive to this type of parental belief.

The third risk involves differences in stress that may be linked to psychological internal problems. In this study, as in others, females score higher on experiencing internal problems like depression, anxiety, and somatic symptoms. In this study, family structural differences proved to be a unique source of stress for females particularly during adolescence. If girls were conceived when their mothers were teenagers, then the demographic combination of a young mother and older teen (up to 16 years of age) was linked to a strong explanation of psychological problems. A "gender competent" service system should be sensitive to the potential problems of female adolescents who were born when their mothers were also teenagers.

The final gender difference pertains to the finding that mothers were more likely to be pro-active in seeking help on behalf of their sons, in comparison to their daughters. This was a surprising finding, since the help-seeking literature contains many studies that document how females are more likely to seek help for themselves, in comparison to males. Functioning as third-party help-seekers, mothers are probably more pro-active than fathers—but they appear to play this role more assertively on behalf of their sons. The sources of this gender bias are worth exploring in a service system that attempts to become "gender competent."

Encouraging Youths to Be Help-Seekers

One of the major tenets of the help-seeking professions rests on the assumption that persons who seek help on their own behalf are more likely to use the service provided most effectively. If the helping agency in the ECYS study had waited for youth to refer themselves for assistance, then they would have had no clients. According to the parent reports about who suggested the agency, or whose idea it was to come to the agency, none of the responses mentioned youth. While it would be easy to accept this outcome as an agency "fact of life," and continue to work with youth as involuntary clients, there exist alternative models of providing youth services that can be considered. One is the telephone "hot line" and the second is the school-based clinic.

Telephone hot lines have been used in many communities since the 1970s. They are usually associated with suicide prevention (Hinson, 1982). However a recent study of an adolescent help line that emphasizes suicide prevention, in Los Angeles, revealed that a wide array of problems were discussed by youth with adult-supervised, peer counselors (de Anda and Smith, 1993). In the Los Angeles study only about 5% of the problems involved just suicide. Adolescents sought out help for the following kinds of other problems: family conflict; love problems; abortion for pregnancy; depression; alcohol or drug use; sexual problems, and others. While a disproportionate number of cases were female, it is useful to note that males were also willing to use this helping resource (about 30%). To the best of our knowledge, hot lines were not available to Newark youths.

A less anonymous way of seeking help is the school-based health clinic. Besides providing on-site advice about birth control and health care, high school clinics have also offered physical examinations for athletes, immunizations, and weight control programs. In the process of using these desired services, youth began to use the staff for advice about a variety of personal problems. Starting in St. Paul in 1971, the number of school-based clinics had grown to 85 in 25 states by 1987. Most of the clinics offered easy physical and psychological access for comprehensive health services. A number offered special efforts to follow-up or reach out to high-risk youth. All emphasized confidentiality (Schorr, 1988).

The ability of the new service models to attract youths with sexual, personal, and psychological problems is well documented. Communities that wish to provide services in a format that is attractive to youth should re-examine the older service models. This re-examination should focus on ease of access, broader services, stricter confidentiality, and real crisis availability. If the services are wanted, and delivered in a manner attractive to youth, they will come. In order to formulate a reasonable social policy for dealing with the multiple problems presented by youths, it is important to specify the targets of any proposed actions. Relying on parents' reports, this study has provided empirical support for the proposition that many problems co-exist together in distinct patterns.

Rather than addressing single problems on an *ad hoc* basis, it is strategically useful to identify the patterns and attempt to discuss critical targets for public and private policy-oriented activities. This study has identified and concentrated on understanding three distinct patterns—legal delinquency, non-legal aggression, and internal, psychological problems.

Assumptions of a Pro-Social Youth Policy

Virtually all of the efforts by parents in our study to seek and utilize help offered by human service agencies were aimed at controlling and/or remediating existing problems. While it is possible to empathize with these efforts and the attempts by the agencies to provide help, a creative public policy ought to be able to go beyond addressing problems from a remedial or re-socialization perspective (a tertiary prevention strategy, according to public health authorities). If our goal is to reduce the rates of occurrence of initial problems, then a strategy involving primary or secondary prevention should be considered.

A primary prevention policy could attempt to set forth proposals that would aim to change the social, cultural, and economic conditions—on a societal level—that appear to be associated with high rates of youth problems in urban areas, such as Newark. Given the distinct patterns of problems as well as the influences associated for each type, this strategy may be a utopian prospect. The problems are complex, as we have demonstrated. In addition, the social technology (and the political will) to engage in societal-level social reconstruction seem to be lacking. It appears more realistic, and therefore useful, to pursue a secondary prevention strategy—policies aimed at reducing the rate of occurrence of initial problems without assuming that major societal changes will occur soon. We propose to address the two major anti-social problems—legal delinquency and non-legal aggression—by providing extra resources to expand and promote pro-social youth and family activities. The aim of a pro-social youth policy would be to expand the number of youths who would be participants in, and supportive of, pro-social attitudes, norms, and behaviors. In brief, we propose to promote a pro-social youth subculture to compete with the deviant youth subculture that is prevalent in many inner-city areas. By targeting specific neighborhoods, with a focused use of resources, we would aim to reduce the rates of the component elements of the mixed delinquency patterns.

If this could be accomplished then high rates of physical aggression could also be reduced. In addition, if the mixed delinquency rates were reduced, then we could expect a reduction in rates of teenage parenting; if this were to occur, then future daughters of teenage mothers would experience less stress in living with young mothers. A clear focus on competing with the deviant youth culture could have a maximum impact if the secondary prevention strategy targeted specific high-risk areas.

To the best of our knowledge, the areas of highest risk are inner-city neighborhoods where the concentrated effects of poverty and the legacy of discrimination are linked to major threats to youth development. In areas of concentrated poverty—where 40% or more of the persons in a census tract are poor—the rates of youthful (and adult) anti-social behaviors are disproportionately high (Wilson, 1987; Jencks and Peterson, 1991; and Jargowsky and Bane, 1990). While our Essex County Youth Study (ECYS) sample is drawn from an agency population, rather than a geographic location, a disproportionate number (63%) live in Newark—which had one of the highest concentrations of poverty in the nation in 1990 and continues today (Jargowsky and Bane, 1980, p. 59); a disproportionate number of ECYS youths lived in households that received one or more types of welfare (46%), and 77% lived in a female-headed household. If we targeted high poverty areas in cities like Newark—rather than agency households—we would be including many of the youths who where included in ECYS-type samples (especially blacks and Hispanics). In addition, we would be including many of the households that probably contain youths who were not referred to ECYS type agencies, but who exhibited core patterns of the major problems.

Specific census tracts in Newark, for example, could be primary candidates for a secondary prevention strategy. From 1970 to 1980 the number of Newark census tracts with 40% or more poor persons grew from 9 to 39 tracts. In 1970 about 18% of all poor blacks lived in a high poverty, ghetto-type neighborhood. By 1980 the percent of poor blacks living in a high poverty, ghetto-type tract increased to 37%. For Hispanics, the rate of poor persons living in a concentrated poverty area grew from 4 to 33%. These are precisely the neighborhoods where we would expect—based on our accumulation of knowledge about concentrated poverty areas—the rates of truancy and school drop out, unemployment of 16–21-year-olds, and teenage pregnancies to be disproportionately high in comparison to other areas in a metropolitan region (Jargowsky and Bane, 1990; and Jencks and Peterson, 1991).

A middle range type of social policy would attempt to reinforce and expand the pro-social attitudes and behaviors promoted by the two primary adult-sponsored institutions—the family and the school. As noted, the policy goal would be devoted to creating a more potent pro-social subculture that could adequately compete with a deviant youth subculture in high-risk areas. Specifically, the goal of such a secondary prevention policy would be to assist families to realize positive goals they would like to see youth accomplish: school achievement and higher graduation rates; respect for parents and adult authority; adherence to ethical norms of honesty, respect for others, and a sense of guilt about misdeeds; regulation of sexual behavior to reduce teen pregnancy and premature fatherhood; the capability to provide friends with support for acceptable recreational activities; and competencies and skills to deal with interpersonal conflicts without relying on cruelty, bullying, or assaultive behaviors.

Based on ECYS data, we believe these kinds of pro-social goals would be supported by an overwhelming majority of parents in high-risk areas of our urban centers. If we could find and promote a broad array of activities that could provide an attractive alternative to the deviant youth culture that supports disaffection from the primary institutions of socialization, then it is quite conceivable that the rates of anti-social behaviors could be reduced. We would also hope that some of the sources of psychological stress—like the number of young mothers with teenage daughters—could also be influenced by a pro-social policy strategy that targets both sexes on an equal basis.

A full secondary prevention strategy would begin with a brand-new generation of youth—and expose them to a concentrated series of experiences that would reinforce and expand the socialization of youth on behalf of pro-social norms and attitudes. While we are willing to discuss an improved remediation policy for the current generation (i.e., a tertiary prevention strategy), we believe that a reasonable preventive strategy would have to be conceived on a generation of youths who could become carriers of a pro-social subculture in high-risk, ghetto-type, areas. This means that our policy proposal is based on a minimum cycle of 20 years—or an entire youth generation growing up in high-risk areas.

In order to promote a pro-social youth policy, it is necessary to provide extra resources for a lengthy period on a neighborhood level in order to compensate for the documented socialization deficiencies of high-risk, ghetto-type, areas. Since a new generation of children are hardly to blame for the deviant activities of an existing generation of adolescents, they can morally lay claim to the extra resources necessary for them to be compensated for their neighborhood handicaps. In accord with one of Brickman's approaches to social policy, we can offer compensatory resources without any attribution of blame towards a growing generation or their parents. We expect, however, that the parents, and later the children, will take the responsibility for using the extra resources on their own behalf. If the resources are deemed useful, and presented in a culturally acceptable fashion, we could expect high utilization rates without an accompaniment of social stigma—since extra resources would be expended on the basis of residence, rather than by a means test.

Ingredients of a Pro-Social Youth Policy

An adequate pro-social policy would be based on utilizing the best available knowledge about what types of programs, at specific stages of the life cycle, can improve the capabilities and competencies of a new generation of youth and their families. Rather than singling out one particular program, or age-range, we propose to provide a sequence of promising programs for each stage of child development—beginning with pre-natal services and ending with subsidized college and / or vocational technical training. Instead of one magic program-bullet, we propose that a coherent set of programs be available on a sequential basis to targeted high-risk communities. We also propose that the effects of the components of the programs be systematically studied with experimentally controlled research designs with comparison groups as minimum requirements.

The specific ingredients of a generational prevention strategy would include, for illustrative purposes, the following types of programs in targeted elementary school neighborhoods:

1. Pro-active family planning for all youths in order to reduce unwanted, as well as teenage, pregnancies;

2. Pro-active pre-natal care for all new pregnancies in order to assure optimal physical, cognitive, and emotional development;

3. Continued child health services and related parent education for all new-born children and their families;

4. Day care/head start programs for all new-born children that include a socialization milieu for learning accepted standards of ethical behavior and respect for others, as well as cognitive and emotional experience to prepare youngsters for school;

5. Continued involvement of parents in all pre-natal health, and day care/head start activities, including formal and informal lessons in parent effectiveness training;

6. Follow through of head-start experiences in elementary grades, including adequate tutoring services within and after school;

7. A full range of recreational and cultural opportunities that include sports, games, the arts, dramatics, dance, music, group activities, camping, and excursions;

8. Availability of health services for teenagers within junior and secondary high schools, including sex information, advice, and referrals to family planning clinics;

9. Provision of fully funded college and/or vocational scholarships for all high school graduates desirous of further schooling or training;

10. Availability of part-time jobs (including transportation) equal to the opportunities available for suburban youth, for all youths interested in such activities; and

11. Organization of neighborhood parent groups to decrease blatant adult anti-social activities—like prostitution and drug sales—and their removal to non-residential "red light" areas.

Models for most of these programs (as well as others) can be found in Lisbeth Schorr's book *Within Our Reach: Breaking the Cycle of Disadvantage.* As Schorr points out, we have the ability to conceptualize and implement pro-social programs since we have many promising examples of what is possible. The critical challenge is to choose specific high risk areas—where the proportion of poor families is 40% or more—and progressively fund *all* of these types of programs in a sequential fashion (with adequate resources), so that a generation of youth could experience a pro-social package of experiences and activities that could compete with the existing older youth culture. Our proposal is a reasonable extension of Schorr's emphasis on helping individuals break the cycle of disadvantage. We are interested in connecting successful youths and families so they can reinforce each other with subcultural support.

Potential Objections to a Pro-Social Youth Policy

There are, of course, a number of potential objections that could be constructed against such a broad-gauged effort at generational change. Not surprisingly, we might expect objections about the amount of new funds that would be required to fund the multi-program strategy over a period of 20 years. We are used to subsidizing with public funds—over many years—a variety of projects that benefit specific communities or interests: dams and reclamation projects; seaports; roads and bridges; anti-pollution facilities; savings and loans bailouts; and space stations. The relative availability of funds and their commitment over a long period of time is probably not the critical issue. Rather, the issue is mobilizing the political will and leadership to entertain a serious prevention strategy that could have multiple social and individual benefits and a reduction in future criminal justice costs.

Besides the willingness to make the necessary public investment in a pro-social youth policy—on a focused geographical basis—there is also little doubt that many current efforts at assisting high-risk areas are poorly targeted or inefficiently administered. Besides the infusion of new funds, it would be extremely useful to inventory all of the current federal, state, local, and private funds that are currently being spent in high-risk areas and calculate how "old funds" could be targeted in a more focused, integrated manner towards promoting generational change. This kind of social accounting would, in the case of Newark (and perhaps other cities), have to be conducted by independent auditing organizations, since critical public agencies—like the Newark schools—have been accused of gross mismanagement by state authorities or independent groups. The public support for a "new generation investment strategy" might be capable of being mobilized and sustained, provided taxpayers were assured that the funds would not be wasted by inefficiency, incompetence, redundant personnel, and bloated administrative salaries. Proponents of pro-social youth policies might have to learn how to play the role of "fiscal watch-dogs," as well as investment advisors.

A second criticism could be made that we are writing off the current generation. Our proposal does not involve any reduction of current levels of resources or a fair-share of annual increases for inner-city programs. What we advocate is that the new generation have an improved chance of "breaking the cycle of disadvantage" that is disproportionately associated with high rates of family and education alienation, as well as a deviant peer culture that inhibits the realization of individual potential. If we are unwilling to expend extra resources on these youth who have yet to misbehave or drop-out from school, we are even less likely to recruit extra funds for youth who misbehave with minimal guilt and fail to take advantage of existing opportunities.

Another objection to this pro-social policy proposal might be that success would have to wait a full 20 years, in order to determine whether the strategy has worked. While we do have a few long-term evaluations of the positive long-term effects of early school programs (see Schorr, pp. 192–197), it is not necessary to wait a generation in order to obtain feedback on the progress. We believe that it would not be difficult to utilize existing data or to create new baseline measures in order to document the following: 1) reductions of teenage births in an area; 2) births with higher weights and fewer complications; 3) indicators of physical child development; 4) indicators of cognitive social and emotional development; 5) lower rates of deviant behaviors based on parent CBCL reports of 4–5, 6–11, and 12–16-year-olds; 6) improved scores on standardized achievement tests and lower reports of school problems, based on teacher forms and independent observations; 7) shifts in the use of leisure time by youth; 8) reductions in official truancy and dropout rates; 9) increased part-time job rates; 10) higher high school and post-high school achievement rates and accomplishments; 11) lower rates of police events and juvenile court involvement; 12) lower rates of detention and juvenile corrections; 13) reduced rates of imprisonment after the age of 16; 14) increased scores on measures of self-esteem and locus of control by youths; and 15) sociometric choices of close friends. Each of these measures could provide evidence of whether the specific aims of the pro-social programs were being accomplished at critical stages of the life-cycle of youths.

In addition to the objections we have discussed, it is useful to be aware that previous efforts at reforming high-risk areas have concentrated on organizing adults to control their neighborhoods and to become more involved in administering social restraints on youths' behavior. In the 1930s, public authorities subsidized the Chicago Area Project, under the leadership of Clifford Shaw, with the aim of expanding indigenous efforts of adults and local organizations to monitor neighborhood youths. The major evaluative criteria focused on a reduction of illegal behaviors with virtually little attention to providing activities and improving pro-social attitudes, norms, and behaviors (outside of sports for males). A recent re-analysis of the Chicago Area Project provides evidence that the anti-delinquent results are still uncertain (Schlossman and Sedlak, 1983).

A current generation of urban community development specialists are also working to improve the capacity of adults to control their neighborhoods against deviant activities. For the past two years such an effort has been underway in Newark and other cities, with the explicit aim of reducing alcohol and drug abuse in high risk communities. Funded by a private foundation, virtually all of the new resources are being spent on "building community capacity" (Chavis, Speer, Resnick, and Zippay, 1993). After two years, this effort at community development in Newark is in the throes of an administrative reorganization and an attempt to re-define the specific goals of the "neighborhood coalitions"(private communication, 1993).

Despite the difficulties being experienced by the Newark effort, it is important to contrast their underlying assumptions to improve the lives of inner city residents with our set of assumptions—since millions of dollars are currently being spent by private sources on behalf of a community development strategy. According to community theorists, the goal of their efforts is to seek change in the setting and enforcement of new "community norms." From their perspective "norms are established and reinforced in communities through a complex web of institutions that impact on personal lives"(Chavis et al., 1993, p. 255). By supporting a "process of empowerment whereby citizens re-established strong community norms in the schools, communities of faith, service agencies and civic organizations," communities can develop solutions to their problems.

Instead of attempting to influence a "complex web of institutions" and developing a "process of empowerment," we are proposing that two existing institutions—the family and the schools—be supported with a set of specific pro-social activities. New and old resources are to be directed on behalf of specific program models at distinct stages of the life cycle for a specific generation of youth in targeted high-risk areas. Besides improving the life-chance of specific youths in measurable ways, we expect that participating in the array of pro-social activities will have beneficial consequences for youths and their families. An expansion of pro-social attitudes and norms would be expected to occur *after* continued participation in a sequence of activities that emphasizes improved competencies and skills. The increased number of more successful youths would become the carriers of a competing, broader, pro-social, youth culture within high-risk areas.

The targeted outcomes of our proposed strategy are possible to achieve without directly confronting a "complex web of institutions" or reforming adults so they can engage in a "process of empowerment." Our secondary prevention strategy calls for a maximum amount of funds to be directed at the delivery of expanded services to youths and their families. These additional resources are needed in order to compensate for the deficiencies associated with youths growing up in high-risk, ghetto-type areas. Instead of an infusion of additional compensatory resources on behalf of non-deviant youths and their families, the community development strategy spends money for other activities to pay for staff and an infra-structure to organize adults. Strange as it may seem, the current community development strategy proposed for inner-city area emphasizes "renovating the social infra-structure" without adding any appreciable amount of resources to low-income areas.

Although we believe that a pro-social youth policy would prove to be more effective than a community development strategy, a careful reading of our proposed set of "ingredients" will show that the last item includes community organization for a specific objective. We believe that helping neighborhoods to reduce open drug sales and prostitution, to some degree, would improve the quality of life for all residents, as well as reduce the array of deviant occupations and role models presented to children and youth. However, we are well aware that excluding the sale of drugs and prostitution in a neighborhood is linked to social, political, and police tolerance of these deviant activities in low-income neighborhoods. Forcing these deviant activities outside of low-income areas into neighboring areas would involve a great deal of conflict with interests that are more powerful than the residents of high-poverty areas. A reasonable solution would be for deviant services to be provided in areas away from children and families—in "red light" areas, as used to occur in American cities in the nineteenth century and still occurs in many European cities. If adult citizens can be mobilized to confront the "web of institutions" that support drug sales and prostitution in low-income areas and push them into other parts of the urban ecology we would consider this to be a useful challenge for a community developmental effort. The target is clear and the results can be easily measured. If local residents of inner-city areas cannot rid their neighborhoods of activities that they deplore—like open drug sales and prostitution—it is difficult to believe that they have become "empowered." Since our secondary prevention strategy does not rely on citizen empowerment, this failure would not be fatal to the pro-social design—even if it would continue to make life more difficult for youths and their families.

Researching a Pro-Social Youth Policy

Services are variables that can be manipulated (unlike age, sex or intelligence, for example) so they can be systematically tested. Because a pro-social youth policy would include a number of services, it is crucially important to study the services systematically in as much detail as possible in future research.

If we are to prevent or reduce the occurrence of urban youth problems, we have to develop and test the effectiveness of specific services. As Burns and Friedman (1990) and Curry (1991) point out, ongoing evaluative and comparative research in a matrix of services ranging from most to least restrictive is a crucial direction for the development of policy for children and adolescents with serious problems. Obvious improvements in methods are required. Larger samples across different settings are necessary to avoid spurious selection effects. Longitudinal studies offer our only hope that predictors of outcomes can be disentangled over time. Random assignment of individuals to different treatments or services is imperative to control the influence of extraneous variables. In other words, systematic, experimentally controlled research designs with comparison groups are minimum requirements.

These design factors are necessary to advance our knowledge, but good study design, by itself, is not sufficient. The broad, non-specific definitions of services used in the literature (e.g., inpatient milieu treatment, outpatient counselling, social casework, family therapy, partial care or case management) conceal much variation within categories of treatment. We need a much more precise, more detailed level of analysis to specify exactly what happens to children and adolescents in programs and services. Research in social work on direct practice outcomes, and in psychology on psychotherapy outcomes, and in education on educational outcomes, has taught us a lesson: effectiveness cannot be adequately tested using gross, definitional categories. We suggest developing more refined, theory-driven descriptions and typologies of specific services received by specific individuals to help us understand individual treatment outcomes.

Theory-driven research on the effectiveness of pro-social youth interventions may lead to significant improvements in the service delivery system for urban adolescents.

Bibliography

Achenbach, T.M., Conners, C.K., Quay, H.C., Verhulst, F.C., & Howell, C.T. (1989). Replication of empirically derived syndromes as a basis for taxonomy of child/adolescent psychopathology. *Journal of Abnormal Child Psychology, 17*, 299–323.

Achenbach, T.M. & Edelbrock, C. (1983). *Manual for The Child Behavior Checklist and Revised Child Behavior Profile.* Burlington: University of Vermont, Department of Psychiatry.

Achenbach, T.M. & Edelbrock, C. (1987). Behavioral problems and competencies reported by parents of normal and disturbed children aged four to sixteen. *Monographs of the Society For Research in Child Development, 46,* (I, Serial No. 188).

Achenbach, T.M., Howell, C.T., Quay, H.C., & Conners, C.K. (1991). National survey of problems and competencies among four to sixteen year olds: Parents reports for normative and clinical samples. *Monographs of The Society For Research in Child Development, 56,* (III, Serial No. 225).

Achenbach, T. M., Verhulst, F.C., Baron, G.D., & Akkerhuis, G. W. (1987). Epidemiological comparisons of Dutch and American children. *Journal of the American Academy of Child and Adolescent Psychiatry, 26,* 317–325.

Adam, B.S., Kashani, J.H., & Shulte, F.J. (1991). The classification of conduct disorders. *Child Psychiatry and Human Development, 22,* 3–16.

Agnew, R. (1991). A longitudinal test of social control theory and delinquency. *Journal of Research in Crime and Delinquency, 28,* 126–156.

American Psychiatric Association. (1987). *Diagnostic and Statistical Manual of Mental Disorders* (3rd ed. rev.). Washington, DC: American Psychiatric Association.

Ames, R. (1983). Help-seeking and achievement orientation: Perspectives from attribution theory. In B.M. DePaulo, A. Nadler, and J.D. Fisher

(Eds.), *New Directions in Helping*, Vol. 2. (pp. 165–186) New York: Academic Press.

Avison, W.R., & MacAlpine, D.D. (1992). Gender differences in symptoms of depression among adolescents. *The Journal of Health and Social Behavior, 33*, 77–96.

Backeland, F., & Lundwall, L. (1975). Dropping out of treatment: A critical review. *Psychological Bulletin, 82*, 738–783.

Barton, W.H., & Butts, J.A. (1990). Viable options: Intensive supervision programs for juvenile delinquents. *Crime and Delinquency, 36*, 238–256.

Behar, L. (1991). *Close to Home: Community Based Mental Health For Children.* Raleigh, N.C.: N.C. Division of Mental Health/ Developmental Disabilities. Presented as testimony to the U.S. House of Representatives Select Committee on Children, Youth and Families on April 29.

Bell, D. (1953). Crime as an American way of life. *Antioch Review, 12*, 131–153.

Benjamin-Bauman, J. (1984). Increasing appointment keeping by reducing the call-appointment interval. *Journal of Applied Behavior Analysis, 17*, 295–301.

Breckenridge, S.P., & Abbott, E. (1912). *The Delinquent Child and The Home.* New York: Macmillan.

Bremner, R.H., Barnard, J., Haraven, T.K., & Mennel, R.M. (1970). *Children and Youth in America: A Documentary History*, 2 Vols. Cambridge, MA: Harvard University Press.

Brickman, P., Rabinowitz, V.C., Karuza, Jr., J., Coates, D., Cohn, E., & Kidder, L. (1982). Models of helping and coping. *American Psychologist, 37*, 368–384.

Burchard, J.D., & Clarke, R.T. (1990). The role of individualized care in a service delivery system for children and adolescents with severely maladjusted behavior. *The Journal of Mental Health Administration, 17*, 48–77.

Burgess, R.L., & Akers, R.L. (1966). Differential reinforcement theory of criminal behavior. *Social Problems, 14*, 128–147.

Burns, B., & Friedman, R. (1990). Examining the research base for child mental health services and policy. *The Journal of Mental Health Administration, 17*, 87–98.

Camasso, M.J., & Geismar, L. (1992). A multivariate approach to construct reliability and validity assessment: The case of family functioning. *Social Work Research and Abstracts, 28*, 16–26.

Chavis, D.M., Speer, P.W., Resnick, I., & Zippay, A. (1993). Building community capacity to address alcohol and drug abuse: Getting to the heart of the problem. In R.C. Davis, A.J. Lurigio, and D.P. Rosenbaum (Eds.) *Drugs and The Community: Interviewing Community Residents in Combatting the Sale of Illegal Drugs* (pp. 251–284). Springfield, IL: Charles C Thomas.

Cloward, R.A., & Ohlin, L.E. (1960). *Delinquency and Opportunity: A Theory of Delinquent Gangs.* New York: Free Press.

Cohen, A.K. (1955). *Delinquent Boys.* New York: Free Press.

Cohen, R., Parmalee, D.X., Irwin, L., Weisz, J.R., Howard, P., Purcell, P. & Best, A.M. (1990). Characteristics of children and adolescents in a psychiatric hospital and a correction facility. *Journal of the American Academy of Child and Adolescent Psychiatry, 29,* 909–913.

Curry, J.F. (1991). Outcome research on residential treatment: Implications and suggested directions. *American Journal of Orthopsychiatry, 61,* 348–357.

deAnda, D., & Smith, M.A. (1993). Differences among adolescent, young adult, and adult callers of suicide help lines. *Social Work, 38,* 421–429.

Dembo, R., Williams, L., Whitke, W., Schneider, J., Getrell, A., Berry, E., and Wish, E.D. (1992). The generality of deviance: Replication of a structural model among high-risk youths. *Journal of Research in Crime and Delinquency, 29,* 200–216.

DePaulo, B.M., Nadler, A., & Fisher, J.D. (Eds.). (1983). *New Directions in Helping.* Vol. 2: *Help-Seeking.* New York: Academic Press.

Devins, G.M., & Orme, C.M. (1985). Center for Epidemiologic Studies Depression Scale. In D.J. Keyser, and R. C. Sweetland, (Eds.), *Test Critiques,* Vol.2 (pp. 140–150). Kansas City, MO: Test Composition of America.

Dillman, D.A. (1978). *Mail and Telephone Surveys: The Total Design Method.* New York: John Wiley and Sons.

Donovan, J.E., & Jessor, J. (1985). Structure of problem behavior in adolescence and young adulthood. *Journal of Consulting and Clinical Psychiatry, 53,* 890–904.

Edelbrock, C., Costello, A.J., Duncan, M.K., Kalas, R., & Conover, N.C. (1985). Age differences in the reliability of the psychiatric interview of the child. *Child Development, 56,* 265–275.

Eisenberg, N. (1983) Developmental aspects of recipients reactions to aid. In J.D. Fisher, A. Nadler, and B.M. DePaulo, (Eds.), *New Directions in Helping.* Vol. 1: *Recipient Reactions to Aid.* New York: Academic Press.

Elliott, D.S., & Ageton, S.S. (1980). Reconciling race and class differences in self-reported and official estimates. *American Sociological Review, 45,* 95–110.

Elliott, D.S., Ageton, S.S., Huizinga, D., Knowes, B.H., & Carter, R.J. (1983). *The Prevalence and Incidence of Delinquent Behavior: 1976–1980.* Boulder, CO: Behavioral Institute.

Elliott, D.S., & Huizinga, D. (1983). Social class and delinquent behavior in a national youth panel. *Criminology, 21,* 149–177.

Elliott, D.S., Huizinga, D., & Ageton, S.S. (1985). *Explaining Delinquency and Drug Use.* Newbury Park, CA: Sage Publications.

Elliott, D.S., Huizinga, D., & Menard, S. (1989). *Multiple Problem Youth: Delinquency, Substance Use, and Mental Health Problems.* New York: Springer-Verlag.

Empey, L.T. (1978). *American Delinquency: Its Meaning and Construction.* Homewood, IL: Dorsey.

Fisher, J.D., Nadler, A., DePaulo, B.M. (Eds.) (1983). *New Directions in Helping.* Vol. 1: *Recipient Reactions To Aid.* New York: Academic Press.

Fulkins, E. (1983). Waiting time and no-show rate in a community mental health center. *American Journal of Community Psychology, 11,* 121–123.

Gore, S., Aseltine, Jr., R.H., & Colten, M.E. (1992). Social structure, life stress, and depressive symptoms in a high school aged population. *The Journal of Health and Social Behavior, 33,* 97–113.

Gross, A.E., & McMullen, P.A. (1983). Models of the help-seeking process. In B.M. DePaulo, A. Nadler, and J.D. Fisher, (Eds.), *New Directions in Helping,* Vol. 2 (pp. 47–72). New York: Academic Press.

Gutterman, E.M., O'Brien, J.D., & Young, J.G. (1987). Structured diagnostic interviews for children and adolescents: Current status and future directions. *Journal of the American Academy of Child and Adolescent Psychiatry, 26,* 621–630.

Hawkins, J.D. (1985). Executive summary. In *Drug Abuse, Mental Health and Delinquency.* Washington, DC: U. S. Department of Justice.

Hinson, J. (1982). Strategies for suicide intervention by telephone. *Suicide and Life-Threatening Behavior, 12,* 176–184.

Hirschi, T. (1969). *Causes of Delinquency.* Berkeley, CA: University of California Press.

Huizinga, D., Esbensen, F.A., and Weiher, A. H. (1991). Are there multiple paths to delinquency? *The Journal of Criminal Law and Criminology, 82,* 83–118.

Ingersoll, G.M. (1989). *Adolescents* (2nd ed.). Englewood Cliffs, NJ: Prentice Hall.

Institute of Medicine (1989). *Research on Children and Adolescents with Mental, Behavioral, and Developmental Disorders.* Washington, DC: National Academy Press. Report of a Study by a Committtee of the Institute of Medicine Division of Mental and Behavioral Medicine.

Interviewer's Manual (1977). Ann Arbor, MI: The University of Michigan Institute for Social Research.

Isaacs, M.R. and Benjamin, M.R. (1991). *Towards a Culturally Competent System of Care.* Washington, DC: Georgetown University Child Development Center.

Jargowsky, P.H., & Bane, M.J. (1990). Ghetto poverty: Basic questions. In L.E. Lynn, Jr. and M.G. McGeary (Eds.), *Inner City Poverty In The United States* (pp 16–67). Washington, DC: National Academy Press.

Jencks, C. (1992). *Rethinking Social Policy: Race, Poverty, and The Underclass.* Cambridge, MA: Harvard University Press.

Jencks, C., & Peterson, P. (Eds.). (1991). *The Urban Underclass.* Washington, DC: Brookings Institute.

Jessor, R. (1987). Problem-behavior theory, psychosocial development, and adolescent problem drinking. *British Journal of Addiction, 82,* 331–342.

Jessor, R., & Jessor, S.L. (1977). *Problem Behavior and Psychosocial Development: A Longitudinal Study of Youth.* New York: Academic Press.

Jessor, R., Graves, T.D., Hanson, R.C., & Jessor, S.L. (1968). *Society, Personality, and Deviant Behavior*. New York: Holt, Rinehart and Winston.

Jessor, R., & Jessor, S.L. (1984). Adolescence to young adulthood: A twelve-year prospective study of problem behavior and psychosocial development. In S.A. Mednick, M., Harnam, and K.M. Finello (Eds.), *Handbook of Longitudinal Research*. Vol 2: *Teenage and Adult Cohorts*. (pp. 34–61) New York: Praeger.

Kandel, D. (1978). *Longitudinal Research on Drug Use: Empirical Findings and Methodological Issues*. New York: Hemisphere-Halsted.

Kandel, D.B., Simcha-Fagan, D., & Davies, M. (1986). Risk factors for delinquency and illicit drug use from adolescence to young adulthood. *Journal of Drug Issues, 16*, 67–90.

Kaplan, S.L., & Busner, J. (1992). A note on racial bias in the admission of children and adolescents to state mental health facilities versus correctional facilities in New York. *American Journal of Psychiatry, 149*, 768–772.

Lerman, P. (1967). Argot, symbolic deviance and subcultural delinquency. *American Sociological Review, 32*, 210–224.

Lerman, P. (1977). Delinquency and social policy: An historical perspective. *Crime and Delinquency, 24*, 281–298.

Lerman, P. (1984). Child welfare, the private sector, and community-based corrections. *Crime and Delinquency, 30*, 5–38.

Lerman, P., & Camasso, M. (1992). The alternative living arrangment waiting list: A pilot study. New Brunswick, NJ: Rutgers University School of Social Work.

Lerman, P., & Pottick, K.J. (1988). Interviewing inner-city parents as help-seekers: Procedures for improving agency-based research. *Social Work Research and Abstracts, 24*, 3–6.

Leveson, H., & Pope (1981). First encounters: effects of intake procedures on patients, staffs, and the organization. *Hospital and Community Psychiatry, 32*, 482–485.

Lewis, D.O. (1980). Race bias in the diagnosis and disposition of violent adolescents. *The American Journal of Psychiatry, 137*, 1211–1216.

Lewis, D.O., Lewis, M., Unger, L., & Goldman, C. (1984). Conduct disorder and its synonyms: Diagnoses of dubious validity and usefulness. *American Journal of Psychiatry, 141*, 514–519.

Loeber, R. (1988). Natural Histories of Conduct Problems, Delinquency, and Associated Substance Use. In B.B. Lahey and A.E. Kazdin (eds.). *Advances in Clinical Child Psychology* (pp. 73–124). New York: Plenum.

Loeber, R., Stouthamer-Loeber, M., Kammen, W.V., & Farrington, D.P. (1991). Initiation, escalation and desistance in juvenile offending and their correlates. *The Journal of Criminal Law and Criminology, 82*, 36–82.

Mann, B.J., & Borduin, C.M. (1991). A critical reviw of psychotherapy outcome studies with adolescents: 1978–1988. *Adolescence, 26*, 505–541.

McMullen, P.A. & Gross, A.E. (1983). Sex differences, sex roles, and health-related help-seeking. In B.M. DePaulo, A. Nadler, & J.D. Fisher (Eds.), *New Directions in Helping*. Vol. 2 (pp. 233–263).

Matsueda, R.L., & Heimer, K. (1987). Race, family structure, and delinquency: A test of differential association and social control theories. *American Sociological Review, 52,* 826–840.

McManus, M. (1984). Psychiatric disturbance in serious delinquents. *Journal of the American Academy of Child and Adolescent Psychiatry, 23,* 602–615.

Meyers, W.C. (1990). DSM-III diagnoses and offenses in committed female juvenile delinquents. *Bulletin of the American Academy of Psychiatry and Law, 18,* 47–54.

Miller, W.B. (1958). Lower-class culture as a generating milieu of gang delinquency. *Journal of Social Issues, 14,* 5–19.

Nadler, A. Fisher, J.D., & DePaulo, B.M. (Eds.). (1983). *New Directions in Helping*. Vol 3: *Applied Perspectives on Help-Seeking and Receiving.* New York: Academic Press.

National Institute of Mental Health. (1986). Series CN, No. 11, *Specialty Mental Health Organizations, United States, 1983–1984.* Washington, DC: Superintendent of Documents, U.S. Government Printing Office, DHHS Pub. No. (ADM), 86–1490.

Osgood, D.W. (1989). Covariations of risk behaviors during adolescence. Washington, DC: U.S. Government Printing Office. Prepared for the U.S. Office of Technology Assessment.

O'Sullivan, M.J., Peterson, P.D., Cox, G.B., & Kurkeby, J. (1989). Ethnic populations: Community mental health services ten years later. *American Journal of Community Psychology, 17,* 17–30.

Patterson, G.R., Chamberlain, P., and Reid, J.B. (1982). A comparative evaluation of a parent training program. *Behavior Therapy, 13,* 638–650.

Piliavin, I. (1972). A model of help utilization. Paper presented at the annual meeting of the American Psychological Association, Honolulu, Hawaii.

Piliavin, I., & Briar, S. (1964). Police encounters with juveniles. *American Journal of Sociology, 70,* 206–214.

Pottick, K.J., & Lerman, P. (1991). Maximizing survey response rates for hard-to-reach inner-city populations. *Social Science Quarterly, 72,* 172–180.

Pottick, K.J., Hansell, S., Gaboda, D., & Gutterman, E. (1993). Child and adolescent outcomes of inpatient psychiatric services: A research agenda. *Children and Youth Services Review, 15,* 371–384.

Quay, H.C. (1965). Personality and delinquency. In H.C. Quay, (Ed.), *Juvenile Delinquency: Research and Theory.* New York: D. Van Nostrand.

Quay, J.C. (1986). Classification. In H.C. Quay and J.S. Werry (Eds.), *Psychopathological Disorders of Childhood* (3rd Ed.) (pp. 1–34). New York: Wiley.

Quay, J.C., & Werry, J.S. (Eds.). (1986). *Psychopathological Disorders of Childhood* (3rd Ed.). New York: Wiley.

Radloff, L.S. (1977). The CES–D scale: A self-report depression scale for research in the general population. *Applied Psychological Measurement, 1,* 385–401.

Reiss, A.J., and Roth, J.A. (Eds.). (1993). *Understanding and Preventing Violence.* Washington, DC: National Academy Press.

Richardson, T.R. (1989). *The Century of the Child: The Mental Hygiene Movement and Social Policy in the United States and Canada.* Albany, NY: State University of New York Press.

Robins, L.N. (1991). Antisocial Personality. In L.N. Robins and D. Regier (Eds.) *Psychiatric Disorder in America.* New York: Macmillan/Free Press.

Robins, L.N., & McEvoy, L. (1990). Conduct problems as predictors of substance abuse. In L.N. Robins, & M. Rutter (Eds.), *Straight and Devious Pathways From Childhood to Adulthood* . Cambridge, MA: Cambridge University Press.

Rutter, M. (1986). The developmental psychopathology of depression: Issues and perspectives. In M. Rutter, C. Izard, & P.B. Read, (Eds.), *Depression in Young People: Developmental and Clinical Perspectives.* New York: The Guilford Press.

Schlossman, S., & Sedlak, M. (1983). *The Chicago Area Project Revisited.* Santa Monica, CA: The Rand Corporation (Publication N–1944 NIE).

Schorr, L.B. (1988). *Within Our Reach: Breaking The Cycle of Disadvantage.* New York: Doubleday.

Shannon, L.W. (1982). Assessing the relationship of adult criminal careers to juvenile careers: A summary. Washington, DC: U.S. Government Printing Office. Prepared for the U.S. Office of Juvenile Justice and Delinquency Prevention.

Shanok, S.S. (1983). A comparison of delinquent and nondelinquent adolescent psychiatric inpatients. *The American Journal of Psychiatry, 140,* 582–585.

Shaver, K.G. (1985). *The Attribution of Blame: Causality, Responsibility, and Blameworthiness.* New York: Springer-Verlag.

Shaw, C.R., & McKay, H.D. (1942). *Juvenile Delinquency and Urban Areas.* Chicago: University of Chicago Press.

Shell, R. & Eisenberg, N. (1992). A developmental model of recipients' reactions to aid. *Psychological Bulletin, 111,* 413–433.

Short, Jr., J.F., & Nye, F.I. (1958). Extent of unrecorded delinquency: Tentative conclusions. *Journal of Criminal Law, Criminology, and Police Science, 49,* 296–302.

Smith, D.A., Visher, C.A., & Jarjoura, G.R. (1991). Dimensions of delinquency: Exploring the correlates of participation, frequency, and persistence of delinquent behavior. *Journal of Research in Crime and Delinquency, 28,* 6–32.

Stroul, B.A., & Friedman, R.M. (1988). Caring for emotionally disturbed children and youth: Principles for a system of care. *Child Today, 17,* 11–15.

Sue, S. (1977). Community mental health services to minority groups: Some optimism, some pessimism. *American Psychologist, 43*, 301–308.

Sue, S. (1988). Psychotherapeutic services for ethnic minorities: Two decades of research findings. *American Psychologist, 43*, 301–308.

Sue, S., Fujino, D.C., Hu, L., Takeuchi, D.T., & Zane, N.W.S. (1991). Community mental health services for ethnic minority groups: A test of the cultural responsiveness hypothesis. *Journal of Consulting and Clinical Psychology, 59*, 533–540.

Sunshine, J.H., Witkin, M.J., Atay, J.E., & Manderschied, R.W. (1986). *Psychiatric Outpatient Care Services in Mental Health Organizations.* Washington, DC: U.S. Department of Health and Human Services, Public Health Service.

Sutherland, E.H. (1947). *Principles of Criminology* (4th ed.). Philadelphia: Lippincott.

Sutherland, E.H., & Cressey, D.R. (1955). *Principles of Criminology* (5th ed.). Philadelphia: Lippincott.

Sutton, J.R. (1988). *Stubborn Children: Controlling Delinquency in the United States, 1640–1981.* Berkeley, CA: University of California Press.

Thornberry, T.P., Krohn, M.D., Lizotte, A.J., & Chard-Wierschiem, D. (1993). The role of juvenile gangs in facilitating delinquent behavior. *Journal of Research in Crime and Delinquency, 30*, 55–87.

Thornberry, T.P., Lizotte, A.J., Krohn, M.D., Farnsworth, M., & Jang, S.J. (1991). Testing interactional theory: An examination of reciprocal causal relationships among family, school, and delinquency. *The Journal of Criminology, 82*, 3–35.

Tracy, P.E. (1987). Race and class differences in official and self-reported delinquency. In M.E. Wolfgang, J.P. Thornberry, & R.M. Figlio, (Eds.), *From Boy to Man, From Delinquency to Crime.* Chicago: University of Chicago Press.

Truax, C. (1973). Effective ingredients in psychotherapy. In A. Mahren & L. Pearson (Eds.), *Creative Developments in Psychotherapy.* New York: Jason Aronsen.

Turner, R.J. (1981). On social support as a contingency in psychological well-being. *Journal of Health and Social Behavior, 22*, 357–67.

Turner, A.J., & Vernon, J.C. (1978). Prompts to increase attendance in community mental health centers. *Journal of Applied Behavior Analysis, 9*, 141–145.

Veroff, J., Douvan, E., & Kulka, R. (1981). *The Inner American: A Self-Portrait From 1957 to 1976.* New York: Basic Books.

Viale-Val, G., Rosenthal, R.H., Curtiss, G., & Marohn, R.C. (1984). Dropout from adolescent psychotherapy: A preliminary study. *Journal of the American Academy of Child Psychiatry, 23*, 562–568.

Wakefield, J.C. (1992). Disorder as harmful dysfunction. A conceptual critique of DSM-III-R's definition of mental disorder. *Psychological Review, 99*, 232–247.

Weisman, M., & Klerman, G.L. (1977). Sex differences and epidemiology of depression. *Archives of General Psychiatry, 34,* 98–111.

Wells, V.E., Deykiw, E.Y., & Klerman, G.L. (1985). Risk factors for depression in adolescence. *Psychiatric Development, 3,* 83–108.

Westendorp, F., Brink, K.L., Roberson, M.K., & Ortiz, I.E. (1986). Variables which differentiated placement of adolescents into juvenile justice or mental health systems. *Adolescence, 21,* 23–37.

White, H.R. (1992). Early problem behavior and later drug problems. *Journal of Research in Crime and Delinquency, 29,* 412–429.

White, H.R., Johnson, V., & Garrison, C. (1985). The drug-crime nexus among adolescents and their peers. *Deviant Behavior, 6,* 183–204.

White, H.R., & LaGrange, R.L. (1987). An assessment of gender effects in self report delinquency. *Sociological Focus, 20,* 195–213.

White, H.R., Pandina, R.J., & LaGrange, R.L. (1987). Longitudinal predictors of serious substance use and delinquency. *Criminology, 25,* 715–740.

Whyte, W.F. (1943). *Street Corner Society.* Chicago: University of Chicago Press.

Williams, S., Anderson, J., McGee, R., & Silva, P.A. (1990). Risk factors for behavioral and emotional disorders in pre-adolescent children. *Academy of Child and Adolescent Psychiatry, 29,* 413–419.

Wills, T.A. (Ed.). (1982). *Basic Processes in Helping Relationships.* New York: Academic Press.

Wilson, W.J. (1987). *The Truly Disadvantaged: The Inner City, The Underclass, and Public Policy.* Chicago: University of Chicago Press.

Wolfgang, M.E., Figlio, R.M., & Sellin, T. (1972). *Delinquency in a Birth Cohort.* Chicago: University of Chicago Press.

Wolfgang, M.E., Thornberry, T.P., & Figlio, R.M. (1987). *From Boy to Man, From Delinquency to Crime.* Chicago: University of Chicago Press.

Wu, I.H., & Windle, C. (1980). Ethnic specificity in the relative minority use and staffing of community mental health centers. *Community Mental Health Journal, 16,* 156–168.

Zill, N., & Schoenborn, C.A. (1990). Developmental, learning, and emotional problems: Health of our nation's children, United States, 1988. *Advanced Data From Vital and Health Statistics,* No. 190. Hyattsville, MD.: National Center for Health Statistics.

Appendix A

Essex County Youth Study

THE STATE UNIVERSITY OF NEW JERSEY
RUTGERS

ESSEX COUNTY YOUTH STUDY

PARENT/CAREGIVER SURVEY OF OPINION

Interviewer's Name _____

Place of Interview:

Date of Interview _____   Age of Child _____

Research Case #_____

PARENT/CAREGIVER SURVEY OF OPINION

FACE SHEET INFORMATION

0. First name of child _____

1. Sex of child _____

2. Agency case number (if assigned) _____

3. Day and date of intake interview _____

4. Scheduled time of intake interview _____

5. Name of agency intake worker _____

6. Place of survey interview _____

7. Date of survey interview _____

8. Parent permission obtained? _____

9. Child permission obtained? _____

<u>INTRODUCTION</u>:   <u>READ</u> <u>TO</u> <u>EVERYONE</u>

    Hello, I'm (Iwer's name)_____ and I'm working for
the Rutgers University research study on young people in Essex
County.

    Thank you for giving us permission to ask you some
questions.   We want to find out how parents think about young
people--and the problems youth might have while growing up.

    Everything we talk about will be strictly private and
confidential.   Nobody in your family will ever be identified by
name.

    If we should come to any question you don't want to answer,
just let me know and we'll skip over it.   I think you will find
the questions interesting and will want to give them careful
thought.

    At the end of the interview we would like to fill out a form
so Rutgers can send you a $5.00 check for taking the time to talk
to us.

SECTION A: NECESSARY INFORMATION

A1.   First, we are interested in knowing how you are related to
       (NAME)_____. Are you (HIS/HER) parent, a relative,
       or not a relative?

       1. Mother

       2. Father

       3. Aunt/Uncle

       4. Sister/Brother

       5. Other relative (SPECIFY) _____

       6. Non-relative (SPECIFY) _____

A2.   How old was (NAME)_____ on (HIS/HER) last birthday?

       1. 12 years

       2. 13 years

       3. 14 years

       4. 15 years

       5. 16 years

Appendix A

A3.　　Does (NAME)_____ go to a public, private, or parochial school?

　　　1. Public

　　　2. Private

　　　3. Parochial

　　　4. Other (SPECIFY) _____

A4　　In what year of school is (NAME)_____?

　　　1.　5th or less　　　　7.　11th

　　　2.　6th　　　　　　　　8.　12th

　　　3.　7th　　　　　　　　9.　Graduated H.S.

　　　4.　8th　　　　　　　10.　Ungraded

　　　5.　9th　　　　　　　11.　Not sure

　　　6. 10th

SECTION B: LIST OF ACTIVITIES AND BEHAVIORS

B1.   I am going to show you a list with many examples of differ-
      ent kinds of youth behavior. Some of the items I will ask
      you about may be true for your child, but others may not.
      First let's talk about the sports your child may take part
      in. (HAND THE RESPONDENT THE CHECKLIST TO LOOK AT WHILE YOU
      FILL IT OUT).

CHILD BEHAVIOR CHECKLIST FOR AGES 4–16

I. Please list the sports your child most likes to take part in. For example: swimming, base-
ball, skating, skate boarding, bike riding, fishing, etc.

☐   None

a.   _____

b.   _____

c.   _____

Compared to other children of the same age, about how much time does he/she
spend in each?

	Don't Know	Less Than Average	Average	More Than Average
a.	☐	☐	☐	☐
b.	☐	☐	☐	☐
c.	☐	☐	☐	☐

Compared to other children of the same age, how well does he/she do each one?

	Don't Know	Below Average	Average	Above Average
a.	☐	☐	☐	☐
b.	☐	☐	☐	☐
c.	☐	☐	☐	☐

II. Please list your child's favorite hobbies, activities, and games, other than sports. For
example: stamps, dolls, books,, piano, crafts, singing, etc. (Do not include T.V.)

☐   None

a.   _____

b.   _____

c.   _____

Compared to other children of the same age, about how much time does he/she
spend in each?

	Don't Know	Less Than Average	Average	More Than Average
a.	☐	☐	☐	☐
b.	☐	☐	☐	☐
c.	☐	☐	☐	☐

II. (Continued)

Compared to other children of the same age, how well does he/she do each one?

	Don't Know	Below Average	Average	Above Average
a.	☐	☐	☐	☐
b.	☐	☐	☐	☐
c.	☐	☐	☐	☐

III. Please list any organization, clubs, teams, or groups your child belongs to.

☐ None

a. _____

b. _____

c. _____

Compared to other children of the same age, how active is he/she in each?

	Don't Know	Less Active	Average	More Active
a.	☐	☐	☐	☐
b.	☐	☐	☐	☐
c.	☐	☐	☐	☐

IV. Please list any jobs or chores your child has. For example: paper route, babysitting, making bed, etc.

☐ None

a. _____

b. _____

c. _____

Compared to other children of the same age, how well does he/she carry them out?

	Don't Know	Below Average	Average	Above Average
a.	☐	☐	☐	☐
b.	☐	☐	☐	☐
c.	☐	☐	☐	☐

VIII. Below is a list of items that describe children. For each item that describes your child **now or within the past 6 months**, please circle the **2** if the item is **very true** or **often true** of your child. Circle the **1** if the item is **somewhat** or **sometimes true** of your child. If the item is **not true** of your child, circle the **0**. Please **answer all items** as well as you can, even if some do not seem to apply to your child.

   0 = Not True (as far as you know)
   1 = Somewhat or Sometimes True
   2 = Very True or Often True

0	1	2	1.	Acts too young for his/her age	16
0	1	2	2.	Allergy (describe): _____	
0	1	2	3.	Argues a lot	
0	1	2	4.	Asthma	
0	1	2	5.	Behaves like opposite sex	20
0	1	2	6.	Bowel movements outside toilet	
0	1	2	7.	Bragging, boasting	
0	1	2	8.	Can't concentrate, can't pay attention too long	
0	1	2	9.	Cant get his/her mind off certain thoughts; obsessions (describe):	
0	1	2	10.	Can't sit still, restless, or hyperactive	25
0	1	2	11.	Clings to adults or too dependent	
0	1	2	12.	Complains of loneliness	
0	1	2	13.	Confused or seems to be in a fog	
0	1	2	14.	Cries a lot	
0	1	2	15.	Cruel to animals	30
0	1	2	16.	Cruelty, bullying, or meanness to others	
0	1	2	17.	Day-dreams or gets lost in his/her thoughts	
0	1	2	18.	Deliberately harms self or attempts suicide	
0	1	2	19.	Demands a lot of attention	
0	1	2	20.	Destroys his/her own things	35
0	1	2	21.	Destroys things belonging to his/her family or other children	
0	1	2	22.	Disobedient at home	
0	1	2	23.	Disobedient at school	
0	1	2	24.	Doesn't eat well	
0	1	2	25.	Doesn't get along with other children	
0	1	2	26.	Doesn't seem to feel guilty after misbehaving	
0	1	2	27.	Easily jealous	
0	1	2	28.	Eats or drinks things that are not food (describe); _____	
0	1	2	29.	Fears certain animals, situations, or places, other than school (describe): _____	
0	1	2	30.	Fears going to school	45

0 = Not True (as far as you know)
1 = Somewhat or Sometimes True
2 = Very True or Often True

0	1	2	31.	Fears he/she might think or do something bad	
0	1	2	32.	Feels he/she has to be perfect	
0	1	2	33.	Feels or complains that no one loves him/her	
0	1	2	34.	Feels others are out to get him	
0	1	2	35.	Feels worthless or onferior	50
0	1	2	36.	Gets hurt a lot, accident-prone	
0	1	2	37.	Gets in many fights	
0	1	2	38.	Gets teased a lot	
0	1	2	39.	Hangs around with children who get in trouble	
0	1	2	40.	Hears things that aren't there (describe): _____	
				_____	55
0	1	2	41.	Impulsive or acts without thinking	
0	1	2	42.	Likes to be alone	
0	1	2	43.	Lying or cheating	
0	1	2	44.	Bites fingernails	
0	1	2	45.	Nervous, highstrung, or tense	60
0	1	2	46.	Nervous movements or twitching (describe); _____	
0	1	2	47.	Nightmares	
0	1	2	48.	Not liked by other children	
0	1	2	49.	Constipated, doesn't move bowels	
0	1	2	50.	Too fearful or anxious	65
0	1	2	51.	Feels dizzy	
0	1	2	52.	Feels too guilty	
0	1	2	53.	Overeating	
0	1	2	54.	Overtired	
0	1	2	55.	Overweight	70
0	1	2	56.	Physical problems without known medical cause:.	
0	1	2		a. Aches or pains	
0	1	2	.	b. Headaches	
0	1	2		c. Nausea, feels sick	
0	1	2	.	d. Problems with eyes (describe): _____	
0	1	2		e. Rashes or other skin problems	75
0	1	2	.	f. Stomachaches or cramps	
0	1	2		g. Vomiting, throwing up	
0	1	2	.	h. Other (describe): _____	
0	1	2	57.	Physically attacks people	

0 = Not True (as far as you know)
1 = Somewhat or Sometimes True
2 = Very True or Often True

0	1	2	58.	Picks nose, skin, or other parts of body (describe): _____	
					80
0	1	2	59.	Plays with own sex parts in public	16
0	1	2	60.	Plays with own sex parts too much	
0	1	2	61.	Poor school work	
0	1	2	62.	Poorly coordinated or clumsy	
0	1	2	63.	Prefers playing with older children	20
0	1	2	64.	Prefers playing with younger children	
0	1	2	65.	Refuses to talk	
0	1	2	66.	Repeats certain acts over and over; compulsions (describe):	
0	1	2	67.	Runs away from home	
0	1	2	68.	Screams a lot	25
0	1	2	69.	Secretive, keeps things to self	
0	1	2	70.	Sees things that aren't there (describe): _____	
0	1	2	71.	Self-conscious or easily embarrassed	
0	1	2	72.	Sets fires	
0	1	2	73.	Sexual problems (describe): _____	
					30
0	1	2	74.	Showing off or clowning	
0	1	2	75.	Shy or timid	
0	1	2	76.	Sleeps less than most children	
0	1	2	77.	Sleeps more than most children during day and/or night (describe):	
0	1	2	78.	Smears or plays with bowel movements	35
0	1	2	79.	Speech problem (describe): _____	
0	1	2	80.	Stares blankly	
0	1	2	81.	Steals at home	
0	1	2	82.	Steals outside home	
0	1	2	83.	Stores up things he/she doesn't need (describe): _____	
					40
0	1	2	84.	Strange behavior (describe): _____	
0	1	2	**85.**	Strange ideas (describe): _____	

0 = Not True (as far as you know)
1 = Somewhat or Sometimes True
2 = Very True or Often True

0	1	2	86.	Stubborn, sullen, or irritable
0	1	2	87.	Sudden changes in mood or feelings
0	1	2	88.	Sulks a lot
0	1	2	89.	Suspicious
0	1	2	90.	Swearing or obscene language
0	1	2	91.	Talks about killing self
0	1	2	92.	Talks or walks in sleep (describe): _____
0	1	2	93.	Talks too much
0	1	2	94.	Teases a lot
0	1	2	95.	Temper tantrums or hot temper
0	1	2	96.	Thinks about sex too much
0	1	2	97.	Threatens people
0	1	2	98.	Thumb-sucking
0	1	2	99.	Too concerned with neatness or cleanliness
0	1	2	100.	Trouble sleeping (describe): _____
0	1	2	101.	Truancy, skips school
0	1	2	102.	Underactive, slow moving, or lacks energy
0	1	2	103.	Unhappy, sad, or depressed
0	1	2	104.	Unusually loud
0	1	2	105.	Uses alcohol or drugs (describe): _____
0	1	2	106.	Vandalism
0	1	2	107.	Wets elf during the day
0	1	2	108.	Wets the bed
0	1	2	109.	Whining
0	1	2	110.	Wishes to be of opposite sex
0	1	2	111.	Withdrawn, doesn't get involved with others
0	1	2	112.	Worrying
			113.	Please write in any problems your child has that were not listed above:
0	1	2		_____
0	1	2		_____
0	1	2		_____

45

50

55

60

65

70

PLEASE BE SURE YOU HAVE ANSWERED ALL ITEMS
PLEASE UNDERLINE ANY YOU ARE CONCERNED ABOUT

B2.   Are there any behaviors that you might be concerned about that do <u>not</u> seem to be on this list?

     1. Yes, (PROBE FOR ADDITIONAL ITEMS AND WRITE IN HERE)

               _____

               _____

               _____

     2. No, None to add

B3.   Here is the list of behaviors that you told me to circle. Could you look over the ones we circled as "True" or "Very True" and tell me which ones you think of as problems and are most concerned about? (<u>UNDERLINE</u> ON YOUR CBCL-- INCLUDING ANY ADDED BY R)

     1. One or more items underlined

     2. No items underlined

B4.   Do you think of any of the problems that we <u>underlined</u> as being tied together in some way? Are any of them a connected set of problems, or are they separate and distinct?

     1. Separate and distinct (GO TO B6)

   * 2 a. Some are connected (ASK *b)

       * b. Which ones?_____

           _____

           _____

B5.   Are there any others that you see as a connected set of problems?

     1. No others

   * 2 a. Yes, there are others (ASK *b)

       * b. Which ones? _____

           _____

           _____

B6.   Out of the problems you are concerned about--either
       separate or as a set of problems--which <u>one</u> is the main
       problem or is most important to you?

       1. Separate and distinct problem #_____

       _____

       2. One problem within a set (SPECIFY)_____

       _____

       _____

       3. Entire set of problems noted in:

          a. B4 set   (FIRST SET)

          b. B5 set   (OTHERS SET)

B7.   What is there about the main problem that particularly
       concerns you--could you tell me <u>why</u> you are concerned?

       _____

       _____

       _____

       _____

       _____

       _____

B8.   When did you first find out that (NAME)_____ had
       this problem--within the past month, 1-3 months ago, 3-6
       months ago, 6-12 months ago, 1-2 years ago, or more than 2
       years ago?

       1.   Within the past month

       2.   1-3 months ago

       3.   3-6 months ago

       4.   6-12 months ago

       5.   1-2 years ago

       6.   More than 2 years ago

7

B9.   How did you find out about the main problem--did you
       notice it or did someone else notice it and tell you?
       (PROBE, "WHO WAS IT?", IF SOMEONE ELSE).

       1. You (RESPONDENT)

       2. Father

       3. Child's brother/Sister

       4. Other relative (SPECIFY)_____

       5. Adult friend/Neighbor

       6. Child's friend

       7. School staff

       8. Juvenile officer or other police

       9. Medical doctor/Nurse

       10. DYFS worker (Div. of Youth and Family Services Worker)

       11. Other social worker

       12. Someone else (SPECIFY)_____

B10.   Did you personally ever have this kind of problem when
       you were growing up?

       1. Yes

       2. No

       3. Not sure

B11.   Have you ever known anyone else--in or outside your family
       --who has had this kind of problem?

       1. Inside Family (SPECIFY)_____

       2. Outside Family (SPECIFY)_____

       3. No one

       4. Not sure

8

B12. Have you ever read or heard anything before about this kind
      of problem--like from TV, newspapers, books or magazines?

      1. Yes (SPECIFY)_____

      _____

      2. No

      3. Not sure

B13. In your opinion is this the kind of problem that almost
      everybody has while growing up, a lot have, some have, or
      very few have while growing up?

      1. Almost everybody has

      2. A lot have

      3. Some have

      4. Very few have

      5. Not sure

9

SECTION C: PARENT/CAREGIVER OPINIONS ABOUT PROBLEMS

C1 a. Looking back to when the main problem first got <u>started</u>, why do you think it began?

_____

_____

_____

_____

_____

   b. Was anybody responsible for the main problem getting started?

       1. Yes

       2. No (GO TO C2)

       3. Don't know (GO TO C2)

  *c. Who was that? (IF MORE THAN ONE PERSON MENTIONED, ASK *d)

_____

       * d. Who would you say was <u>mainly</u> responsible?

_____

C2 a. Is there anything that happened that made the main problem get <u>worse</u> than when it first got started?

       1. Yes

       2. No (GO TO C3)

       3. Don't know (GO TO C3)

   b. Like what?

_____   _____

_____   _____

_____   _____

_____   _____

C2 c. Was anybody responsible for it getting worse?

    1. Yes

    2. No (GO TO C3)

  *d. Who was that? (IF MORE THAN ONE PERSON MENTIONED, ASK *e)

_____

    * e. Who would you say was <u>mainly</u> responsible?

_____

C3. Considering everything you know about what caused (NAME)_____'s main problem to get started or get worse, how responsible would you say the following people are--a lot, some, a little, or not at all?

<u>List</u> <u>of</u> <u>Persons</u>	A <u>Lot</u>	Some	A <u>Little</u>	Not <u>At</u> <u>All</u>
a. (NAME)_____	1	2	3	4
b. (NAME)_____'s friend	1	2	3	4
c. You (RESPONDENT)	1	2	3	4
d. Father	1	2	3	4
e. Brother or sister	1	2	3	4
f. Other relatives living in house (SPECIFY) _____	1	2	3	4
g. Other relatives living outside (SPECIFY) _____	1	2	3	4
h. Anybody else (SPECIFY) _____ _____	1	2	3	4

C4.   If (NAME)_____ had been asked this question would (HE/SHE) have answered (HE/SHE) was responsible a lot, some, a little or not at all?

1. A lot

2. Some

3. A little

4. Not at all

C5.   Besides the reasons we have been talking about, some people think that other things could play a part in causing youth problems or making them worse. How responsible would you say the following things are for causing (NAME)_____'s problem--a lot, some, a little or not at all?

Other Things	A Lot	Some	A Little	Not At All
a. Bad health	1	2	3	4
b. Family heredity	1	2	3	4
c. TV, movies, newspapers	1	2	3	4
d. Type of neighborhood	1	2	3	4
e. Kind of school (HE/SHE) goes to	1	2	3	4
f. Not having enough religious faith	1	2	3	4
g. Family income not enough	1	2	3	4
h. Discrimination	1	2	3	4
i. Crowded apartment or house	1	2	3	4

C6.   Now let's talk about how you personally have tried to do something to solve or improve the main problem before you came to this place. What kinds of things have you personally tried to do?

_____

_____

_____

_____

12

C7.   Before you came here, did you ever talk about the main
        problem with any of the following people? (READ LIST AND
        IF ANSWER IS "YES", CIRCLE LETTER ON LEFT).

People Talked To	Really	Only Partly	Hardly
a. (NAME)_____'s father	1	2	3
b. Your mother	1	2	3
c. Your sister or brother	1	2	3
d. Other relatives (SPECIFY) _____			
_____	1	2	3
e. Personal friends	1	2	3
f. Friends at work	1	2	3
g. Neighbors	1	2	3
h. None of the above (GO TO C10)	-	-	-

C8.   How well do you think each person you talked with under-
        stood your ideas and feelings about the main problem--do
        you think you were really understood, only partly under-
        stood, or hardly understood by _____. (READ FOR EACH
        PERSON CIRCLED AND CODE 1, 2, OR 3, ON RIGHT)

C9 a.   Did any of the people you talked with suggest that you
        come here to this place--or a place like this--to help
        (NAME)_____ with the main problem?

        1. Yes

        2. No (GO TO C10)

   b.   Who suggested it? (PROBE FOR "ANY OTHERS?")

        _____

        _____

        _____

        _____

13

C10.   And before you came here, did you ever talk about the main
       problem with other people--like any of the following?
       (READ LIST AND IF ANSWER IS "YES", CIRCLE LETTER ON LEFT).

Other People Talked To	Really	Only Partly	Hardly
a. Teachers or school staff	1	2	3
b. Juvenile officers or other police	1	2	3
c. Probation officers or judges	1	2	3
d. DYFS workers or Division of Youth and Family Services workers	1	2	3
e. Other social workers	1	2	3
f. Psychologists or mental health counselors	1	2	3
g. Ministers or clergy	1	2	3
h. Medical doctors or nurses	1	2	3
i. None of the above (GO TO C13)	-	-	-

C11.   How well do you think each one of these other people you
       talked with understood your ideas and feelings about the
       main problem--Do you think you were really understood,
       only partly understood, or hardly understood by _____.
       (READ FOR EACH PERSON CIRCLED AND CODE 1, 2, OR 3 ON
       RIGHT).

C12 a. Did any of these other people you talked with suggest that
       you come here to this place--or a place like this to help
       (NAME)_____ with the main problem?

       1. Yes

       2. No (GO TO C13)

   b. Who suggested it? (PROBE FOR "ANY OTHERS?")

       _____

       _____

       _____

14

C13. Now looking to the future, how much responsibility should the following people have in solving or improving the main problem--a lot, some, a little, or not at all?

Persons Taking Part	A Lot	Some	A Little	Not At All
a. (NAME)_____	1	2	3	4
b. You (RESPONDENT)	1	2	3	4
c. (NAME'S)_____ father	1	2	3	4
d. Other relatives (SPECIFY)_____				
_____	1	2	3	4
e. Teachers or school staff	1	2	3	4
f. Probation officers or court officials	1	2	3	4
g. Family Crisis Intervention Unit counselors	1	2	3	4
h. Mental health counselors	1	2	3	4
i. Ministers or clergy	1	2	3	4
j. Medical doctors or nurses	1	2	3	4
k. Anybody else (SPECIFY) _____				
_____	1	2	3	4

C14. If (NAME)_____ had been asked this question do you think (HE/SHE) would have answered (HE/SHE) was responsible a lot, some, a little, or not at all?

1. A lot

2. Some

3. A little

4. Not at all

C15 a. Taking everything into consideration, do you think the main problem will definitely get better, maybe get better, or do you think the main problem might not get better?

1. Definitely get better (ASK *b)

2. Maybe get better (ASK *b)

3. Might not get better (GO TO SECTION D)

*b. Do you think the main problem will get better within 6 months, 12 months, 1 to 2 years, 2 to 3 years, 4 to 5 years, or 6 years or more?

1. Within 6 months

2. 12 months

3. 1 to 2 years

4. 2 to 3 years

5. 4 to 5 years

6. 6 or more years

SECTION D: PARENT/CAREGIVER IDEAS ABOUT AGENCIES

D1 a.   And now I would like to ask you some questions about
        trying to get help for problems from places like this
        agency. Has (NAME)_____ ever gone to an agency
        like this before?

        1. Yes

        2. No (GO TO D3)

   b.   Do you remember the name of the agency or the kind of
        place the last one was? (SPECIFY)

        _____

        _____

        _____

D2.   Do you think that (NAME)_____'s going to that
        agency helped a lot, some, a little, or not at all?

        1. A lot

        2. Some

        3. A little

        4. Not at all

D3.   Whose idea was it that (NAME)_____ should come to
      this particular agency at this time--rather than go some-
      place else?

a. You (RESPONDENT)

b. Father

c. Other relative (SPECIFY)_____

d. DYFS worker (Division of Youth and Family Services worker)

e. Social worker (not from DYFS)

f. Minister or clergy

g. Teacher or other school staff

h. Juvenile or other police officer

i. Probation officer/Court official

j. Medical doctor/Nurse

k. Mental health professional

l. Any other person (SPECIFY)_____

D4.   Why was this agency picked--rather than someplace else?
      (PROBE "ANY SPECIAL REASON?")

      _____

      _____

      _____

      _____

      _____

D5.   Is this a place where you personally think your ideas and
      feelings have been really understood, only partly under-
      stood, or hardly understood?

      1. Really

      2. Partly

      3. Hardly

D6 a. Do you think this agency will be able to offer (NAME)
       _____ some help with the main problem, arrange for
       another agency to help, or won't they be able to help?

       1. Offer help (ASK *b)

       2. Arrange for another agency to help (ASK *b)

       3. Won't be able to help (ASK **c)

   *b. What kinds of help will they probably offer or
        probably arrange for another agency to give?

        _____

        _____

        _____

        _____

   **c.   (IF WON'T BE ABLE TO HELP) Why do you feel this way?

        _____

        _____

        _____

        _____

D7.   I am going to read you a list of the kinds of help that
       might be offered to (NAME)_____. You may or may
       not want (NAME)_____ to have one or more of these
       types of help. Please tell me whether you would answer
       definitely yes, maybe, or definitely not for each type of
       help that might be offered to (NAME)_____.

   a. Work with a counselor who can figure out what is wrong
       with (NAME)_____ and then tell (HIM/HER) exactly
       what to do to overcome the main problem.

       1. Definitely yes   2. Maybe   3. Definitely not

   b. Work with a counselor who can encourage (NAME)_____
       to use (HIS/HER) own will to try harder to overcome the
       main problem by (HIMSELF/HERSELF).

       1. Definitely yes   2. Maybe   3. Definitely not

19

D7 c. Work with a counselor who can lead and provide (NAME)
       _____ with a disciplined program that (HE/SHE) can
       follow to overcome the main problem.

       1. Definitely yes   2. Maybe   3. Definitely not

   d. Work with a counselor who can offer to teach
       (NAME)_____ new ways of acting so (HE/SHE) can learn
       to use the new ways to overcome the main problem by
       (HIMSELF/HERSELF).

       1. Definitely yes   2. Maybe   3. Definitely not

   e. Work with a counselor who can figure out what is wrong
       with (NAME)_____ and then discuss with him/her what
       could be done to overcome the main problem.

       1. Definitely yes   2. Maybe   3. Definitely not

D8.   Out of all the types of help that might be offered, which
       one would you want the most for (NAME)_____?

       1. _____ (SELECT A LETTER)   2. None

D9.   And how would you feel about (NAME)_____ living
       away from home for a short time in order to help overcome
       the main problem? Would you answer definitely yes, maybe,
       or definitely not to any of the following places?

Outside Places	Definitely Yes	Maybe	Definitely Not
a. Youth shelter	1	2	3
b. Foster home	1	2	3
c. Detention center	1	2	3
d. Group home	1	2	3
e. Psychiatric hospital	1	2	3
f. Residential treatment center	1	2	3
g. Residential school	1	2	3

D10.   Taking everything into account, would you say (NAME)_____ came to this agency because (HE/SHE) wanted to come, wanted to please somebody in the family, because (HE/SHE) felt afraid or threatened, or for some other reason?

1. Wanted to come

2. Wanted to please somebody in the family

*3 a. Felt threatened   (ASK *b)

     *b. How?   By whom? _____

     _____

4. Other reason (SPECIFY) _____

    _____

    _____

    _____

D11.   And how did you feel about coming here--did you come because you wanted to come, wanted to please somebody in the family, felt afraid or threatened, or for some other reason?

1. Wanted to come

2. Wanted to please somebody in the family

*3 a. Felt threatened   (ASK *b)

     *b.   How?   By whom?_____

     _____

4. Other reason (SPECIFY) _____

    _____

    _____

    _____

D12 a. Are you or your child supposed to come back here soon, go
       to another agency, or not come back at all?

       *1. Yes, come back here (ASK *b)

           *b. Who is supposed to come? _____

           _____

       *2. Yes, go to another agency (PROBE FOR EXACT NAME AND
            ASK *c)

            (SPECIFY)_____

            *c. Who is supposed to go? _____

            _____

       3.   Not come back (GO TO D15)

       4.   Not sure (GO TO D15)

   d. What date are you or (NAME)_____ supposed to come
      back or go to another agency? (APPROXIMATE DATES ARE
      ACCEPTABLE).

           _____
              month   day   year

D13 a. Looking ahead to the future just for you, how likely is it
       that you will actually be able to come (ON THAT DATE/WHEN
       A DATE IS SET)--very likely, somewhat likely, not too
       likely, or not likely at all?

       1. Very likely

       2. Somewhat likely

       3. Not too likely

       4. Not likely at all

   b. Is there anything that might keep you from coming (ON THAT
      DATE/WHEN A DATE IS SET?) (SPECIFY)

      _____

      _____

      _____

D14 a. And how likely is it that you will be able to arrange for
       (NAME)_____ to come--very likely, somewhat likely,
       not too likely, or not likely at all?

       1. Very likely

       2. Somewhat likely

       3. Not too likely

       4. Not likely at all

    b. Is there anything that might keep (NAME) _____
       from coming on that date? (SPECIFY)

       _____

       _____

       _____

       _____

D15.   Now I would like to ask whether there are any types of
       help that you personally might want if they were offered
       to you by agencies like this. You may or may not want to
       have one or more of these types of help. Please tell me
       whether you would answer definitely yes, maybe, or
       definitely not for each type of help that might be
       offered.

    a. Work with a counselor who can figure out how you can act
       differently as a parent and then tell you exactly what to
       do to act differently.

       1. Definitely yes   2. Maybe   3. Definitely not

    b. Work with a counselor who can encourage you to use your
       own will to try harder by yourself to act differently as a
       parent.

       1. Definitely yes   2. Maybe   3. Definitely not

    c. Work with a counselor who can lead and provide a
       disciplined program that you can follow to act differently
       as a parent.

       1. Definitely yes   2. Maybe   3. Definitely not

D15 d. Work with a counselor who can offer to teach you new ways
of acting so you can learn how to act differently as a
parent by yourself.

   1. Definitely yes   2. Maybe   3. Definitely not

   e. Work with a counselor who can figure out how you can act
differently as a parent and then discuss with you what
you could do to act differently.

   1. Definitely yes   2. Maybe   3. Definitely not

D16.   Out of all the types of help that might be offered which
one would you want the most?

   1. _____ (SELECT A LETTER)

   2. None (GO TO SECTION E)

D17 a. If you had your choice which day during the week or weekend would be the most convenient to take part in the types
of help you would want the most for (NAME)_____
and you?

   1. Monday   5. Friday

   2. Tuesday   6. Saturday

   3. Wednesday   7. Sunday

   4. Thursday   8. No day (GO TO SECTION E)

   b. Which hour or time during the day or evening would be most
convenient for the types of help you would want the most
for (NAME)_____ and you?

   (GET A SPECIFIC HOUR)_____

SECTION E. IMPORTANT FACTUAL INFORMATION

E1.   We're almost through--but we need a few facts like age, occupation, and so on, so we can compare the ideas and answers of older parents with younger parents and one group with another. First, what is your date of birth?

    _____
         Month   Day   Year

E2.   Where were you born?

    1. Town and State _____

    2. Outside U.S.A. (SPECIFY COUNTRY)_____

E3.   And (NAME)_____, where was (HE/SHE) born?

    1. Town and State_____

    2. Outside U.S.A. (SPECIFY COUNTRY)_____

E4.   What religion is (NAME)_____, or doesn't (HE/SHE) have any?

    1. Protestant--Baptist

    2. Protestant--Methodist

    3. Protestant--Other (SPECIFY)_____

    4. Roman Catholic

    5. Jewish

    6. Muslim

    7. Other (SPECIFY) _____

    8. None

E5.   Does (NAME)_____ live with you or someone else?

    1. With respondent

    2. Someone else (SPECIFY)_____

    _____

E6. How many people actually live together in your child's
     household--counting all the adults and all the children?
     And how many of these are 21 years and over, and how many
     are under 21?

     1. Total number   2. No. of adults   3. No. of children
                           (21 and over)   (under 21)

     _____   _____   _____

E7 a. What relationship--if any--does each adult in the house-
      hold have with your child? (INCLUDE PARENT/CAREGIVER)

                                   A   B
                              Relationship   Marital Status

      Adult #1 (PARENT).... _____   _____

      Adult #2 ....   _____   _____

      Adult #3 ....   _____   _____

      Adult #4 ....   _____   _____

   b. Are any of the adults married or remarried, separated,
      divorced, widowed, or never married? (SPECIFY IN COLUMN
      B)

E8. It's important to know how close (NAME) _____ feels
     to adults in (HIS/HER) life. Here's a picture of circles
     with (NAME) _____ in the middle. As you can see,
     the first circle is very close to (NAME) _____, the
     second is fairly close, the third is not as close, and
     there's space outside all the circles. Where would you
     place the following adults in this picture? (USE HOUSE-
     HOLD NUMBERS)

     1. You (RESPONDENT) (USE NUMBER #1)

     2. (NAME) _____'s father (USE F IF NOT IN HOUSEHOLD)

     3. The other adults living in the household (USE #2,3,& 4)

     4. Any adults not living in the household (HE/SHE) feels
        close to (USE LETTERS A, B, C, D, ETC. AND SPECIFY)

        A_____   D_____

        B_____   E_____

        C_____   G_____

WHO IS CLOSE? HOW CLOSE?

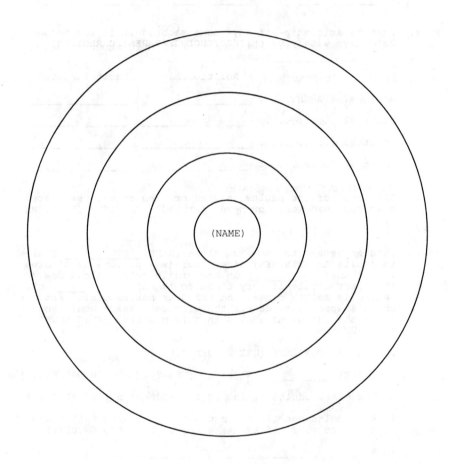

E9.   Do any of the adults in--or outside--the household take part in disciplining (NAME)_____? Which ones?

   1. Yes, (SPECIFY BY NUMBER OR LETTER) _____

   _____

   _____

   2. No

E10. Who would you say is the head of the household where (NAME)_____ lives?

   1. You (RESPONDENT)

   2. Father

   3. Mother's mother/Father's mother

   4. Mother's father/Father's father

   5. Foster mother/stepmother

   6. Foster father/stepfather

   7. Other relative (SPECIFY)_____

   8. Other non-relative (SPECIFY) _____

   9. Not sure

Ell a. How many years of schooling did you complete?

    1.   8 yrs. or less

    2.   1 or more years of high school--did not graduate

    3.   12 years--graduated high school

    4.   GED certificate

    5.   1 year college

    6.   2 years college--no degree

    7.   2 years college--Associate's Degree

    8.   3 years college

    9.   4 years college--graduated college

   10.   4 years college plus

   11.   Don't know/not sure

Ell b. (IF RESPONDENT IS <u>NOT</u> THE HEAD OF HOUSEHOLD, ASK). And
how many years of schooling did the head of the household
complete?

    1.   8 yrs. or less

    2.   1 or more years of high school--did not graduate

    3.   12 years--graduated high school

    4.   GED certificate

    5.   1 year college

    6.   2 years college--no degree

    7.   2 years college--Associate's Degree

    8.   3 years college

    9.   4 years college--graduated college

   10.   4 years college plus

   11.   Don't know/not sure

   12.   Respondent head of household, does not apply

29

E12 a. Do <u>you</u> get paid for any of the work you do?

    1. Yes

    2. No (GO TO E13)

  b. What type of paid work do you consider to be your main
    job? (GET SPECIFIC JOB NAME AND PROBE FOR TYPES OF JOB
    TASKS)

    _____

    _____

    _____

    _____

    _____

  c. What kind of business or industry is that in?

    _____

    _____

    _____

    _____

  d. Do you work for someone else or are you self employed?

    _____

    _____

    _____

E13 a. (IF RESPONDENT IS <u>NOT</u> THE HEAD OF HOUSEHOLD, ASK). Does
       the head of the household get paid for any of the work
       (HE/SHE) does?

       1. Yes

       2. No (GO TO E14)

       3. Respondent head of household, does not apply (GO TO E14)

   b. What type of work does (HE/SHE) consider to be (HIS/HER)
       main job? (GET SPECIFIC JOB NAME AND PROBE FOR TYPES OF
       JOB TASKS)

       _____

       _____

       _____

       _____

       _____

   c. What kind of business or industry is that in?

       _____

       _____

       _____

       _____

       _____

   d. Does (HE/SHE) work for someone else or is (HE/SHE) self-
       employed?

       _____

       _____

       _____

31

E14.   During the last month, did anyone in (NAME)_____'s
        household receive <u>any</u> money from any of the sources on
        this list I will read to you?

Source List	Yes	or	No
a. Your job	Yes		No
b. Job of another adult in house	Yes		No
c. Child support for any child	Yes		No
d. Welfare assistance or AFDC	Yes		No
e. Unemployment insurance	Yes		No
f. Social Security Retirement Insurance	Yes		No
g. Social Security Disability Insurance	Yes		No
h. Workmen's Compensation	Yes		No
i. Supplementary Security Income--SSI	Yes		No
j. Veterans' benefits	Yes		No
k. Private pension	Yes		No
l. Family gift or trust	Yes		No
m. Any other (SPECIFY)_____	Yes		No

E15.   Last month about how much take-home income did <u>each</u> adult
        in the household actually get for the whole month from one
        or more of the sources--after taking off for any state and
        federal taxes and Social Security deductions? (USE LIST
        OF HOUSEHOLD MEMBERS FROM E7).

                                    Take <u>Home</u> $ <u>Last</u> <u>Month</u>

        1.   Adult #1 (RESPONDENT)   _____

        2.   Adult #2   _____

        3.   Adult #3   _____

        4.   Adult #4   _____

E16. Just a few more questions and we're almost through. Besides
     receiving cash income, did anyone in (NAME)_____'s
     household receive any benefits during the past month from
     Food Stamps, Medicaid, a Rent Subsidy, or Public Housing?

	Benefits	Yes or No	
a.	Food Stamps	Yes	No
b.	Medicaid	Yes	No
c.	Rent Subsidy	Yes	No
d.	Public Housing	Yes	No

E17. How long has (NAME)_____ lived in this household?

0.	less than one year	6.	6 years
1.	1 year	7.	7 years
2.	2 years	8.	8 years
3.	3 years	9.	9 years
4.	4 years	10.	10 years or more
5.	5 years	11.	Not sure

33

E18 a. One last question. If someone from our research team at
       Rutgers University wanted to contact you to clear up any
       misunderstanding about your answers,   could they call
       you on the telephone?

       1. Yes

       2. No   (GO TO E19)

       3. Not sure (GO TO E19)

    b. Could you give us a phone number and a good time to
       call?

       1._____   2._____
              Telephone number   Time to call

E19.   Thank you very much for your time. We would like to mail
       you a $5.00 check for taking the time to be interviewed.
       Could you give us the address and name where you would
       like the check mailed? After the study is completed, the
       head researchers will throw away the name, address, and
       phone number. That way your interview will stay private
       and confidential.

       1. _____
          (NAME ON CHECK)

       2. _____
          (STREET ADDRESS AND NUMBER)

       3. _____   4. _____
          (TOWN)   (ZIP CODE)

       RESEARCH CASE #_____   EXACT TIME NOW:_____

35

SECTION F: INTERVIEWER OBSERVATIONS
(COMPLETE AS SOON AS YOU HAVE FINISHED THE INTERVIEW)

F1.   Respondent's sex is:

1. Male

2. Female

F2.   Respondent's racial or ethnic group is:

1. White

2. Black

3. Oriental

4. Hispanic

5. Other (SPECIFY)_____

F3 a. Were any other people present at the survey interview?

1. None   (GO TO F4)

2. Child under 6

3. Other child

4. Spouse

5. Other relative

6. Any others (SPECIFY) _____

   b. How much do you feel the presence of other person(s)
       influenced the answers given by the respondent?

       _____

       _____

       _____

       _____

37

F4.   Overall, how strong was the respondent's interest in the
      interview?

      1. Very high

      2. Above average

      3. Average

      4. Below average

      5. Very low

F5.   Which questions gave the respondent the most trouble in
      <u>understanding?</u> (LIST ALL NUMBERS)

      _____

      _____

F6.   Which questions gave the respondent the most trouble in
      <u>answering</u>--even though (HE/SHE) seemed to understand
      the question? (LIST ALL NUMBERS)

      _____

      _____

F7.   General observations and comments about respondent--or
      interview situation.

      _____

      _____

      _____

      _____

      _____

      _____

      _____

      _____

F8.   **Please sign below after you have reviewed and edited the
       entire interview**

                                            _____
                                            Interviewer's Signature

—— Appendix **B** ——
Scoring the Achenbach Child Behavior Checklist (CBCL)

The CBCL consists of a total of 119 items referring to an array of behaviors and descriptions of emotional problems. Examples of some of the specific behavioral items are: argues a lot; destroys things; disobedient at school; lying or cheating; steals at home; truancy; and runs away from home. Examples of emotional problems are: can't concentrate; clings to adults; confused; doesn't feel guilty; easily jealous; too fearful; anxious; daydreams; feels worthless; and unhappy or sad. A list of seven specific physical problems occurring "without known medical cause," when added to the 111 behavior and emotional items increases the actual number of items to 118 items. One general item, referring to "any other problem" not on the list, increases the total to 119.

Parents are asked to respond to each item of behavior for their child as occurring "now or within the past 6 months" and to respond to one of the following scoring categories: "not true"(0); "somewhat or sometimes true"(1); or "very true or often true"(2). Parents can circle a 0, 1, or 2 for each item by themselves, or an interviewer codes the CBCL on the basis of parents' responses. An unknown number of Achenbach's clinical and normal respondents filled out the CBCL form themselves, while others were filled out by agency intake workers or research interviewers. In the Essex County Youth Study (ECYS) all items were read to parents and the responses were circled by trained interviewers. This was done to insure uniformity of data collection for literate, semi-literate, and illiterate respondents.

The *Manual* published by Achenbach and Edelbrock (1985) presents three methods for scoring the CBCL. These methods generate three distinct types of scores: a total behavior score; a specific factor or scale score; and a general internal and external score. The total behavior score uses the 118 specific items plus one general "any other problem" item. Each of the 119 items is scored as 0, 1, or 2, and the results added together for a final score. The procedures are the same for all ages and sexes, and do not differentiate between types of behaviors. It is meant to be a general measure of the total number of behavior problems that also includes a weighting for the frequency of occurrence.

The specific factor—or scale—score relies on the results of distinctive factor analyses conducted for each sex, according to the age groups of 4–5, 6–11, and 12–16. The procedures are the same for each age group, but this discussion will refer only to the 12–16 year olds. The factor analysis is conducted by first scoring each item as having occurred or not; the frequency distinction between sometimes and often is ignored. The scored items (i.e., 0 vs 1 or 2) are then entered into a statistical factor analysis that attempts to identify those items that share a sufficient commonality that distinguishes them from other groupings. This commonality—or factor—is a hypothetical construct that can be best described by the items that share a high proportion of the variance of this commonality. For example, delinquency is an idea—or construct—that could refer to many specific legal violations. But in the Achenbach factor analysis, it was found that non-legal, as well as legal, forms of deviance were statistically associated and formed a factor. The empirically derived factor was labeled "delinquency" in order to capture the dominant content of the specific items. Once the items are categorized for each factor they are scored, using the frequency weights of 0, 1, 2. Duplicate scoring of items is permitted for specific scales, as long as there are no duplicates within the scale. Each sex, according to the Achenbach procedures, yields distinct factors and specific scale scores.

A third mode of assessing the items uses the specific scales to determine if there is any commonality between scales that occurs in a new factor analysis. For each sex, the specific scales are entered into a second-order factor analysis to determine whether the weighted scores of the scales behave in a common manner—so that Achenbach obtained second-order factors that successfully grouped most of the scale scores into two distinct dimensions: internal and external. Internal scales are behaviors and feelings that refer to "fearful, inhibited, or over controlled" items. External scales refer to aggressive, antisocial or " under controlled" behavior. Scales that could not be statistically distinguished as internal or external are labeled as "mixed".

The internal and external factor scoring is based on the results of the second order factor analysis for each sex. Items are scored as 0, 1, 2 on an internal, external, or mixed dimension. Duplication of items is permitted between dimensions, but not within a second-order factor. An item can be scored an internal and external, but not twice within an internal or external dimension score.

—— Appendix C ——
Factor Analysis Results

TABLE C–1. Factor Analysis Results For Seven Legal Violation Items, Both Sexes

		Loadings on Rotated Factor	
Legal Items		Legal Property Factor	Legal Assaultive
(#82)	Steals outside home	77	02
(#81)	Steals inside home	72	09
(#106)	Vandalism	68	19
(#72)	Sets fires	46	21
(#57)	Physically attacks people	10	83
(#97)	Threatens people	07	83
(#21)	Destroys things of family or others	23	60
Percent of variance accounted for		34.8%	17.6%

TABLE C-2. Factor Analysis Results For Six Status Offense Items, Both Sexes

		Loadings on Rotated Factors	
Status Offense Items		Disobedience	Truant/Runaway
(#86)	Stubborn, Sullen	80	–04
(#22)	Disobedient at home	77	11
(#23)	Disobedient at school	69	36
(#101)	Truancy	–01	80
(#67)	Runs away	17	64
(#195)	Uses alcohol/drugs	09	55
Percent of variance accounted for		34.9%	19.3%

TABLE C-3. Second Order Factor Analysis of 12 Factors, Both Sexes

	Loadings on Rotated Factors			
Factors	Multi-aggression	Mixed Delinquency	New Internal	Unduplicated Number of Items
1. Multiaggression				
Verbal agression	82	21	27	12
Fearful perfectionist	77	–03	29	06
Unliked/cruel	76	19	17	05
Legal assault	71	28	12	03
			(Subtotal)	(26)
2. Mixed Delinquency				
Legal property	10	79	–03	04
Truant/runaway	–03	73	11	03
Hyperactive	37	70	20	05
Disobey	48	66	10	03
			(Subtotal)	(15)
3. New Internal				
Withdrawn	–01	28	83	05
Depressed	41	01	71	09
Strange ideas/behavior	38	32	62	06
Somatic	32	17	49	07
			(Subtotal)	(27)
Percent of variance	41.2%	13.9%	8.7%	

Index